ACADEMIC VALUES AND MASS EDUCATION
The Early Years of Oakland and Monteith

Academic Values and Mass Education

The Early Years of Oakland and Monteith

DAVID RIESMAN
JOSEPH GUSFIELD
ZELDA GAMSON

DOUBLEDAY & COMPANY, INC., GARDEN CITY, NEW YORK
1970

TO EVERETT CHERRINGTON HUGHES

Contents

Preface

The intellectual origins of this book go back to the years when Everett C. Hughes in the Sociology Department at the University of Chicago was encouraging his students to study institutions, educational and otherwise, and to observe the dialectical relations between occupational guilds and customers, clients, or sponsors.[1] Gusfield had written his dissertation on the WCTU under Everett Hughes, viewing that institution historically in terms of a shift of its leadership away from earlier evangelism toward more up-to-date and moderate professionalism. Riesman's interest in higher education was stimulated by his close colleagueship with Hughes and by the opportunity to report and reflect on a national survey of academic institutions.[2] In 1958, when plans were being laid for founding two new colleges as offshoots of major state universities in Michigan, Gusfield and Riesman decided that they should study their development from the beginning. It was already evident that the forty-five per cent of all undergraduates who were then educated in

[1] See Everett C. Hughes, *Men and Their Work;* for a sampling of the concerns of men and women who consider themselves students of Hughes, see Howard Becker, Blanche Geer, David Riesman, and Robert S. Weiss (eds.), *Institutions and the Person: Essays in Honor of Everett C. Hughes.*

[2] See Paul F. Lazarsfeld and Wagner Thielens, Jr. (with a field report by David Riesman), *The Academic Mind: Social Scientists in a Time of Crisis.*

private institutions would continue to decline (by 1968, it was down to twenty-nine per cent) and that, among the public institutions, the fastest-growing segment would continue to be the commuter colleges. These two new colleges would offer the chance to see how such institutions developed in response to the vision of their founders, to the outlook and talents of their faculty and administration, to the values and capacities of the students who were attracted, sifted, or fenced off, and to the local communities in which they were located. Zelda Gamson had independently become interested in one of these colleges, Monteith, and recounted the development of its early years in her doctoral dissertation at Harvard.[3] As a onetime student at Antioch College (as well as the University of Michigan), she shared the concern of many Antiochians with educational experiment and was curious about a setting where students helped define the institution, rather than one where students arrived to become socialized in an already well-defined collegiate culture. Though not a student of Hughes, she, too, had been influenced by his work. In 1962–63, as the charter class of Monteith students was finishing, she was interviewing faculty and administrators, collecting statistics, and attending classes and faculty meetings.

Riesman had first learned of the college that Michigan State University was planning in Oakland County (just outside Detroit) at the time that the newly appointed Chancellor, D. B. Varner, came to Harvard to consult with academicians. At about the same time, he and Gusfield were told of the plans for Monteith College of Wayne State University through friends recruited for Monteith's social science program and through a meeting between Riesman and President Clarence Hilberry of Wayne. The offspring were being launched at a time when both the parent universities were principally preoccupied with improving their programs in graduate and professional instruction and research. State systems of higher education are constantly launching two-year and four-year commuter colleges to meet anticipated traffic densities of students. But Oakland and Monteith were intended to be beacons of a sort, high-

[3] For further details on the methods used and the data gathered, see Zelda F. Gamson, "Social Control and Modification."

quality places, not mere extrapolations. Such a focus of privileged faculties on unselected commuter students seemed a new departure. We wanted to discover what sort of faculty could be attracted to such institutions, and what hopes these particular men and women had brought with them for themselves, their prospective students, and the new colleges.

In the calendar year 1960, when both colleges had been in existence for a year, we began our interviewing with faculty and administrators. Gusfield, then Professor of Sociology at the University of Illinois, spent periods at each college doing most of the interviewing; he also visited classes and examined records of student test scores and performance on examinations. Riesman made many brief trips to both colleges, talked with student and faculty informants, "interviewed" by extensive correspondence, sought out Oakland and Monteith administrators and faculty at various professional meetings, and followed faculty publications and student journalism. Zelda Gamson joined Gusfield and Riesman's project after she had finished her thesis in 1965 and moved to the Institute for Social Research at the University of Michigan. She helped Gusfield and Riesman to re-examine their own work in terms of her findings, and did further work on Oakland as well as on Monteith. By continuous rewriting and exchanging of drafts in the past five years, interspersed with occasional reunions, we have sought to make the educational outlooks that we started with more explicit.

Ours was never a systematic study of students. The Monteith Program Study followed students from the outset, and in Chapter XI we report on some of this material. But our principal concern has been with faculty. Gusfield and Riesman interviewed virtually all the faculty of both colleges in the first two years; Zelda Gamson interviewed almost all faculty members at Monteith in the academic year 1962–63. Undoubtedly, the intensive concentration on the early years has colored our work, although it should be added that these same years provided the legend and imagery that continue to influence both institutions—surprisingly in Oakland's case since it is now incomparably larger and more diversified than the small liberal arts college it was in its early years. It is possible that we have insufficiently corrected our earlier mental sets, and in any case it has proved impossible to bring our account up to date: as we reluctantly close the covers on our work in the academic year 1969–70, both institutions are facing succession crises as their leaders depart, their boards of trustees change, and Michigan, like other states, seeks to pare down the soaring costs of its educational enterprises.

In such circumstances, as throughout our work, we have been anxious that nothing we have said about these two institutions would influence their opportunity to compete for the never fully adequate state resources or for students and faculty members inside and outside Michigan. Although Michigan state colleges and universities are nominally under the supervision of a State Board of Education, this does not prevent Monteith College from having to compete for funds and backing with the rest of Wayne State University, which in turn is in competition with Oakland, Michigan State, the University of Michigan, and all the other public colleges of Michigan. Hence, when we first wrote preliminary articles about these colleges, we hesitated to use their actual names and decided on pseudonyms as a protection, for we do not think institutions that generously make themselves available to researchers should be punished and their vulnerability exploited.[4] The representatives of neither college insisted on anonymity, and we ourselves finally concluded that pseudonyms make readers' understanding more difficult. "Midwest City" is not the same thing as Detroit and does not carry the same connotations. Indeed, we ourselves have had the experience of reading about pseudonymous colleges and getting our signals mixed so

[4] Vassar College made itself available for extensive studies in the 1950s by Nevitt Sanford and his collaborators; this allowed some snide critics to jibe at the sex life and personal values of Vassar girls. Yet Vassar made a genuine contribution both to its self-understanding and to wider awareness through its encouragement of this research. (Cf. Nevitt Sanford, "Personality Development During the College Years.") Bennington College deserves similar credit for allowing Theodore Newcomb to use its name in his study *Personality and Social Change: Attitude Formation in a Student Community* and his restudy with Koenig, Flacks, and Warwick, *Persistence and Change: Bennington College and Its Students After Twenty-five Years.*

that we added what we knew about "College A" when in fact we were reading about "College B." Moreover, to the limited degree to which the experiences of Oakland and Monteith can instruct would-be educational reformers elsewhere, names should be given as an aid to others who are looking for advice.

When it came to individual faculty members, we felt that the balance between caution and candor tilted the other way. We have left unchanged the names of chancellor and president, the chief executive officers, which are in the public domain. For all others, we have altered names, while doing our best to preserve gender, class, and ethnicity in the pseudonyms; sometimes we have changed identifying details while still trying to maintain reasonable proximity to reality.

We have circulated earlier drafts of this book to faculty and administrators of the two colleges; these colleagues have been conscientious and generous with their criticisms and help in correcting misapprehensions, and we are indebted to them for this—as well as for their willingness to be interviewed (and often observed in class) in the first place. Naturally, we have sought to take account of their criticisms, but there are still many things we say with which insiders disagree, both with us and among themselves.[5]

Our work has intensified our conviction of the idiosyncracy of institutions, as of individuals. Nevertheless, while we think that only a modest amount can be learned as a "lesson" of history, we try, especially in the two concluding chapters, to generalize about educational reform. For example, while articulate faculty members and students in many institutions tend to denigrate administrators, in our study the administrators come off well. In some cases, their very preoccupation with institutional survival makes them readier to innovate. They tend to be exposed to a wider network

[5] Since our manuscript was completed, Sally Whelan Cassidy and others at Monteith have published a report, *Impact of a High-Demand College in a Large University on Working Class Youth*, which describes in detail the evaluations pursued by the Program Study, which compared Monteith students to those in Wayne State College of Liberal Arts. We have drawn on some of this work in its earlier stages, but the report came too late to be taken account of in our own work.

of constituencies than are many faculty members and they are, of course, subject to all the competing pressures from faculty. What is surprising is that paralysis does not result more often.

It is understandable that administrators are generally better read in the literature on higher education than are faculty members or students.[6] Whatever their original field of specialization, higher education is now the administrators' "field," and their meetings and journals are occupied with its problems. But we hope that a number of faculty members and students will also read this book, whether or not they have a particular interest in undergraduate educational reform. We are talking about what happens when a commitment is made to near-universal higher education in more than a pro forma way. We are asking how academic and intellectual values can come alive for students, most of them commuters, who are the first in their families to attend college and are there mainly because it has become the thing to do. In some ways, this issue is even more grave today than it was when Monteith and Oakland began. Commuter students have often been passive saboteurs of the educational ambitions of their teachers, but today many have learned from the radical and avant-garde students a new ideology of resistance against constraints, including those of grades, degrees, and required curricula. A new coalition encourages both the children of the elite and those who come from inadequate high schools to want to do their own thing in college. Thus the old Philistinism and the new radicalism combine to make even more difficult the achievement of the ambitions with which Oakland and Monteith began.

Both colleges opened with a high proportion of young faculty. We sought to assess the impact of what for many was their first experience of teaching outside the place where they had gotten their graduate training. How had student reactions affected them? Had they been sensitive to the feelings about education and acade-

---

[6] To this generalization there are exceptions both ways. In 1968–69, for instance, Ira Magaziner and his student colleagues at Brown University prepared a report showing a thorough coverage of the literature on educational innovation.

micians in the local community? How had original hopes and ideals been refracted by experience? The experience relevant here is, of course, not only that of individual faculty members but of collectivities as interpreted by the mutual encounters of faculty, students, and local residents.

We have not been able to give an account of the microclimates that arose within each individual discipline at each of the two colleges, but instead have generalized about groups of faculty in the natural sciences, the social sciences, and the humanities. To do more would have involved a biographical effort that would be rewarding but enormous. Since we have not done this, we have constantly had to guard against the dangers of overgeneralization, for in every discipline there are men who do not fit its more representative styles, which have some of the quality of ethnic stereotypes. When we began our work, we noticed in ourselves a tendency to polarize the two institutions: to see Oakland as square and correct, Monteith as groovy and loose. The more we learned, the less were we satisfied with such oversimplification. We want to emphasize again that no one should suppose that he understands these two colleges as they are now simply from what he reads about them in this book. They always were, and they now are, more complicated and various than our description of them.

More important still, we are not recounting the story of non-literate tribes for a metropolitan audience. The conflicts between the claims of traditional culture and egalitarian values on which we touch in this book are conflicts that have been thoroughly explored on both campuses by sophisticated and devoted scholar-teachers. Our own abilities as teachers and our own educational philosophies have been enriched by our colleagueships with faculties at both institutions. Monteith began with the mandate of bringing to its students something of the intellectual style and content of the best liberal arts colleges. It intended to do this through a revival of General Education at a time when elsewhere such programs were giving way to more specialized departmental course work. Oakland, although it did not consider itself an experiment, was self-consciously designed to bring rigorous academic standards and high

culture to commuter students who for the most part had had no
previous acquaintance with either. In the dozen years since the
planning of these colleges began, questions have been increasingly
raised about the class and cultural biases that may have been built
into the definition of standards and the passing on of particular
cultural styles. Efforts that were avant-garde in 1958 may now seem
quaint, even regressive. But the dilemmas remain as to how to
respond to the new student clienteles of higher education. Kingsley
Amis rejected British university expansion with the phrase "More
means worse." Few Americans, either radical or reactionary, would
openly say that about higher education as such, whatever elitism
may lurk in their criticism of particular versions of education. Increasingly, such questions tend to be drowned in rhetoric. We hope
that a somewhat closer look at how students and faculties responded
to each other's aspirations at two new colleges may help the discussion move closer to actuality.

David Riesman
Center for Advanced Study in the
Behavioral Sciences
and
Harvard University

Joseph Gusfield
University of California, San Diego

Zelda Gamson
Institute for Social Research
University of Michigan

June 1969

Acknowledgments

Our work put a great burden on the two institutions, for without the co-operation of faculty members and administrators we could neither have carried on our research nor felt confidence in the results. Because we follow the policy of not identifying individuals, we acknowledge them here by name but without reference to location. By listing them alphabetically, we group together those who read one or another chapter with those many friends who read the entire manuscript; we trust they realize, in addition, the extent of our obligation to them from what we have said and written privately.

At the very beginning of our work, we benefited from conversations with the late Clarence Hilberry, President of Wayne State University, and toward the end of it from discussions with President William R. Keast, his successor. At Oakland University, we had from the outset the full and frank co-operation of Chancellor D. B. Varner, and the opportunity for conversations with John Hannah, former President of Michigan State University.

Turning now to those who helped us at Oakland and Monteith, we would like to thank: Sheldon L. Appleton, Thomas H. Atkinson, Carol Ballingall, Betty J. Beardslee, David C. Beardslee, Paul Bluemle, Glen Brown, W. Royce Butler, Sally Cassidy, Melvin

xvi   *Acknowledgments*

Cherno, Kenneth H. Coffman, Max Coral, Thomas B. Dutton, Kay Engle, Kenneth Feigenbaum, Otto Feinstein, John E. Gibson, James C. Haden, Laszlo J. Hetenyi, Edward J. Heubel, Dorothy Hope, Sara Leopold, Clifford L. Maier, George T. Matthews, Nahum Medalia, Frederick W. Obear, Donald D. O'Dowd, Jesse Pitts, Henry Rosemont, Jr., Woodburn O. Ross, Richard H. Schell, William F. Sturner, Paul Tomboulian, Nola H. Tutag, Paule Verdet and Robert Hoopes.

Many friends outside Oakland and Monteith read and commented on the manuscript. We had exceptionally helpful and detailed comments from Howard Becker, Department of Sociology, Northwestern University; Bennett Berger, Department of Sociology, University of California, Davis; Robert T. Blackburn, Department of Higher Education, University of Michigan; Donald Brown, Center for Research on Learning and Teaching, University of Michigan; Alden Dunham, Carnegie Corporation; John Elmendorf, President of New College (Sarasota); Clarence Faust, formerly of the Fund for the Advancement of Education; Kenneth Feldman, Department of Sociology, State University of New York at Stony Brook; Walter Feinberg, College of Education, University of Illinois; William Gamson, Department of Sociology, University of Michigan; Andrew M. Greeley, National Opinion Research Center; Conrad Hilberry, Department of English, Kalamazoo College; Everett C. Hughes, Department of Sociology, Boston College; Judson Jerome, Antioch College; Kenneth Keniston, Departments of Psychiatry and Psychology, Yale University; William Meyers, Division of Community Psychiatry, Harvard Medical School; Barry Munitz, Staff Associate of the Carnegie Commission on the Future of Higher Education, Berkeley; Evelyn T. Riesman, Kenneth Roose, American Council on Education; Martin Trow, Department of Sociology, University of California, Berkeley; Donald Warwick, Department of Social Relations, Harvard University; Robert S. Weiss, Laboratory of Community Psychiatry, Harvard Medical School.

Carol Kaye, originally a member of the Program Study at Monteith, now of the Jewish Board of Guardians and the William Alanson

White Institute, was of particular assistance to our work at the very beginning, as well as in later stages.

Martha Glazier not only typed many drafts of the manuscript but checked tables and references and helped see the book through the press; her intelligence and grace made onerous burdens seem light.

From the outset, our work has been supported by a grant of the Carnegie Corporation to Harvard University for Riesman's study of higher education; as grantor, the Corporation manifested its characteristic restraint and patience.

Without the freedom of the academic year 1968–69 at the Center for Advanced Study in the Behavioral Sciences at Stanford, Riesman could not have brought his work on the manuscript to completion. Discussions of the work there, especially with Michael Maccoby, proved clarifying.

List of Tables and Charts in the Text

List of Tables and Citations in the Text

List of Appendixes

ACADEMIC VALUES AND MASS EDUCATION
The Early Years of Oakland and Monteith

I The Move Toward Universal Higher Education

As late as the 1960s only eight per cent of the adult population in the United States had attended college, and only three per cent of the total population were in college. This was despite the fact that in 1961 thirty-eight per cent of high school students were entering college, and by 1966 half of those who completed high school continued into some form of postsecondary education.[1] Martin Trow, in a stimulating essay, speaks of this era as one of mass education. Indeed, he sees the United States as moving presently even further toward universal higher education, in which three quarters or more of the age grade would continue through the thirteenth grade and beyond.[2] He notes that the shift, first toward mass and now toward near-universal higher education, has proceeded at a faster rate than did expansion of high school enrollments in the first part of this century.[3] In California, the forerunner in this as in other respects,

---

[1] Since there are great regional variations, there are states where half of the relevant age group are in college, and others where the proportion drops to a third. See U. S. Department of Health, Education, and Welfare, "Reference Facts on Health, Education, and Welfare," p. 30; A. M. Cartter and R. Farrell, "Higher Education in the Last Third of the Century"; see also Clark Kerr, "New Challenges to the College and University."

[2] See "Reflections on the Transition from Mass to Universal Higher Education."

[3] See Carl Kaysen, *The Higher Learning, the Universities, and the Public*, p. 12.

a high school diploma is not necessary to attend a community college: it is enough to be eighteen years old. Many other educational systems are rapidly expanding their network of community colleges, and many efforts have been made to assure federal support so that no one is deprived by financial stringency of the chance to attend college, although the lack of provision of income foregone leads young people in the poorest families, to regard college as not at all for them. Nevertheless, the agendas for our society drawn up not only by educators but by other elites take for granted the continuing expansion of higher education.

It is true that presently there has been a slight slowing down of the expansion of faculties and facilities, reflecting inflation, resistance to staggeringly increasing costs, and resentment of student turbulence. And it is possible that, if the Vietnam War draft eventually is removed, college may seem less attractive to young men who can get well-paying blue collar jobs without it. Indeed, some elite college students are already mounting an attack against what they call credentialism: some see the dropout as morally superior to the docile, persistent student. Yet on the whole, what David Plath has written of Japan could be said equally well of the United States: "As industrial techniques have greatly expanded the supply of Disraeli's 'two great civilizers of men'—increased means and increased leisure—at the same time, democratic vistas have greatly increased the demand. All of us have become, simultaneously, workers and aristocrats."[4] Aristocratic disdain for the routines of college has not prevented tipping most middle class and lower-middle class neighborhoods in the direction of college, making it harder for the majority of young people not to go to college than to go.

What happens to faculties as more and more students are drawn into the colleges, beyond the very large numbers already there? For years, they have complained about the dilution of academic

[4] David Plath, *The After Hours: Modern Japan and the Search for Enjoyment.* The only industrial country that has resisted extremely rapid expansion has been the United Kingdom. Cf. the discussion in David Riesman, "Notes on New Universities, British and American."

quality by the emphasis on mere quantity. These misgivings are quite different from Martin Trow's concerns, in the article already mentioned, that the prevailing compromises between egalitarian or populist functions of higher education and more autonomous and elite ones will come unstuck in the years ahead. Yet until just recently, the short-term effect on academic culture of the fantastic expansion of undergraduate enrollment has been to expand graduate enrollments even more rapidly and to enhance faculty bargaining powers as colleges scramble to staff themselves. Faculty bargaining power has in turn been reflected in a dramatic decline in the number of teaching hours (though this says nothing about their intensity), thus leading to still further increases in the demand for faculty.

Faculty members have responded in an enormous variety of ways to their greater affluence and saliency. Like other previously underprivileged groups, they have not always wanted to believe in their present and future good fortune. Thus the nostalgic fantasy persists that the liberal arts college was in earlier epochs the enclave of a common culture and a sense of shared purpose, whereas today it is dominated by Philistines, the military-industrial complex, and other despots. Our own reading of college histories, however, suggests to us that American colleges have never been strictly elitist, nor, with rare exceptions, have they shared an insular cohesion. At least since Federalist times, the United States has not had a self-conscious, national elite, trained in the same schools and colleges and sharing the same cultural style and conviction. Higher education in the United States has never been a monopoly of the well born (although it has helped to prevent the downward mobility of the well born). Like the military academies and the theological seminaries, higher education has also been a route for young men of modest background and at least modest aptitude to enter a profession, to make contacts, and to attain new occupational and social orbits. In the small colleges not so long ago, restless students, barely pacified by athletics and chafing under rigid rules, were subsidized by faculty members still largely engaged in discipline and "character building." Meanwhile, on the other side of the tracks, the land-grant institutions attempted to follow private university models not only in campus architecture but also in extracurricular life and in classroom formulas—despite the egalitarian rhetoric that initiated and sustained them. Faculty members struggled for community respect and personal autonomy and, like Thorstein Veblen, complained that they were dominated on the one hand by tycoons and on the other by the student barbarians for whom they were obliged to act as baby sitters until the latter were old enough to enter their real careers.[5]

The attitude toward students and society of a good many older faculty members reflects their memories of a period when academic careers were not so highly valued by most undergraduates as were the professions, business, and journalism. The books cited in the preceding footnote illustrate how difficult it has been to import to the United States the German, or Continental, model of the autonomous graduate school, without a large undergraduate base; the problems faced by universities designed on the European model, such as Clark University, John Hopkins, and Chicago, testify to this. Only since the Second World War has the federal government taken responsibility for the development of a system of world-class, research-oriented universities, by subsidizing research in the natural and later the health sciences (and still later in the other fields of knowledge) by individual scholars and groups of scholars, at the same time that the vast expansion of undergraduate enrollments was intensifying the demand for Ph.D.s. Even the elite private universities, which at the undergraduate level have remained fairly stable in size, have grown at the graduate level, while in many fields of the arts and sciences the most distinguished universities and those that offer the best research training are the great state universities with massive undergraduate enrollments and a great scatter of professional schools of high, medium, and low quality.[6]

[5] One of the best of the college histories is Richard J. Storr, *Harper's University;* Frederick Rudolph, in *The American College and University*, portrays the vicissitudes of academic careers and institutions; Laurence Veysey, *The Emergence of the American University*, describes the slow emergence of departments, of academic professionalism, and of research.
[6] See Allan M. Cartter, *An Assessment of Quality in Graduate Education.*

Graduate students are drawn to these state universities by the distinction of their research-oriented faculties; they are subsidized during their graduate work by jobs as teaching assistants for lower-division undergraduate courses. This then frees their professors to supervise them and to get on with what they call their "own work." One of the justifications of this arrangement has come from the sense of grievance vis-à-vis the indolent Philistines that developed in many academicians in the early stages of their careers. And of course, one consequence has been a devotion to advancing the discipline rather than the local institution where one happens to be working, a development reflecting a general decline in provincialism as well as the increase in faculty bargaining power we have already noted. In addition to the three dozen major American universities, there are said to be 150 institutions of lesser rank that seek to become full-fledged universities granting the doctorate; probably for a majority of these, the aim is to become what the leaders already seem to be. These institutions provide jobs for young Ph.D.s turned out by the major universities, which cannot re-employ all their own graduates in spite of their own continuing expansion. In both the established state universities and those that are following their model, a division of labor exists, so that the engineering school and some departments in the college of liberal arts and sciences will attract more capable students, while education, home economics, undergraduate business administration, and perhaps agriculture will take in the less academically talented. This allows some graduate school professors to teach undergraduate majors without having to make too many concessions to human frailty and lack of interest.

Such generalizations, which emphasize the similarity of academic models throughout the United States (as we ourselves have done in other writings), should not prevent awareness of substantial differences that remain. Thus, some of the major state universities (Michigan, Minnesota, and Illinois, for example) pay a good deal more attention to undergraduate teaching and probably have more faculty who combine institutional with guild loyalties than other eminent state universities (such as Berkeley). Moreover, between these institutions and their upwardly mobile imitators there is always the slippage that occurs when a model is carried across a boundary line, whether between regions or between social strata. The chances are that "research" is defined in more quantitative terms in the upwardly mobile than in the already arrived universities, that the former have a greater spread of salaries at the same academic rank because of their effort to import a few luminaries, and that they are generally more dependent on federal funds for expansion: lacking endowments, they are federal-grant universities par excellence. Correspondingly, there are very great variations among departments in the same institution in terms of what colleagues regard as "research," and what kinds of responsibilities for teaching are expected.

Since their inception, the state and land-grant universities have sought to serve scholarship and high culture, while at the same time doing enough to satisfy local interests so as to justify their claims on local resources. In that sense, they were "multiversities" from the first. Correspondingly, they were attacked for their elitism by the Populists even while some local citizens took pride in cathedrals of learning where their children would never worship and whose liturgies they themselves would never understand. Today, the vociferous demand that universities serve not only some but all the public has led to a new combination of attacks on what Martin Trow speaks of as the autonomous functions of universities —attacks from both Right and Left. In some states, such as Texas, legislators have introduced measures that would require state college and university faculty members to teach twelve or fifteen hours a week—rather than, as legend has it, jetting off to Washington to advance socialism, or leading radical students to the barricades, or in any event having an easier life, longer vacations, and higher salaries than any other civil servants, including the governor. Angry Left-wing students also want faculty members to teach and not to do research, which is believed to support mere technological progress at best and imperialism and racism at worst. Both groups have taken up the lament that faculty members are trained to do research rather than teaching and are rewarded only for the former. We shall return to this issue in Chapter XIII, but here want to emphasize that the complaint misses the crucial differences among departments and institutions already mentioned, as well as the fact that for most faculty members the question is not *whether* but *which* students are to be taught, for only very rarely do academic men reject teaching altogether.[7]

Most departments want to be well regarded by students, and they also need such regard if they are to expand. Within the available limits, most professors prefer to teach their own disciples or potential disciples, not bored undergraduate captives or uncommitted shoppers. A professor of English or political science hopes to teach his specialty to those who might carry it further; he does not want to have to dilute or simplify the insights and subtleties that are the fruits of his competence. Moreover, mammoth student loads mean mammoth examinations, many conferences, and long lines of students with their personal and curricular problems. Under these conditions, only the most missionary-minded have resisted letting teaching assistants carry a major burden.[8] The teaching assistants have gotten the message that, if they are good, they should as soon as possible imitate their professors, abandoning lower-division students in favor of upper-division majors, and attract their own comet's tail of graduate students. This ambition to teach one's own potential disciples does not seem simply careerist and mean-spirited in the light of frequent experience with ordinary, uncommitted students who are or may appear collegiate, frivolous, and unwilling.[9]

[7] See the report on a survey of faculty members' preferences for teaching *and* research in Talcott Parsons and Gerald M. Platt, "Considerations on the American Academic System."

[8] In the course of a political movement largely directed off-campus, the Free Speech Movement in Berkeley in 1964 and subsequent years made propagandistic use of the impersonality of Berkeley and of the disparagement of lower-division teaching by eminent faculty. Ironically, faculty members at Berkeley now teach considerably less than they did in 1964. In part, it is said, this decline reflects the concessions that had to be made to recruit or keep faculty in such a troubled institution; in part, it also reflects the shift from a term to a quarter system, which was originally proposed as an economy measure.

[9] A dozen years ago, many faculty heads nodded when Philip Jacob, examining the impact of college, contended that undergraduates were cheerfully insulated

There have always been some eminent faculty who resisted this division of academic labor and who chose to work with some of the less preferred clients of academic men. The General Education movement represents one aspect of this resistance. At present, many teaching assistants are rejecting what they regard as unworthy and careerist academic games in favor of teaching at the undergraduate level; some drop out of Ph.D. programs altogether to teach in community colleges or in the offbeat colleges that do not ask for the Ph.D. Most institutions, however, need Ph.D.s for purposes of accreditation; most want them for prestige. Many faculty members use the dissertation as a Rorschach to discover something about a man's interests, his pertinacity, his general ability and even his likely promise as a teacher. The new anti-research and, to some degree, anti-academic movements have not yet appreciably reduced the national demand for Ph.D.s, a demand that, as we have seen, has been built largely on the mass base for higher education (as well as on the demands of industry and government for men with Ph.D.s in many physical sciences and some social sciences). Since this demand is increasingly felt nationally, individual academicians, visible through their research or their sponsors, have the chance to move to places with more favorable conditions for both research and teaching. Though there are other desiderata, such as climate and colleagueship, access to better students is a principal attraction—"better," that is, in terms of aptitudes and attitudes and, at the undergraduate level, often in terms of their desire and potential for pursuing academic careers.

It follows that vastly expanded undergraduate enrollments have increased the power of a minority of faculty to choose the conditions

---

from the impact of the faculty, going through routines that would locate them securely in the occupational structure after a college career of fun and games. See Philip E. Jacob, *Changing Values in College: An Exploratory Study of the Impact of College Teaching;* see, however, Riesman's critique of this conclusion, "The 'Jacob Report.'" For a more subtle examination than Jacob's of the way in which the grading system and student responses to it undercut faculty efforts to involve the students in the academic world, see Howard S. Becker, Blanche Geer, and Everett C. Hughes, *Making the Grade: The Academic Side of College Life.*

of and the clients for their teaching. Jencks and Riesman contended in *The Academic Revolution* that this increasing faculty power has been good not only for professors, but on the whole for America. It has helped make this country the world leader in more than research and has made it possible for some universities to become patrons of high culture, interpreters of the meaning of existence, and, on rare occasions, problem-solvers.[10] It has created the expanded graduate schools, which in turn have made it possible to increase the proportions of students attending undergraduate colleges. Yet the very fact that some visible faculty members have had such large opportunities for choice has brought with it many costs. It is likely, as we have already noted, that many young faculty, in securing their Ph.D.s from major research-oriented institutions, would want to imitate their own professors and make only minimal adaptations when they go out to teach students quite unlike themselves. Students today are probably no worse than those who attended college in earlier generations, and perhaps they are even better prepared and more sophisticated, but faculty standards and expectations have greatly risen, so that to teach indifferent and inept students now becomes a source of bitterness rather than being taken for granted as a way of life.[11] To the degree that faculty have expectations of virtual autonomy from donors, local communities, churches, and students, they will attempt to shift the

[10] Christopher Jencks and David Riesman, *The Academic Revolution.*
[11] An exception must be made for those junior colleges, very unevenly located the country over, that have been staffed largely by teachers from high schools and colleges or departments of education. These faculty members are further away from the great graduate models and are willing enough to teach students only somewhat more selectively screened than those in public high schools. Yet it should not be supposed that junior and community colleges cater to the very poor and deprived. They often cater to the less motivated or capable children of the modestly well off. See for further discussion *The Academic Revolution,* Chapters Two and Three.

Furthermore, the vocational and technical programs in junior colleges often have less standing with students and their parents than the transfer programs, so that many declare a wish to go on to a full four-year college even though, in perhaps the majority of cases, they do not in fact transfer. See, for example, Robert H. Fenske, "Who Selects Vocational-Technical Post-High School Education?"

institutions where they are teaching in the direction of the models they have learned to admire during their own socialization in graduate school.

Over the years, many public universities have worked out strategies for adapting on the one hand to demands for an open-door admissions policy and on the other hand to faculty judgments as to who can profitably be taught.

Thus, many state universities that are required by law or public relations to admit high school graduates use the freshman year as a *de facto* College Entrance Board examination and flunk out a large number; some students read the portents correctly and leave even before they are failed out, sometimes with the first mid-term exams. Sometimes, as Burton Clark noted with reference to community colleges, students are "cooled out" rather than flunked out.[12] A curriculum may be seen as a rough-and-ready bargain between what faculty members are willing or prepared to teach and what a sufficient body of students are willing or prepared to learn. We have expanded to mass higher education without many ideas about how to reach the unprepared students who are simply there as bodies or absent as semi-truants. Faculty members in general know little about what, if anything, might interest such students, and understandably fear that exploring this might lose them their more wide-awake and sophisticated students. Given both the pattern of curricula and the time budgets of faculty, it is difficult, for example, for a professor to tell an undergraduate that he will help him learn something about blues music if the student will prepare himself by acquiring both a basic musical literacy and some historical understanding of folk cultures. What generally occurs in place of such an intricate negotiation is a tacit over-all bargain based on the mutual indifference of uncommitted students and overworked faculty, in which the former learn to put out a certain amount of effort to grab the grades necessary to practice committee work, marriage, and subtle reprisals against employers and institutions, thus allowing the faculty to feel justified in their neglect of such students. Under such arrangements, some

---

[12] See Burton R. Clark, "The 'Cooling Out' Function in Higher Education."

students become active dropouts, often leaving with a feeling of defeat, while others become psychic dropouts who, with whatever resentment or self-blame, feel that high culture is not for them.[13]

Two Experiments in Non-elite Education

The apparent lack of impact on the uncommitted student of the programs of the great state universities has led in recent decades to a variety of proposals for reform. Occasionally, the assumption is challenged that a college education is everyone's right (or even duty), and it is argued that the state universities should follow the lead of the elite private ones in restricting undergraduate enrollment to the academically adept and motivated.[14] But even the private universities are not able to hold entirely to this restriction, particularly where black and other minority students are concerned. Proposals for restricting access, going as they do against the egalitarian grain, seem to us to have extremely limited political prospects of success. Furthermore, egalitarianism has the ironic consequence of making it difficult to give status to post-secondary alternatives such as vocational and technical education, home study, and in-service training. High school graduates in general want to attend a "real college," just as on graduation from college they want to find white collar jobs which retroactively justify their having gone to college. If blue collar occupations lack status even though they may carry high incomes, their educational programs are not likely to confer status, no matter how well they may be run. Indeed, if the educational preparation for a particular calling is much superior to life in that calling, the result will not be to raise the

[13] The "dropout" could instead be defined by how far he got rather than where he left off. One could imagine a society in which people did not feel the pressure to attend college and in which there was no stigma to dropping out. A subsociety of this sort already exists among highbrow anti-intellectuals and Bohemians, who glorify those who do not attend college and denigrate those who are too well educated. For one expression of such attitudes, see Peter Marin, "The Open Truth and Fiery Vehemence of Youth: A Sort of Soliloquy"; Paul Goodman's position is more ambivalent, as in "The Present Moment in Education."

[14] For an unsparing critique of the "service-station university," see Jacques Barzun, *The American University: How It Runs, Where It Is Going.*

prestige of the calling but to disorient and disillusion many of its practitioners.

While some post-secondary programs have moved in the direction of professionalization in the hope of providing another avenue toward careers outside of regular collegiate programs, some massive state universities have taken another tack: believing that the answer to the question, "Who shall be educated?" is "Almost everybody," they have developed programs of General Education in the hope of connecting with freshman and sophomore students who have not yet decided on a vocation or enrolled in a professional school. Minnesota and Michigan State set up what were in effect separate colleges for these students, hoping that interdisciplinary programs might attract such students until they could find themselves academically. A somewhat less specialized and often less senior faculty, although not necessarily one more ingenious in awakening the undergraduates, was recruited for these programs—a faculty that, as at the private universities of similar organization, has tended to become second-class in prestige.[15]

One of the two institutions analyzed in this book, Monteith College of Wayne State University, represents a late dedication to the General Education movement. That movement seems to us to rest on the assumption that, if students are not enlightened, it is the fault of the faculty, not of such alibis as the poor motivation or incompetence of students. (Robert Hutchins seems to have been impartial in blaming both students and faculty for the failure of the American people to take part in the Great Conversation.) This attitude had a certain appeal in the great state universities, which from principle or politics felt it necessary to accept local students without requiring College Boards or similar screening.

But in some of the state universities another response to the problem of numbers and quality has been the development of

[15] For a discussion of the desuetude of traditional General Education programs at Columbia, Chicago, and Harvard, and of the problem of having a teaching faculty at the same institution as a research- or graduate-oriented faculty, see Daniel Bell, *The Reforming of General Education: The Columbia College Experience and Its National Setting;* see also Martin Trow, "Notes on Undergraduate Teaching at Large State Universities."

honors programs or honors colleges, which collect a minority of talented students to nourish each other and to provide at least a few faculty with the opportunity to teach students as talented as those to be found in an elite private college. Occasionally the honors program provides residential facilities, more commonly a center and special counseling, and commonly also relative freedom from curricular requirements. Michigan State, Texas, Kansas, Oregon, and other universities have used their honors programs to recruit National Merit Scholars and other capable students, and hold these out as bait for talented faculty. In the less distinguished and sometimes in the merely massive state universities, such programs have served to give shy academically inclined students the feeling that they are not alone, not oddballs, as well as to give some faculty the opportunity to move at a faster and more exciting pace.

But there have always been critics of the honors approach who say that it removes from the classroom some of the most stimulating students and thus has no effect or perhaps even a negative effect on the great majority of non-honors, average students. Especially after Sputnik, in 1957, there was a crescendo in the academic chorus that contended that students had insufficient demands made on them and were going soft. A post-Sputnik movement wanted in effect to bring the honors college model to non-honors students to see whether, by intensive teaching in small classes, such students could not be brought a long way from their mindless and relaxed frivolities. The aspiration given visibility in the founding of Oakland University as an offshoot of Michigan State was the redemption of the average student in terms defined by the post-Sputnik critique of American educational laxity.

A dominant cadre of the founding social science faculty at Monteith had been influenced by the University of Chicago program and indirectly by the ideals of the Hutchins College although with a less restrictive view of content (all books did not have to be Great) and a greater openness concerning classroom styles. The initial Oakland faculty had no particular academic model, but many admired the curricular and the academic intensity of such elite liberal arts colleges as Columbia, Oberlin, Swarthmore, Wesleyan —all primarily residential institutions. One way of defining the idealism of both new colleges is to say that they hoped to bring to commuter education some of the high academic status generally associated with the New England private colleges that in turn modeled themselves on Oxford and Cambridge.

Indeed, it has been a widespread assumption in public as well as private institutions that distinguished education would have to be residential education. Many private, once-commuter colleges have built dormitories to recruit a national clientele; for example, Boston College and Boston University have moved in this direction, thus drawing students of higher incomes and usually higher SAT scores. A few institutions have remained distinguished although dependent principally on local commuters: UCLA and the University of Minnesota are examples. And before the development of what amounts to a national market for able students and faculty, some urban commuter colleges in the 1930s benefited from the poverty and élan of local residents—notably the New York City colleges and, to a lesser degree, Wayne State. (Today, of course, the children of CCNY graduates move easily into selective colleges in the Ivy League and elsewhere.) Oakland and Monteith accordingly began with the recognition that they would not appeal to the most talented students from their immediate surroundings, let alone students from elsewhere; the ablest students would continue to seek out residential institutions, including the University of Michigan.[16] But the new colleges rejected the apparent corollary—that they would have to resign themselves to an imitation collegiate life, a low-level vocationalism, and a generally unintellectual atmosphere.

[16] There is a small proportion of elite students who could get into selective colleges and who could afford to go to residential ones but prefer to attend a local commuter institution; a few such students would be found at Oakland and Monteith. Perhaps they turn against the status struggle of parents and peers or have personal ties in the local area. Sometimes such students move into off-campus digs in their home city (as with Bay Area students who move to Berkeley). This pattern is more likely where the local university has a distinguished faculty. For some students from elite families, it may seem less shameful to commute to the local college than to admit that one did not get into one's ancestral Princeton or Mount Holyoke.

In the aspirations of the two new colleges, there was an element of revivalism, both in an effort to return to plain living without frills and in a perfectionist hope that a mass of unselected students might somehow be redeemed. Monteith would go back to a smaller scale of things and to a more coherent curriculum, Oakland to the supposedly sterner discipline of a hardier, less affluent America. As we shall see in more detail in Chapter IV, not all the recruits interpreted the ideals in the same self-denying way. Yet the ideals did provide one basis for recruiting and selecting faculty, including some who had struggled in vain on behalf of similar ideals, at more established and inert institutions. It was clear that, at least in the initial years, all the students at Monteith and the vast majority at Oakland would be undergraduates, and the majority of these, underclassmen. There is little overlap between missionary idealism and sainthood, however, and those faculty members drawn to these two institutions shared the self-doubts, the narcissism, and the resentments common to academic and other people who are supposed to be creative, independent, and original. Often they fought within themselves and with each other, and despaired both of their students and of their joint efforts. Even so, their degree of involvement in building a new institution served to reduce somewhat their chances for personal visibility through publication and through circulation in their disciplines. We believe that both fiction and social science have tended to overstate the marketplace careerism of academic men and to understate the elements of idealism, the interest in teaching, and the missionary spirit.

Of course there are many different missionary spirits. The post-Sputnik rationale for rigorous, ascetic education has considerably receded, along with the waning in academic and liberal circles of concern with the Cold War. (At times it almost looks as if hedonism has become a new crusade. Today the idea prevails that effort and production are no longer needed to keep the economy and society going, and indeed may be antithetical to more humane values and to greater social justice at home and abroad.) It will become clear in what measure Oakland has changed to respond to the new mood. Monteith's mission turned out to be more in line with today's moral imperatives, particularly with the demand for a manageable undergraduate community with highly personal faculty-student interaction. Many of the faculty at Monteith sought to create a vivacious peership between students and faculty, which would be divorced from academic departments and the ways in which knowledge has traditionally been organized in the university. Yet by the same token, Monteith presented its students with a highly structured and, for the most part, entirely required curriculum. It was, of course, recognized that students might resist the program, "voting" with their feet to indicate their span of attention, the amount and intensity of work they would do, and the careers they would choose. It was not anticipated that students would become a visibly politicized lobby for attacking educational requirements, often winning the right to go their own way and offering new ideological justifications for the old elective system.[17]

Because it was self-consciously conceived as an experiment, Monteith College in a number of ways adumbrated the contemporary cultural climate. Many of its faculty, unlike Oakland's, were early recruits in the war against what they considered academic specialism, unalleviated meritocracy, and mindless technologism. They were concerned with "the whole student," with his affective life and his local roots as well as with his disciplined learning and his future career. And because Monteith is a collegiate option in a large state university rather than, like Oakland, a separate institution altogether, it could afford a kind of experimentation that Oakland never attempted, with the assurance that students for whom this was unsuitable could find alternatives within other parts of the same university.

Indeed, Oakland did not begin as a self-conscious experiment but was initially planned to become a full-fledged university in an area previously without any institutions of public higher education. It was intended by its Michigan State University founders to be

---

[17] Of course the student revolt goes well beyond this, rejecting even the mild constraints of the elective system in favor of the free universities and programs that reduce the authority of the instructor and of the institution to grade, sift, certify, and evaluate.

distinguished rather than distinctive. In practice, this meant going East to recruit some of the first faculty. For the most part, these were scholars who would have been acceptable at leading American institutions, private or public, but mostly, in fact, with backgrounds in selective private education. What then turned into a *de facto* experiment was the encounter or, more appropriately, the collision between this faculty and their commuter students.[18]

Both institutions have succeeded with some of their students in transforming the aspirations with which they came so as to permit movement to a new level of competence and sophistication. Both colleges have failed with large numbers of students, either through savage standards and high flunk-out rates (Oakland's early problem) or through selective attention to some sorts of students as opposed to others (in some measure, Monteith's problem). The difficulties that both colleges have experienced indicate how wide is the gap between the dream of education for all and the reality. That gap has always been wide, but larger and more massive institutions can hide it from themselves, as Monteith and Oakland could not.

We have already indicated our judgment that the dream is unlikely to be surrendered, at least in the immediate future. To the extent that Americans seek college as virtually the only route to a good job and to a feeling of personal worth, limited entry will be regarded as morally intolerable. Every effort is now being made by cultural stimulation and financial inducement to increase enrollment of previously deprived cadres, notably ghetto blacks, but also Hispano-Americans and, to a very small degree, American

[18] Michigan State, like many good state universities, is highly selective of out-of-state students and also highly attractive to them (including many National Merit Scholars and Finalists). Wayne State admits students with a "B" average in high school, which of course means different things in different high schools. Both Michigan State and Wayne, like the still more selective University of Michigan, are less accessible academically than the community colleges and regional universities such as Eastern Michigan University, which were until recently teachers colleges. Eastern Michigan University in Ypsilanti was too far for commuting for many of the students who turned up in the first years at Oakland, as was the two-year college in Flint. Other than Wayne, the city of Detroit has no public institution within its borders, having repeatedly voted in referenda against establishing community colleges.

Indians. While it will take a longer time for poor rural whites
and urban Italians to press for the same opportunities, such awakening seems likely. Furthermore, state universities are in competition
within their own state systems with newer and more local institutions,
and if they insist on restricting access only to the enterprising
and the talented, they will suffer in the competition for state funds.
Indeed, if they want to be able to accept any considerable number
of out-of-state students, and most of them do, they must remain
reasonably open to in-state students. To the degree that the federal
government steps in to help finance the increasingly high cost of
higher education, it is likely to do so on a per capita basis or
through grants and loans given directly to students, thus further
facilitating open access.

Yet as higher education inches toward universality, it faces even
more the unsolved problem of how to cope with massive semi-
captive audiences of semi-adept students. One procedure, already
being followed in some measure, is to assume that serious and
esoteric studies will not be pursued until after the baccalaureate
degree, justifying college as a rite of easy passage either for cynical
reasons or as a kind of distributive justice. Another answer is to
attempt what Oakland and Monteith have done: to expect more of
the faculty and students and to take seriously the possibility that
with greater effort and intensity a process of mutual assimilation and
influence could occur.

II Origins: Oakland University and Post-Sputnik Education

The Initiating Actions

The University of Michigan at Ann Arbor has been the pre-eminent academic leader throughout Michigan's history, the institution to which citizens have looked for social prominence, often in preference to Ivy League schools, the place where most of the state's leading lawyers and many other professionals have been trained. In racing to catch up with and even overtake Ann Arbor, Michigan State University is one of the academic success stories of our time. It was established in 1855 as the first land-grant college, and at its centennial published a history recounting its successes in agricultural extension, the related sciences, graduate work in all fields, and recent overseas projects.

The growth of the Detroit metropolitan area quite naturally began to attract the interest of Michigan State—and indeed of all the major Michigan universities, sensitive as they were to possibilities for both their own expansion and that of their academic rivals. Oakland County, bordering Detroit's Wayne County, is typical of many fringe areas that are moving from exurban to suburban uses. There remain gentleman farms with rolling pastures and attractive rail fences owned by wealthy auto makers, the relics of a day when the locale was thought to be too far for regular commuting. One of the most impressive of these farms was Meadow Brook Farm, the estate of Mr. and Mrs. Alfred G. Wilson. In 1932, Mrs. Wilson had become a member of the Michigan State University Board of Trustees, reflecting, perhaps, the fact that she belonged to one of the first families of wealth but not of social prominence in the state; she took her duties very seriously and served a six-year term. In 1956, she and Mr. Wilson offered Meadow Brook Farm to President John Hannah, one of the more visionary, enterprising, and strong-willed of recent academic leaders.

Around the same time, the University of Michigan set up a senior college branch in the city of Flint in which the graduates of Flint Junior College could enter a two-year institution, the University of Michigan at Flint; and acquired a second satellite when the Ford family estate at Dearborn, on the outskirts of Detroit, was offered to it as a site for a college. The launching of Michigan State University at Oakland gave notice that MSU would match any colonizing ventures of its main competitors.

The Wilsons' gift, along with a small amount of land received earlier from another patron nearby, put sixteen hundred acres of attractively landscaped real estate into the University's hands, including several magnificent horse barns. The Wilsons added two million dollars for the construction of classrooms and other buildings, a bonus that allowed their land to be converted quickly into the seat of a college.[1]

So far as we are aware, the Michigan State founders of Oakland did not plan it to be a satellite in any sense, but an independent institution. The tie between the two institutions would allow Oakland to receive funds from the Michigan Legislature in order to

---

[1] Mr. Wilson died in 1963. Before her death in 1967, Mrs. Wilson served Oakland as a *grande dame* and patroness, opening her house (very much a showplace) for student balls and administration receptions—providing a certain link with a vanishing past of baronial munificence. She left this house at her death to the University—the kind of place that is now so often an embarrassment to the legatee.

get started, but it would have to recruit students within commuting range on its own.[2]

In Pontiac, five miles west of Meadow Brook Farm, there is a small denominational college, and in the adjacent small town of Rochester, a denominational junior college; but at Oakland's inception, there was nothing nearby to serve the working class students who were not prepared for the long commuting trip to Wayne State, the University of Detroit, or the University of Michigan. Colleges are not always founded where needed, but frequently, like small businesses, are established more by booster spirit than because of market research. Mrs. Wilson herself, however, according to one of the Oakland administrators, had learned that the Oakland County Planning Commission had uncovered a great need for higher education in the county.

President Hannah has become known as a maker of college presidents; a number of men who worked under him have gone elsewhere, for example, to head the State University System of New York, and Southern Illinois, Hawaii, and West Virginia universities, as well as regional universities in Michigan. He assigned D. B. Varner, then head of off-campus programs at MSU and a man with excellent contacts in the state at large as well as in the Legislature, to take over the new campus.

Consumer Research and Product Planning

At this point, a survey was made to determine the market for higher education in Oakland County. According to the survey's report, there were fifty-four thousand people of college age in Oakland and adjoining Macomb counties in 1954; by 1970, with the expected influx from Detroit and the approaching teen-age wave, there would be one hundred thousand. While the well-to-do upper- and upper-middle class young people of the nearby suburbs would continue to attend Ann Arbor or the leading private colleges

---

[2] Presently, Oakland stands virtually autonomous from the parent, though sharing a common Board of Trustees as well as a supportive but non-interfering common President.

in the nation, the children of the working class and the lower-middle class could not be absorbed into the existing private junior college, the denominational college, or the institutions in Detroit that either required a B average for admission (as Wayne does), were Catholic and costly, or were, before the current net of freeways, too far for commuters.

The years since the end of the Second World War have seen a tremendous growth in free commuter colleges, both two-year and four-year; these colleges have responded to demand but have also helped to create demand. Until Oakland began, the children of the industrial working class of Pontiac seldom went beyond high school; a college nearby, it was believed, would help make higher education seem a possibility for them, as well as for lower-middle class suburbanites beginning to move into the area. It seemed reasonable to assume that these were good conditions and that a college could very well be located there.[3]

The leaders of Michigan State University were ambitious, however, and would not have been satisfied simply to establish another college serving solely locally defined needs, or even another upwardly mobile but still regional college such as Eastern Michigan University. Yet most public colleges must begin with a local base, whatever their larger aspirations. Chancellor Varner needed and wanted to take into account what high school teachers and officials

[3] Careful studies of the market for higher education have shown that, while the physical presence of an available college helps bring in those who would not have gone to college otherwise, it is not always enough; much depends on the way the surrounding culture defines the college. The Chicago Circle campus of the University of Illinois, built on the heavily Negro West Side of the city, has managed to attract until recently only about three hundred Negro students, despite intensive recruiting; it seems too academically and socially forbidding. (However, in spite of the tradition among Negroes to avoid junior colleges, a number of the Chicago junior colleges have become *de facto* black colleges.) When Federal City College opened as the first multipurpose public college in the heart of Washington, D.C., it was flooded with at least three times as many applicants from the black communities of the city as it could accept, and so it decided to choose its entrants by lottery; in this way, Federal City College underscored its academic availability to all comers.

in the area thought; he also wanted to know what prospective Detroit employers thought. But what local leaders think is not totally divorced from what national elites are saying, and recruiting a faculty would depend more on the latter than the former. The Chancellor arranged to meet academic men who had written about higher education to ask them what kinds of programs they thought would be desirable. He asked big businessmen what sorts of qualities they wanted to see in college graduates. Back at his home base, he consulted his Michigan State colleagues about what they would want to see in an institution if they did not have the limitations of traditions, alumni, and tenured faculty.

A Citizens' Advisory Board—which eventually became the Oakland Foundation—was formed in 1957, with members drawn from the local counties and from Detroit. It included businessmen, a lawyer, school superintendents, the Oakland County Supervisor, a former member of the Michigan State University Board of Trustees, two people identified with labor, and the mayor of a nearby community. These people were called upon to lend their financial support (rather modest at the outset) as well as their influence with the Legislature and within the community. The publisher of the Pontiac *Press,* who became chairman of the Board, gave the college the publicity that would help recruit students, and the head of the Pontiac Division of General Motors lent his name and prestige.[4]

Oakland's high degree of independence from the parent university even at the outset reflected the confidence the Trustees and President Hannah had in Chancellor Varner, and the support he could mobilize in the State Legislature. The Citizens' Advisory

---

[4] Pontiac has helped support the *Oakland Observer,* the student weekly, by taking a full-page advertisement in each issue. Business people dominated the Board in the early years. One of the academic planners of Oakland explained to us that at the beginning they feared the bitterness, which still existed, between auto magnates and the UAW. Since then, some important union people have been drawn onto the Board; Ken Morris, UAW Regional Director, is on the Executive Committee of the Oakland Foundation. (A top UAW official has been chairman of the MSU Board of Trustees; another serves on the Wayne State University Board.)

Board was another indication of autonomy vis-à-vis MSU.[5] The
Michigan State Board of Education did not come into existence
until 1965, and up to the present provides only loose supervision
over the network of state institutions. Oakland enjoyed the freedom
of a rather leisurely rate of growth—a situation rarely to be found
among new public colleges in areas of growing population. Thus
somewhat buffered against local and state-wide constraints, Oakland
was relatively free to choose among going educational ideals in
the nation as a whole. Yet as our book will suggest, carrying out
an academic plan runs into many of the same problems as carrying
out any other plan where one must depend on voluntary co-operation. Goals that appear to be shared are variously interpreted; students turn out not to want what they are said to want; the market
situation for both faculty and students changes. On one theme,
Chancellor Varner and the other founders of Oakland felt that
there was a certain amount of consensus in the country at large:
colleges should be more rigorous and demanding; they should make
no concessions to youthful hedonism and slackness, nor to such
symbols of a collegiate culture as athletics and fraternities. This
was the post-Sputnik atmosphere in the media and among businessmen and academicians, but it is probable that it was never as
widespread as it seemed at the time. Moreover, men who are
consulted about other people's academic institutions are very commonly ethnocentric in what they propose: having little sense of
local context, they push their own favorite remedies, which may
not be suitable. (One of the assumptions such consultants often
make is that there will be plenty of money and plenty of time
to try out new ideas, when in general neither can be counted on.)

One influence upon the original cadre from Michigan State was
the sustained interest of President Hannah in improving under-

[5] The branches of the State University of New York are all under the supervision of the Regents and the Chancellor's office in Albany, but are free
to appoint local councils, which, like the Oakland Foundation, permit mobiliz-
ing some local support as well as perhaps transmitting some local pressures.
Similarly, a California state college such as San Diego State has an advisory
board even though it is under the jurisdiction of the State College Board of
Trustees and its Chancellor's office.

graduate education. In the face of MSU's monstrous size (when we last looked, there were forty thousand students at East Lansing), he sought to create residential complexes of modest scale, such as the "living-learning units," that is, dormitories in which under-graduates have classrooms and faculty have offices; later, after Oakland's founding, MSU began to set up non-honors cluster colleges geared to specific areas and organized around a residential base. In the planning of Oakland, however, there was no specific mandate for innovation in undergraduate education, although it was taken for granted that Oakland would care about its teaching mission even if this meant some subordination of research and community service.

The plans began to take shape with a ten-member Program Development Committee chosen from the Citizens' Advisory Board and headed by the vice-president in charge of engineering at one of the major auto companies. Like many of the new breed of managers, he was a believer in general non-vocational education as against narrowly vocational training, an outlook reflecting both the realization by leading businessmen that they could handle vocational deficiencies better through on-the-job training than through often obsolete university courses and the recognition that the grad-uate programs in business administration at Harvard, Carnegie Tech, MIT, Stanford, and elsewhere were superior in quality to their more diluted undergraduate imitators. The Committee members opted for the development of business administration and engineering programs geared to the basic sciences, and for a program in teacher education that would provide the minimum of education courses and the maximum of work in the liberal arts.

It is interesting to see the degree of compatibility between the goals proposed by leading businessmen and those welcomed by both the academicians Varner consulted and those he initially re-cruited. Entirely absent was the notion much in the air today that young people are under excessive pressure, that they need a moratorium to explore their identities, a breathing space before plunging into graduate school or career. However, some of the consultants were hostile to what they regarded as premature vocational commitment, asking for a broad education in the humanities and sciences—not for identity-search but so that students might become cultivated, good citizens. Probably, the businessmen were less hostile to preprofessional undergraduate work than were some of the academicians, but top managers were already opting for the liberal arts. Thus the new college was seen as a place for cultural and academic upgrading.[6]

The Committee arranged a series of meetings, the Meadow Brook Seminars, with men of national stature in adult education and in the four major areas of the curriculum, including such men as Samuel Brownell, former United States Commissioner of Education and later Superintendent of Schools in Detroit, Milton Eisenhower of Johns Hopkins, and Lee A. DuBridge of California Institute of Technology. The Committee took advantage of the momentum that Sputnik provided. Sputnik legitimated arguments that had been around for a long time, against both collegiate indolence and narrowly vocational programs: the achievement of Sputnik was interpreted as the result of hard work and of superiority in basic science as well as in technology. There is perhaps no inherent link between an ascetic view of higher education and a rejection of undergraduate vocational programs, except that in both cases there is a certain snobbery toward what first-generation college students and their families expect. However, the founders' implicit assumption that Oakland's students would not need to be trained for low-level technical jobs took for granted a democratic and non-elitist view of higher education in which there was plenty of room at the top for those whose general education had obliquely prepared them for top managerial positions or the more elevated professions.[7]

[6] One difference, however, was in the attitude taken toward Michigan State itself: members of the Program Development Committee, as an Oakland administrator later put it, "suggested that the new college be named Michigan State University at Oakland," because they thought the prestige of Michigan State useful, whereas for many academicians the tie was viewed as a liability.
[7] In this, Oakland may have outrun its presumptive students and their presumptive employers. Everett Hughes has made the comment that a small business may acquire executives trained at one of the leading graduate schools of business before it can "afford" them. Ways of doing business that may be

At the same time, it was taken completely for granted that Oakland was not to be an elite college, that it would *admit* students rather than *select* them. While some of the original advisers counseled taking in only the top five per cent of high school graduating classes, such an approach would not have brought the new college enough students within commuting radius; and this proposal seems not to have been considered seriously. Indeed, in a later comment concerning Oakland, John Hannah referred to the land-grant tradition as one that had "brought higher education down from the ivory tower and placed it in elbow-contact with the people," changing the course of educational history in this country.[8]

With a commuter population, Oakland had little immediate need for big-time sports. By boasting of absences rather than presences, it appealed to the ascetic streak of American patricians and of some of the less affluent. Furthermore, a "generalist" program is a money saver as compared, for example, to a curriculum cover-

---

efficient in the long run for a large operation may be too elegant for survival in the short run. Furthermore, one might even argue that specialized work in a particular field, provided it is taught with intensity, is at least as good a preparation for high-level executive or professional work as a general education program in the genteel tradition. Assessments here tend to be loaded by the class background or ambiance of students in one or the other kind of program. We do not know any studies that sort out these elements in assessing the impact of education on later careers.

[8] John Hannah as quoted in "A Clean Slate and a Free Hand: Michigan State University—Oakland." It is a common assumption of scholars as well as publicists that the land-grant tradition had the Populist, anti-traditionalist quality that John Hannah ascribes to it. However, it seems evident to us that the land-grant colleges sought to develop the same academic departments as their older private and public competitors. Alvin Johnson describes in his autobiography *Pioneer's Progress,* how he studied the classics at the land-grant University of Nebraska at the turn of the century. Just as it is hard to persuade a Nigerian or Philippine university to concentrate on tropical medicine rather than brain surgery, or on agronomy rather than theoretical physics, so the faculty members of the land-grant colleges found little resistance even from parents and taxpayers to what in moments of Populist rhetoric might be described as esoteric academic frills. The farmers' and mechanics' children who found the land-grant colleges socially and academically accessible seldom planned to return to their parental trades, and accepted a curriculum that looked forward to their hopes rather than one that appeared to condescend to their backgrounds.

ing all the subfields of engineering.[9] Here, the fact that Oakland was planned initially to be a relatively small college, as public colleges go, made possible economies that could be advertised as virtues.

On the liberal arts side, Oakland developed a curricular plan that specified that at least one half of a student's total time would be spent outside his major area of specialized interest. At first, Oakland did not have departments, only divisions of social science, natural science, and humanities. Yet, so far as we are aware, in the original curriculum no effort was made to explore possible experimental or interdisciplinary programs of the sort that foundations are apt to back (and did back at Monteith) or of the sort that had become rather frozen in MSU's General Education program. Rather, there was to be a full roster of liberal arts courses. One faculty member was not too far off when he described Oakland as aiming to be "the Oberlin of public education." Of course, not every faculty member had this aim, or what might be called the Admiral Rickover aim of an all-out attack on slackness and softness in American education. Different missionary strands combined so that in time Oakland developed its own character, which was somewhat more modest, more plausible, and far more pluralistic than the post-Sputnik ideology, which found a resonant audience in 1959.

The Image of Oakland and the Post-Sputnik Mandate

Repeatedly Chancellor Varner has denied that Oakland ever had a reformist bent: it was to be good of its kind, but not of any particularly new kind. His self-effacement is deceptive. Old

[9] Historians teaching a General Education program out of a small array of classics can insist on a large library only in terms of their own research, but only marginally in terms of training lower-division undergraduates. Engineers must begin with the heavy equipment needed in a number of fields, provided that the college starts big enough to try to cover those fields. To be sure, as Beardsley Ruml and Donald Morrison argue, many small colleges do try to cover fields with only minuscule student enrollments, thus dissipating resources and lowering faculty salaries. Ruml, *Memo to a College Trustee: A Report on Financial and Structural Problems of the Liberal College;* see part 4, by Donald H. Morrison, "Achievement of the Possible."

faculty hands at Oakland credit him with guiding the institution in subtle ways while playing down his own role. In the face of objections from some of the men he brought with him from Michigan State, he defended what really was distinctive about Oakland, namely, the effort to bring highbrow academic-intellectual culture to an almost totally commuter student body from non-cosmopolitan backgrounds. At the same time, Chancellor Varner's tendency to self-deprecation allowed his public relations man to play a large part in shaping the national image of Oakland—one that had almost no impact on the recruitment of students, although it may have had some on the recruitment of faculty members and their interpretation of what they were brought to Oakland to do.

Sputnik was launched in October 1957. It gave men like Arthur Bestor, Admiral Rickover, and other long-time antagonists of progressive and permissive education a larger audience for their critiques. In their view, mass education neither sought excellence nor gave it a chance. That Oakland tied itself to this view of things was mainly the work of Tom Fraser, who had become Assistant to the Chancellor on the strength of his experience on the education news staff of a leading newspaper, and who later wrote his own syndicated column on educational news.[10] A more open and avowed idealist than many newsmen, Fraser brought to his work at Oakland a commitment to the post-Sputnik critique; he wanted to see Oakland make a break with traditional indulgence and narrow student careerism. As he declared:

> The only exciting thing about this place is a commitment to a liberal arts education of the highest quality. Since 1875, American education has been going toward career education. We have to move in the direction of liberal arts. We here are marching down a road in the opposite direction from most universities.

Fraser's proclamations of no compromise were what gave the Oakland image its appeal. Americans are easily victimized by the

[10] Here, as stated in the preface, we are using "cover names" to protect individuals.

demand that they should stand for something; similarly, they are easily stampeded by the idea that their institutions should have a single purpose, presumably the original, declared, and pure one. Oakland under Fraser's big public relations drive created a purpose for itself while it was still in the early planning stages.[11] Fraser's articles for Detroit and Chicago papers emphasized the spirit of pioneering and reform with such descriptions as "a new kind of university," "Michigan State at Oakland, a pioneer in education," "the Oakland unit of Michigan State is really new."

It is likely that this kind of overselling would have been checked had Oakland begun with a larger staff for administration and planning. Chancellor Varner characteristically favored a small staff, which made it possible for his newspaperman assistant to portray his dream of Oakland with minimal restraint from a group of colleagues. Long after Fraser departed from Oakland, the legacy he helped to frame remained, a legacy that can perhaps best be described as capitalizing on opposition to what many Americans regard as the effete traditionalism of the Ivy League and also to the muscular mindlessness associated with the collegiate style. Both the Redskin and the Paleface were to be rejected. One unintended consequence was that some Oakland faculty came to believe that their university would forever avoid massiveness, intercollegiate athletics, and similar vulgarities, so that when, for example, Oakland moved into intercollegiate basketball in gingerly steps, this was regarded as a betrayal of the original ideal.

Publicity is always a two-way street, and the reporting in the press on Oakland reflected what made a good story, for example that the Chancellor's office would be only ten by twelve feet and would lack the usual carpeting or drapery. One newspaper story said, "A visitor is given the impression of Athenian ideals and

11 The Meadow Brook Seminars were widely publicized, and the press was called in after each of the five conferences. *Life* mentioned Oakland approvingly in an editorial on mass culture. *Time* gave it sympathetic coverage. Publicity of this sort, though scorned as "Madison Avenue" and "commercialism" by academic and other snobs, is essential to the viability of virtually all non-profit institutions; Oakland's difficulty arose from long-run side effects of a campaign that was spectacularly successful at the outset.

Spartan surroundings." A slightly different note appeared in one Michigan journal's headline: "New Branch of Michigan State Gets Under Way: Strictly Business." In one of his articles, Fraser wrote, "For its students, Oakland will have the appeal of a drugstore that sells only drugs, not even patent medicines." (It would be an interesting question to discover how many of the students who actually came to Oakland had ever seen an apothecary shop!)

It was emphasized that the students would be required to learn either Russian or French, and one news story had it that the engineers would be advised to take Russian (although, so far as we know, they never were). It seems surprising that the stories did not refer to what, from an educator's standpoint, was one of the most significant innovations: lack of any mathematics below the level of calculus. Similarly, the original plan to have no "remedial" or "bonehead" English composition in the freshman year but to begin with the study of literature was in keeping with the post-Sputnik insistence that the colleges force better preparation upon the high schools. Every student was to take a required curriculum of University Courses, consisting of two year-long courses in Western Institutions and Western Literature in the freshman year, a year in Non-Western Studies, a year of science and mathematics, a four-semester sequence in social science, plus a foreign language and one term of music or art. There was also a slot for a Senior Colloquium, which would entail independent work cutting across academic disciplines (the Senior Colloquium did not materialize until 1968).

Incipient Conflicts

In one of his press releases, Tom Fraser spoke of the Renaissance man as Oakland's ideal. Latent in this image was rejection of certain kinds of scientists who wanted to teach their subjects only to those who were going to pursue them as a career and not as part of everyman's equipment. Indeed, although many of the great Renaissance men were, among other things, scientists and even tinkerers, the term today is more often used by men in the humanities to describe their kind of person than by chemists or economists. To be sure, the tough, hard scientist and the cultivated humanist can be allies against narrow vocationalism, the cult of sports, and the other deprecated aspects of American youth culture. Both could defend an Oakland that, as Fraser declared, would stand at "the opposite pole from the life adjustment school." Both could agree with the remark, quoted by *Life*,[12] that the new college was "not interested in producing well-rounded men, but men with sharp, abrasive edges, rebels with clear minds and uncowed consciences, critics of society, not adjusters to it," and the statement in the New York *Times*[13] that Oakland, "reversing the trend to vocational training . . . is to be a liberal arts college of highest quality—but one to develop the abilities of the average good high school graduates rather than of the highly selected elite."

On these issues, most of the faculty could agree. But on others, differences were there from the outset. The Chancellor's own deference to men in the humanities with an Ivy League background influenced his choice of Dean Richard Lane, a professor of English and professional defender of the humanities, who became Varner's first academic superego. Varner's Texas background and lack of the doctorate (he has an MA in economics from the University of Chicago) perhaps made him fear to seem overly practical. Lane stood centrally and polemically for the values Fraser was promoting. Born in Iowa, he had attended Coe College, one of the good, small Iowa colleges, and then had gone on to Yale for graduate work. Like many Midwesterners, he adapted readily to the Ivy League, and when he became vice-president of the American Council of Learned Societies he was a well-established professor of English at Stanford. As a national spokesman for the humanities, he took his place alongside his friend Jacques Barzun in defending the more select and autonomous as against the more sprawling and community-oriented aims of the university.

Both at Oakland and, as we shall see in the next chapter, at

---

[12] October 5, 1959.
[13] June 7, 1959.

Monteith, the phasing of the General Education program has had decisive consequences for the entire flavor of the institution even to this day. Whereas at Monteith the social sciences occupied a large part of the opening year, at Oakland the first-year emphasis was on the humanities. Western Institutions, literature, and languages were all to be started in the freshman year, while most science and social science courses would be taken after the first year. Consequently, of the twenty-three faculty members recruited for the first year, fifteen were in the humanities. While this balance altered in later years, it was one element in the faculty's relentlessly rigorous standards and in their snobbishness toward the local community. The great majority of the faculty were in no way prepared for the students. The Admiral Rickover doctrine assumed that student learning and morale were matters of voluntarism. With enough will, people could be inspired to great achievements— and scared out of failure and slackness. We do not regard the doctrine as completely wrong, certainly no more mistaken than its relaxed opposite; but adhered to fanatically, it presaged a collision course with the expectations of the local community.

Oakland in the Local Community

Chancellor Varner had brought with him a small group of administrators from Michigan State, including a Registrar and a Dean of Students. These men, while not denying that Oakland would differ from its parent institution, remained loyal to the ideals of Michigan State and of the Big Ten in general. Similarly, people nearby, not attuned to the national press, either regarded Oakland simply as the college next door or saw it as a geographically convenient branch of MSU. Thus, the editor of the Pontiac *Press* (whose president and publisher was one of the leading members of the Citizens' Advisory Board and later became an active fund raiser for Oakland) wrote an editorial in January 1958 emphasizing not only the high quality of the prospective college but also its physical proximity, observing that a year's attendance at either Michigan or Michigan State would cost approximately sixteen hundred dollars. "That same boy or girl," he wrote, "can live at home and attend Michigan State at one fourth of the same cost." He concluded that Oakland County would have a college at the same high level of Michigan State.

It may be difficult now for many readers to recall the bitter competitiveness (and the glamour of applied science) during the Cold War, when the Soviet Union was the enemy and Oakland's program could be described as "a Space Age curriculum." Attitudes of this sort helped to promote Oakland nationally, but for Oakland's own students and their immediate circles, the national rhetoric had virtually no impact. The students were a bit like people who might find themselves unexpectedly drafted into the Marine Corps when they had expected to be passengers on a cruise ship. Some students did respond positively to the rigor and toughness, as some Marine recruits do, but those who did not make it seldom felt this way, nor did their friends, relatives, or high school teachers. Fraser later reported how he reacted to their criticism:

> I wrote a letter to the high schools around here asking "Is Oakland too tough?" pointing out that if a college or university is not tough, students are being cheated. The reaction has been good. People are apt to say "Throw it to them! Make them work!" It's the reaction to a too permissive attitude.

To say that the reaction was good, Fraser must have been marching to a different drummer: many of the high schools that had counseled their students to attend Oakland were bitterly resentful of faculty reactions they regarded as snobbish and punitive. The high schools in the area had not been touched by the movement for secondary school reform that has been led by men like Zacharias of MIT, Kemeny of Dartmouth, Holton of Harvard, Biberman of Illinois, and other eminent mathematicians, physicists, and educators, later joined by biologists and social scientists.

The students who came from local high schools[14]—over three

14 Appendix A contains data on the geographical sources, high school ranks, fathers' education, fathers' occupation, and curricular choices of the first Oakland entering class.

quarters of the first entering class came from Oakland County itself—had been prepared in schools of no particular distinction where, in almost two thirds of the cases, they ranked lower than the top twenty per cent of their high school graduating classes. Twelve per cent of the fathers were college graduates, while almost two thirds came from families in which fathers had not attended college; most of the fathers' occupations were working class or lower white collar. In line with these backgrounds, the curricular choices of the students included thirty-five per cent in teacher education and twenty-four per cent in engineering, with twenty-eight per cent in the liberal arts.

Contrary to the implication by the editor of the Pontiac *Press,* many of these students would have had a rough time indeed in the liberal arts programs at Michigan State in East Lansing, even though some might have found more manageable curricula in the undergraduate professional schools. For that editor, Michigan State stood as a beacon of academic repute, but it is not extravagant to say that for most of the faculty attracted to Oakland at the outset, Michigan State's reputation was at best ambivalent: the go-getting, football-happy, cow-college *arriviste.*[15] Since our interviews with Oakland faculty did not take place until the institution's second term, we do not have the most immediate accounts of what drew many of the first group Varner recruited. We have the impression that very few realized that the students they would get would regard Oakland as the available college, much like any other: a means of entry to a white collar occupation such as teaching or accounting or engineering.[16] Faculty members

[15] We trust that it is already clear that we do not share this sort of deprecation. The question must always be asked: What is done with the upward academic mobility that an institution gains, in part by football? Michigan State has done a fair amount; so has Notre Dame. Many private colleges and universities, turning away thousands of underprepared students, can ill afford to sneer at the colleges that accept such students and try to work with them. For an account of a semi-fictional university whose president, very different from John Hannah, sought to transform football prowess into other sorts of eminence, see William Manchester, *The Long Gainer.*
[16] One should not overestimate the ability of upper-middle class children and their parents to make discriminating college choices. Retroactively the

saw a prospective curriculum that looked reasonably familiar in the light of their own liberal arts backgrounds, but failed to appreciate the degree to which students lacking in any cultural sophistication would find such a curriculum alien, even intractable. In the wealthy nearby suburbs such as Birmingham and Bloomfield Hills, young people were not attracted to Oakland at the outset, for even if they could not get into one of the elite colleges or rebelled against them, they would find Colorado or Berkeley more glamorous alternatives.

The small administrative group that came to Oakland from Michigan State knew something about the local high schools and the local outlooks. They were aware that Oakland County was not Detroit and that its high schools were not as good as the best high schools in Detroit (this was before these schools were affected by the exodus of whites from the inner city); they also knew that the county's population contained many migrant southern fundamentalists who had come to the auto plants. They were aware that, except for the Detroit exurbanites, there were very few people of upper-middle class tastes.

To some faculty, all this did not matter, because Oakland was the best job they could get; they would have to take the students as they found them. Others had persuaded themselves that dedicated teaching could awaken the culturally deprived and that it was possible to demand a great deal of such students and to get it. Still others assumed that an unselected student body would not be so very different in academic terms from those at Wesleyan or Columbia—a fantastic error. The conflict of expectations raised the danger that the new intellectual and avant-garde faculty might become so tough and so unintelligible as not to connect at all with the majority of their students. Conversely, had the faculty been fully and realistically briefed on what they were to find, there

choices often look more calculated and sensible than in fact they were. Even at the graduate level, there is often much irrationality in the choices students make in terms of what would be the best match for them; they seldom employ even the limited opportunities for consumer research available in published sources or through knowledgeable insiders.

might have been the opposite danger of overadapting to a mass student body in such a way as to risk too little in terms of confrontation, creating a satellite college that would be smaller and more intimate than Michigan State University but would lack its interest and variety.[17]

Most likely, had they truly known what they were getting into, many of the faculty would not have come to Oakland at all. Once having made the decision to come, however, they were compelled to face the students, and they reacted with almost unchecked intransigence. Here the faculty, not the students, were the confrontationists, and their attitude presented Chancellor Varner with a terrible dilemma. Direct administrative interference with curricula and grades set by individual faculty members would have been considered a scandalous violation of academic freedom, a pandering to community incompetence and self-indulgence, and a surrender of Oakland's initial aspirations. It would have made it difficult, if not impossible, to recruit future faculty at the same level of academic excellence established by the charter group. The relaxation of stringencies that, a decade later, would be made on behalf of black students and others, would in practice have meant that Oakland would become at best another mediocre regional university with a reputation limited to Michigan. Furthermore, the Chancellor, like other administrators, was troubled by the fine line between authoritative and authoritarian leadership and tended to avoid both in seeking to avoid the latter. Only slowly, as we shall see in the discussion in Chapter VIII on the grading crisis and the way it was overcome, did it prove possible to turn Oakland around and reconcile student qualifications and faculty expectations.

[17] Albert O. Hirschman describes development projects in the new nations in somewhat similar terms, arguing that if people had realized the obstacles, they would not have started; but having begun, they often find unexpected ways around the obstacles. This is the paradox not of the invisible, but of the "hiding hand." See Albert O. Hirschman, *Development Projects Observed*.

III Origins: Monteith College and Anti-Departmentalism

The Context for a New College

In the period after the First World War, what is now known as Wayne State University was part of the Detroit public school system. The city colleges of New York, notably CCNY and Brooklyn, sent on to graduate study an extraordinary number of ambitious scholars and were noted for the radicalism of a small but vocal minority of students. In lesser degree, Wayne had something of the flavor of these colleges. Like them, it catered to commuter students from immigrant families of a wide ethnic range—not only Eastern European Jews, but Italians, Poles, and Negroes from a polyglot city. Wayne soon became a university, starting or acquiring colleges of Medicine, Law, Business, Engineering, Pharmacy, Education, and Nursing. After the end of the Second World War, when it was clear that the city could no longer carry the institution financially, a good deal of maneuvering culminated in its conversion to a state university, a process completed by 1956.[1] Freed from the regulations governing secondary schools, Wayne rapidly developed

[1] The incorporation of Wayne into the state university system is part of a more general movement in the state and nationally. In Michigan in recent years, what were once local teachers colleges have become regional universities, such as Western, Central, and Eastern Michigan universities.

a new identity as a university catering not only to local students of relatively underprivileged backgrounds, but also to the state and nation as a competitor in the league of major research-oriented state universities (though in its share of state funds, it has remained behind both Michigan and Michigan State). An engergetic university press was established. New faculty were recruited to the College of Liberal Arts who aspired to develop nationally visible programs of graduate training and research. At the same time, Wayne hoped not to lose the ties of its professional schools and many of its faculty to the Detroit metropolis, which now contains nearly half of the state's population.

The old Wayne had grown in a ramshcakle way by converting run-down houses and office buildings in what, despite the handsome public library and the art museum nearby, was already becoming a slum on the edge of downtown Detroit. However, as part of a process of university renewal, Wayne built in the 1950s the spectacular contemporary buildings designed by Minoru Yamasaki, a Detroit architect who has gone on to do academic buildings elsewhere.

The President of Wayne, Clarence Hilberry,[2] under whose auspices the architectural renovation began, was also the sponsor of Monteith. While Oakland's founding was tied to MSU's state and national ambitions and to national self-criticisms concerning educational deficiencies, Monteith's beginning was somewhat more intramural. Some senior faculty members in the College of Liberal Arts, anxious about changes in emphasis away from undergraduate teaching toward graduate teaching and research, could depend on the support of their friend President Hilberry in a program that would not precisely run counter to Wayne's new look, but that would preserve something they thought valuable in Wayne's old look. Unlike Oakland, Monteith can trace its origins to a founding document or charter, "An Experimental College at Wayne State University" (later, because of its cover, called "the Gray Document"), written by the members of a committee with a strong

[2] Like his predecessor, David Henry, and successor, William Keast, Hilberry had been a professor of English before becoming President.

home-guard commitment to Wayne itself, over and beyond their interest in their specific disciplines. Obviously, this local development also reflected the anxiety that was being generated nationally about the rise of specialization and the neglect of lower-division undergraduates.

New ventures get started in both academic and corporate life by turning to indispensable and overemployed men—on the supposition, frequently correct, that the busiest man will get the most done—and by drawing in men who at a particular point in their careers are looking for a new activity.[3] One of the initiating trio at Wayne, Floyd Murphy, professor of history, was a department chairman with many obligations. But his two colleagues, Donald Pearson, a professor of English, and Sidney Karr, a mathematician, were in situations of somewhat less pressure. All three were senior men without the need to fight for tenure, friends who could draw upon each other for the necessary work.

Academic administration is a calling without a career line, at least at the loftier reaches of the academic procession. The very nature of the academic career provides a certain looseness, symbolized by the absence of time clocks and the (often only apparent) minimal number of required contact hours. Traditional patterns of business or public administration would in any case seem unsuitable as models for the organization of a college or university faculty, for these notably anarchic individualists tend to resent any formal hierarchy, and since the "products" of their work are difficult to measure, especially as teachers, to the point of being impalpable, control would in any case be difficult.[4] In the era when Oakland and Monteith began, men trained in the humanities were common

[3] Only rarely does a university have available a "stockpile" of potential executives such as the peacetime Army may have. In a study of business corporations some years ago, Edith Penrose, a Johns Hopkins economist, concluded that one source of corporate growth was the stockpiling of executives who had to find something more to do and occasionally founded a new division or expanded an old one (personal communication).

[4] For a description of academic organization in these terms, see Talcott Parsons and Gerald M. Platt, "The American Academic Profession: A Pilot Study"; Talcott Parsons, "The Academic System: A Sociologist's View."

choices for presidencies and academic deanships of liberal arts colleges and of many universities. Such men seldom have major grants for research projects, and in subjects like English and history they are as likely to have taught service courses to large undergraduate cadres as to have taught specialized seminars for their research acolytes; they may be somewhat less mobile and more oriented to teaching than natural scientists or the more quantitative or empirical social scientists.[5]

Two of the members of the committee that pioneered Monteith were in the humanities: Donald Pearson, the professor of English who later became Dean of Monteith, and Floyd Murphy. Sidney Karr, the mathematician, later became chairman of the Monteith natural sciences staff and Associate Dean. Mathematicians are the hundred-yard-dash artists of the university, and the "over thirties" often turn to working in applied areas of mathematics or to writing texts; occasionally, some find a renewed interest in educational as against strictly mathematical problems. Karr had many friends in the humanities. Pearson, Karr, and Murphy, while disagreeing in emphases and details, regarded overspecialization at the undergraduate level as a calamity. They remained devotees of General Education when many ambitious new recruits in the College of Liberal Arts at Wayne were seeking to move in exactly the opposite direction. In the Meiji Restoration, the protection of tradition was attempted through the partial incorporation of modernity; in a way, the founders of Monteith could be seen as restorationists in the guise of educational innovators.

In order to understand the intellectual history of the Monteith

[5] Until recently, moreover, men in the humanities were perhaps somewhat more apt to come from Anglo-Saxon backgrounds than were those in the newer fields such as microbiology or sociology. Such recruitments are changing —and such backgrounds are no longer *de rigeur* for college presidents. One can also find a number of political scientists who have become administrators, perhaps in part because they were attracted to the field by an interest in power and because the kind of work they do broadens their ability to communicate with non-academic people. Furthermore, since many natural scientists at an early age pass the point where they enjoy doing firsthand research, a small stream of educational administrators comes from the natural sciences.

idea, it is necessary to see something about the background of the individuals who were responsible for it. Chief among these was Donald Pearson, who was born in Oklahoma, son of a Baptist minister. After attending a local denominational college, he took a master's degree in English at Missouri and a doctorate at Yale. His first teaching job was at Dartmouth, and then for three years he was at the University of North Dakota before coming to Wayne in 1936. Looking back on his experiences, he told us that he felt much more needed at Wayne than in an Ivy League college; at Wayne he found "a lot of bright kids who had been poorly prepared." He arrived at Wayne with "a bright bunch of young [faculty] people," as he put it. "We became a good university at that time." His colleagues included David Henry and Clarence Hilberry, both of whom went on to become university presidents. Staying on during the Second World War, Pearson found himself teaching contemporary American literature to an audience composed principally of undergraduates. After the war, when a new "bright bunch of young people" arrived, Pearson defended General Education against departmental specialists; in doing so, he spoke both for himself and for an earlier Wayne—which had been his Wayne—and he was willing to commit himself to an unfanatical yet sufficiently forceful crusade on behalf of a new academic venture.

Pearson's ally, Sidney Karr, born in Philadelphia, had attended high school in Detroit and then Wayne before it became a university. He took a doctorate in mathematics at the University of Chicago, returning to teach at Wayne, by this time a four-year college. Karr described himself to us as having been a bookish undergraduate, as much interested in philosophy, Lester Ward, or Herbert Spencer, as in mathematics and the sciences; once on the faculty, he joined a book review club whose members included Pearson and the historian Murphy. His concerns were campus-wide, not only departmental.

Further support for innovation at the undergraduate level came from some of the deans of the Wayne professional schools, who, as Donald Pearson later remarked, felt that the faculty in the College of Liberal Arts were more concerned with teaching their own specialties than with giving students a foundation of general education in order to allow them to go on into the college of Law or Medicine or Engineering. Some of the deans may even have hoped that a new undergraduate college would recruit better prospects from the high schools, who would then be inclined to continue their professional education at Wayne. Pearson was encouraged by a Wayne vice-president to look around the country and write a report on General Education; out of this came the committee to which he co-opted Sidney Karr and Floyd Murphy.

Up to this point, the idea of a separate college hardly existed. And without money from outside, it never would have.[6] Wayne's President, confronted with the gap between the institution's growing ambitions and its resources, had been in touch with Clarence Faust of the Ford Fund for the Advancement of Education. (Faust had been Dean of the College of the University of Chicago.) He mentioned to Hilberry his conviction that most Americans were going to be educated in urban state universities; hence it was here that the need for experimentation was greatest. He would like to see General Education and a liberal arts focus within such universities, but he believed that this would require, as at Chicago, an independent college faculty. The officials of the Ford Fund were also interested in encouraging a program of General Education in a commuter institution that would attempt to lower costs through the development of independent studies among advanced undergraduates and thus make it economically feasible to have small freshman and sophomore classes with a staff of average size.[7]

The hint was enough. Plans for a new college were drawn up, primarily by Pearson, Karr, and Murphy, who had formed the earlier Committee on General Education at Wayne; these men produced

[6] For discussion of the role of outside support in inducing change in universities, see David Riesman, "Planning in Higher Education: Some Notes on Patterns and Problems."

[7] While this aspect of Monteith was featured prominently in the Gray Document, its importance was not emphasized in the development of the College beyond the initial planning stages. Only Karr and Pearson ever mentioned this aspect of the plan in our interviews; other faculty were unaware of Monteith as an experiment in university economics.

the Gray Document. The themes expressed in the document are not especially startling to the weary reader of educational prose. Of the new experimental plan, it stated:

> It is an effort to impart to undergraduates, particularly those in training for the professions, that common body of ideas and knowledge that every educated man should possess.[8]

As outlined in the Gray Document, and as it was later carried out, the curriculum was to consist of three sequences, which would account for about half of a student's program in the first two years, one quarter in the junior year, and one half in the senior year: Man and Society; Man and Science; and Man and the Arts. There were to be a two-year sequence in the natural sciences, and year-and-a-half sequences in both the social sciences and the humanities (which would begin in the sophomore year). The timing of these sequences and the amount of time allotted to the entire program reflected complex negotiations to fit into the existing requirements of the other colleges of Wayne. The program would allow students from the very outset to select the rest of their courses from either the preprofessional curricula at the University or from the College of Liberal Arts. The plan specifically eliminated the usual freshman English composition course (as well as a foreign language requirement), since all faculty members in the new college were to be concerned with the quality of students' writing as well as with their own substantive areas. This was innovative, but not unique. In addition to the core courses, students would be required to take an interdisciplinary Senior Colloquium.

It was also anticipated, although only vaguely articulated in the Gray Document, that some students in the new college would have

[8] In his brilliant book *The Reforming of General Education: The Columbia College Experience and its National Setting,* Daniel Bell analyzes the belief that there is such a common body of ideas and knowledge that should be taught in a General Education curriculum; he argues that, with a few exceptions, it is rather process and method that should be taught. See also Martin Trow's discussion "Conceptions of the University: The Case of Berkeley."

no specific program in other colleges but would find a four-year program mainly at Monteith. Such a program would be filled out with specialized tutorials in the new college and with suitable additions from the College of Liberal Arts. Thus a Monteith student who wanted a course in Slavic, Far Eastern history, or in any other specialty, would have to forage for it in the College of Liberal Arts, since Monteith would have no specialized departments. By the same token, the basic Monteith courses would not be any one person's private property, thus departing from the general assumption in elite colleges that academic freedom includes the faculty member's prerogative to determine his own reading lists, the scope of coverage, and the way "his" course is to be run.[9] Following the lead established by Alexander Meiklejohn at the short-lived Experimental College at the University of Wisconsin, the Gray Document proposed that a particular epoch, such as fifth-century Athens or twentieth-century America and Europe, would be the subject matter of all three courses.[10] Thus, in one course the science of a particular period would be discussed, in another the arts and literature, and in still another the cultural, political, and economic structures.

Meiklejohn's Experimental College and its Berkeley analogue,

[9] In such a college, since a course is a professor's own domain, his name is attached to it in the catalogue and it is not given when he is not there or goes on to some other interest. While Oakland in general follows this model and, with the exception of the Western Institutions course, taken from the Columbia College program, has never spelled out specific mandates for the courses faculty members offer, nevertheless the catalogue does not attach names to courses; this reflects the fact that Oakland suffers from cliff-hanger budgets, which make advance scheduling almost impossible. Staffing of the required university courses at Oakland is done by persuasion of individual faculty, not by setting up a two-class faculty—of the indentured, and of the privileged who alone can offer "their own" courses. In non-elite public colleges, in contrast, work is more apt to be organized in terms of assuming certain courses will be taught and leaving it to a hierarchy to commandeer the personnel to teach them.

[10] Joseph Tussman, Professor of Philosophy at Berkeley and a former member of Meiklejohn's Experimental College, created in 1966 the "Tussman College" on a similar ground plan. The College was designed as a two-year program, with an entering class of 150 volunteer freshmen; thereafter, students would enter the upper division as regular academic majors. See Tussman, *Experiment at Berkeley,* and further discussion in Chapter XIII.

Tussman College, have selected from among volunteers. The Wayne and Ford Foundation founders of Monteith were, however, determined that it was to be open to any students eligible for Wayne itself, and not a selected group. A genuine experiment such as the Foundation wanted would require a student body different in no measurable way from Wayne's regular clientele.

At the time that Pearson had come to Wayne and Karr had studied and taught there, it was a homespun commuter institution geared to the children of Detroit's lower-middle and working classes. At that time, however, these young people from working class families who made the conscious choice to attend Wayne may have had a somewhat stronger motivation for college work than their successors, who come at a time when finishing high school and attending college are more common in the same social strata. Thus there was an implicit faith (and an implicit misjudgment) in the Gray Document's assumption that vocationally oriented students of the Eisenhower era could be interested in fifth-century Athens and in the other general courses. The men who drafted it were aware of slippage in the Wayne at which they taught but seemed to feel that this could be overcome by intensive teaching in small discussion classes. Monteith was thus intended, not as a sieve for sorting out students for future academic distinction, but as a step in everyman's emancipation, whatever vocation he might later choose.

Since it was planned for about twelve hundred students, Monteith would be too small for many economies of scale but would seek instead economies of phasing. The freshman classes would be small, with much individual attention at a time in a student's career when it is most needed, while upperclassmen would be put increasingly on their own.[11] By the time of the senior year, classes would be large or eliminated altogether: thus, all students would

---

[11] Although its separate faculty would not in principle imply the absence of teaching assistants, it was clear from the outset that Monteith faculty would share equally in the staff-taught courses, and that those courses that came later in the sequence would not recruit a more senior or in any other way different faculty. (In The College of the University of Chicago, there was some tendency for the staff of the freshman courses to have less prestige than those whose courses came later in the sequences.)

be required to do the final term in one of the three sequences on their own, without the support of the two discussion-group meetings each week.[12]

The Gray Document anticipated contemporary themes in both its discussion of student autonomy through independent work and its insistence that Monteith be kept a small college with small classes,

[12] During the same period, the Fund for the Advancement of Education made a grant to four Connecticut Valley institutions—the University of Massachusetts, Amherst, Smith, and Mount Holyoke—to draw up a blueprint for a new, small college that would explore the economies and possibilities of independent student work. The four-college committee consulted many outsiders (the first author being among them) and produced a widely circulated proposal, *The New College Plan*. An early instance of reaction against large General Education courses and core programs, the report emphasized "training students to teach themselves" by studies in depth in freshman seminars. The student, not a program of courses, should "cover" a subject, his competences to be demonstrated in field examinations and individual research projects. A relatively small course offering, changing constantly in response to faculty and student interests, was to be supplemented by reciprocal opportunities for enrollment in courses at the neighboring institutions. The goal was to avoid tying up faculty time in "complete" departmental offerings—each faculty member offering only one course, of his own choosing—so as to free faculty time for supervision of seminars and independent student work.

After a long hiatus without support for building such a college, substantial funds were pledged by an Amherst alumnus for the creation of a fifth Connecticut Valley college. Some of the original ideas have been revived, together with a new emphasis on involvement with the larger community and on wholeness in human development, in the course of the planning for Hampshire College. (See Franklin K. Patterson and Charles R. Longworth, *The Making of a College: Plans for a New Departure in Higher Education.* Several further planning documents dealing with main subject areas are available from Hampshire College, at Amherst, Massachusetts.)

New College, in Sarasota, Florida, began operation in 1964 with a similar emphasis on independent study. We believe that these institutions are likely to discover that so-called independent study is rarely independent and not inexpensive. Encouraging students ambivalent about independence and torn between antagonism toward and overdependence upon adults to engage in independent work in a sustained way requires a great deal of faculty thought and effort. (For a sympathetic discussion of the dilemmas facing freshmen at Harvard, see "Testing and the Freshman Year.") Indeed, Monteith faculty soon realized that, while independent study had been presented in the Gray Document as not only virtuous educationally, but as economical also, they were often spending more time with students taking independent terms in their divisions than they spent on their "regular" students.

enabling students to identify with a specific community.[13] Small classes, a special Student Center, attention to individual students, close monitoring of student reactions to the College, were all set out in the Gray Document as antitheses to "the great complex of buildings and programs which constitute the large urban institution called 'Wayne State University.' . . ." This insistence on the college as a community is particularly striking in view of the commuter students it would draw. Many such students would have their emotional center of gravity at home or among their non-college friends in the neighborhood; most would have outside jobs; many would think of themselves first of all as prospective teachers or social workers, and not as privileged youth searching for knowledge or identity. Monteith College was expecting a lot from students whose allegiances would be divided.

The Fund for the Advancement of Education had granted Wayne seven hundred thousand dollars to be matched by the University, for the development of Monteith over a five-year period. A program of evaluation and review, the Monteith Program Study, had been embarked upon at the very outset. With enthusiastic backing from President Hilberry, the University Council endorsed the College, fending off opposition from the College of Liberal Arts by declaring that the program would be reviewed by the University faculty when the five-year grant ran out.

As we have seen, some of the deans and other administrators of the Wayne professional schools, sensitive to criticism of "slide-rule morons" and the "trained incapacity" attributed to engineers and businessmen by leaders of the professions, saw Monteith as a way to enlarge the horizons of recruits into their schools. The Department of Civil Engineering (a field with very low prestige in contrast to electrical or aeronautical engineering) made Monteith compulsory for all its entering students, while the Medical School set aside twenty-five places for Monteith students. Neither of these arrangements proved durable. The dean of a professional school might be sympathetic to Monteith while his faculty were indifferent; with

[13] See the discussion in Theodore M. Newcomb, "The Nature and Uses of Peer-Group Influence."

more experience, some professional-school faculty became actively negative. This was true in Engineering, where the original liaison fell apart, and in the Medical School, which found the Monteith intake more problematic than anticipated. Of the major professional schools, only Education has remained committed to the Monteith idea.

Least sympathetic of all were some of the departments in the College of Liberal Arts. Monteith would be a competitor for able and venturesome students and, at least when the Foundation grant ran out, for scarce resources.[14] In some measure, Monteith exists as an implicit critique of the very focus on specialized work and graduate training toward which the Liberal Arts departments have been moving. Monteith was probably less threatening to Liberal Arts faculty as critique, however, than as scandal—it was seen as an embarrassingly amateur enterprise by those seeking to improve Wayne's standing and standards. Perhaps the most outspoken antagonism came from scientists, men over whom President Hilberry had limited or even negative influence. They asked what sort of scientific training students would receive who learned about science in fifth-century Athens, or from nineteenth-century chemistry or physics, but who were not prepared for advanced work on the contemporary frontiers. Floyd Murphy's support prevented outspoken hostility from the History Department, and there were pockets of support elsewhere in the humanities. But the English Department was troubled by the lack of freshman composition courses. This meant that there would be no place for graduate students to pay their way by taking on this teaching; as Pearson said, "We were taking away their bread and butter." To do away with freshman composition seemed at once pretentious and irresponsible. Probably the most receptive and the least threatened were the social science departments. But even there, the desire for professionalism produced

---

[14] Monteith is in fact not frightfully expensive, and the resources Monteith uses would not necessarily go to the College of Liberal Arts if Monteith were abolished. Its students would cost Wayne something to educate anyway, and places would have to be found for its tenured faculty. For the most part, Monteith uses as a joint cost the circumambient facilities already present at Wayne.

skepticism, which the first appointments to the Monteith social science staff did little to dispel.[15]

Without support from President Hilberry and the top administration and what Pearson called "treaties with the professional schools," Monteith might have been prevented from existing by the veto power of the departments. Once it had begun, however, the Dean of Liberal Arts decided that he wanted to be in on the project and agreed that seventy students from among applicants to his College be invited to attend Monteith. These were to be recruited by sending letters of invitation to every fourth or fifth applicant. But this reluctant acquiescence did not dissipate the continuing hostility of Liberal Arts faculty. What was happening was what Gusfield has termed a "symbolic crusade," a struggle to define the kind of place Wayne was to be—and such crusades are the most deadly, because the interests involved cannot be bought off.[16]

Recruitment of Students

Monteith College had no Tom Fraser. At the outset, Donald Pearson preferred to designate himself not Dean, but simply Director of the triumvirate of heads of the humanities, natural sciences, and

[15] In the recent study by Talcott Parsons and Gerald M. Platt of professors in different types of institutions, faculty at universities that are rapidly upgrading themselves experience the most conflict between teaching and research, and generally lead more stressful professional lives than their brethren in more established institutions or in lower-quality and less ambitious ones. Much of the opposition to Monteith from Liberal Arts faculty can be traced to the great pressure—and consequent insecurity—under which Wayne faculty operate. See Talcott Parsons and Gerald M. Platt, "The American Academic Profession: A Pilot Study."

In the undergraduate colleges of some of the elite universities, departments may make an effort to provide a liberal education in their specialty both for majors and non-majors. They are not afraid to do this, because they assume that the necessary technical adeptness will come in due time and that graduates will not be handicapped for lack of expertise. This possibility of General Education in a specialized subject tends to be overlooked when, as at Wayne and generally in the United States, arguments polarize between the proponents of General, that is, non-specialized, Education, and departmentalists insisting on professional competence.

[16] Joseph R. Gusfield, *Symbolic Crusade*, especially Chapter 7.

social sciences staffs. Moreover, he was not present during the first year of the College. He has told us that he felt Monteith would face diminishing antagonism if he took a sabbatical that was coming to him during the initial year. (Since Pearson had suffered a coronary attack during the year of planning prior to Monteith's opening, many assumed that he took a sabbatical abroad on that account, rather than as an exercise in political tact.) On his return, his campaigning on behalf of Monteith, whether in Detroit or nationally, though assiduous, suffered from the fault of much good public relations in academia—pretending to be insouciant and casual. Moreover, Monteith was inhibited from recruiting students outside Detroit by its design as a commuter college within a commuter university, and to push it aggressively within Detroit and its suburbs risked intensifying the competition with the already resentful College of Liberal Arts at Wayne.[17]

To assure the appropriate number of entrants and also to achieve some degree of comparability with students in the College of Liberal Arts, invitations to attend Monteith were sent to a random sample of students who had applied to the various colleges of Wayne. Letters went out under the letterheads of the College of Liberal Arts, the College of Business Administration, and to pre-med and pre-law students, inviting every fourth or fifth student accepted into these programs to attend Monteith. Since students had the option to decline the invitation, it was not clear that the random invitation would work randomly. Yet, despite some unanticipated departures from the original design[18] and the presence of some fifty "self-starters" who had heard about the College and asked to come,

[17] The newly established University of California at Santa Cruz responded to a somewhat analogous dilemma by managing to secure favorable write-ups of its architectural and curricular designs in virtually all the major national media; it sent to prospective students a brilliantly understated pamphlet, "So You're Thinking of Coming to Santa Cruz," and in this way it avoided the gentlemanly ban on competitive recruiting by the branches of the University.
[18] Clerical errors and concern for settling anxieties about whether Monteith would get enough entrants from each college led to several departures from sampling criteria. See Sally Cassidy, Paule Verdet, Richard Schell, and Donald Campbell, "Evaluating an Experimental College Program with Institutional Records: An Interim Report."

the procedure did appear to produce an initial student body that was not too different from that at the College of Liberal Arts in social background and intellectual level.

Monteith students in 1959,[19] like students in the College of Liberal Arts, were drawn from Detroit and its environs and from about the same ranks of their high school classes. Compared to the freshman class at Oakland in 1959, Wayne State University students as a group ranked higher in their high school classes (thirty-six per cent of the Oakland students were in the top fifth of their classes, compared to fifty-two per cent of Monteith and fifty-seven per cent of Liberal Arts students). The fathers of Monteith students were somewhat more likely to be college graduates than the fathers of Liberal Arts students, and Monteith had a slightly higher percentage of students whose fathers were professional men. While it was assumed that a large proportion of the Monteith freshman class would enter one of the professional schools of Wayne as upperclassmen, it turned out to be somewhat smaller than the proportion entering the Liberal Arts programs. The Monteith Program Study examined some of the psychological characteristics of a sample of Monteith and College of Liberal Arts students and concluded that the Monteith students were somewhat more academic in their interests, better prepared,[20] and more adventurous than the average among Liberal Arts students—not particularly astounding in a group of students who viewed themselves as "guinea pigs" in an unknown college.

Some problems in student recruitment appeared early. As we have already noted, the effort to join the Monteith program with civil engineering did not succeed. Analysis of the grades of the charter group of engineers shows that they did less well than their

[19] Appendix B contains data on the geographical sources, high school ranks, fathers' education, fathers' occupation, and curricular choices of the first Monteith entering class and a comparable sample of College of Liberal Arts freshmen.

[20] According to standard Wayne State University placement examinations taken during the first weeks of the fall term 1959, Monteith students placed in the 65th percentile in Verbal Ability and in the 54th percentile in Quantitative Ability, while Liberal Arts students placed in the 53d and 48th percentiles, respectively.

Monteith classmates, even though they had been exempted from the sequence in the natural sciences, which had the most severe grading standards. Most of them transferred out of Monteith and, thereafter, civil engineering students were no longer required to attend Monteith. Few volunteered to do so in the following years. A later study of the academic adjustment of engineers at Monteith revealed that on every indicator—curricular adjustment, personal efficacy, maturity of goals, study skills, and so on—the engineers who did come to Monteith had more problems than either Monteith students in other majors or other students in the School of Engineering.[21] Despite all the efforts by leading spokesmen for engineering to make it a postgraduate profession and to follow the model of MIT and, more recently, of Case, Cal Tech, and Rice, to introduce the social sciences and the humanities to engineering undergraduates in a serious way, the "first generation" students who enter engineering are often allergic to what they regard as cultural bull. (Some of their old-time faculty are likely to give tacit support to this outlook.)

The problem of bridging the "two cultures" did not lie only with the engineers. A number of Monteith instructors were disdainful of engineering, and viewed with triumph the conversion of a bright would-be engineer to a social science or humanities major. They made no effort to encourage engineers to a deeper interest in engineering; and to the extent that these faculty members influenced the student culture, a civil engineer at Monteith must have found himself of as little value as an athlete at Antioch or Reed.[22]

[21] This finding derives from an unpublished report by Marybelle Boyle, "The Measurement of Some Self-Concepts of Entering Students."

[22] It is our impression from observing undergraduates at MIT that somewhat analogous tendencies operate, so that would-be engineers are encouraged to become physics or chemistry majors (and, presently, political science or humanities majors), in the same way that students with initial interest in medical practice were pushed (prior to the advent of medical school activism) toward careers as medical scientists in the research-oriented medical schools. The effort of a profession to make itself more highbrow often runs the risk that neophytes will abandon it altogether, while a failure to meet the aspirations of entering students may run the opposite risk of leading bored students to drop out or to change their fields entirely.

Chance Beginnings

Although we seek in this volume to generalize from two cases, we share the judgment of many historians about the large role that chance plays in human affairs. Macrosociological theories tempt one to generalize about large aggregates, but the life of an individual or of a small institution is less easy to subsume in this way. Chance played an enormous part in the development of both new colleges. Academic administrators in Michigan soon learn how much they depend on the ups and downs of the auto business as well as on the hazards of the two-party system; they must negotiate for both capital funds and annual budgets, not only with legislators but also with the State Board of Education and the Governor's Budget Office. At the outset, Oakland could be somewhat sheltered from these concerns by the umbrella furnished by Michigan State's Board of Trustees. Monteith was more protected still by its Ford grant and by the top administration and trustees of Wayne State. Thus it was possible for Donald Pearson to conclude that Monteith would not suffer and might even benefit if he took his sabbatical overseas; had Monteith been an entirely new college on its own, it could not have begun with a troika and probably not without a search for an experienced administrator-fund-raiser. Pearson was to head the humanities also, but since that sequence was not to commence until the second year of the College, he was free to postpone recruitment of staff and some of the curricular planning in that area. Sidney Karr became acting director in addition to his task of recruiting staff and planning curriculum for the natural sciences. This situation "accidentally" left a partial vacuum for an outsider, Alice Corrigan, whom Karr had discovered when looking for a chairman for the social science division.

Originally, there had been some hope that Floyd Murphy could be drafted to head the social science staff, but he made it clear that he wanted to go back to his writing and to his responsibilities as chairman of the History Department. His place as a draftsman of the Gray Document and hence as an initiator of Monteith had been taken over by a leading scholar in Japanese studies, Eleanor

Philotson, a woman of commanding talent, energy, and personal charm, a friend of the original trio, and a fellow member of the book review club. The possibility arose that she might become the chairman of the social science staff, but she was not interested and it was never pursued. At this point, Pearson (before leaving for Europe) and Karr took off for a tour of universities to see if they could find someone who met their specifications. Three people were eventually invited, and one of these, Alice Corrigan, won approval. She had come to Sidney Karr's attention rather fortuitously because his daughter was a student in the College at the University of Chicago (where, it will be remembered, Karr had done his doctoral work); on a visit to his daughter, Karr attended several classes, including one of Alice Corrigan's, of whom his daughter had spoken as a fine and competent teacher. Karr was impressed. It turned out that Miss Corrigan had had a good deal of experience with Chicago's General Education program and had once been head of the second-year social science staff. When she was invited to head the Monteith social sciences and to recruit a staff, the College acquired a balanced ticket—a Protestant (Pearson), a Catholic (Corrigan), and a Jew (Karr).

It was easier to recruit a social science staff in 1957–58 than it would be now. Alice Corrigan set energetically about the task, drawing on friends and colleagues she had known at the University of Chicago. Six of these met together in Chicago during the summer before Monteith opened to plan the social science curriculum. Later called the "secret six," this group was crucial not only to the social science staff but to the whole College. Several were friends who had known one another for many years, and the six contributed a degree of cohesion to the social science staff that was not equaled in the other divisions—in either numbers or solidarity. Because the humanities staff was not yet on the scene and the natural science staff was small,[23] social scientists constituted two

[23] There was a somewhat reduced need for natural science staff members, owing to the exemption of engineers from the natural science program and the particular ways in which students entering in February of 1960 were able to stagger their programs so as to begin with the social science sequence and postpone their natural science course.

thirds of the faculty in the first year. The implications of this fact rapidly became apparent; the social science staff moved immediately into a position of dominance. This meant that early decisions at Monteith were determined by a group of outsiders, none of whom (with the exception of Miss Corrigan) had been selected by the absent Director. The first action taken by the social scientists was to abandon completely the Gray Document's historical focus.

Even if Donald Pearson had been on hand the first year, it is likely that his unbusinesslike charm would have been no match for Alice Corrigan's energy in developing Monteith's particular atmosphere. Alice Corrigan and her group of lively intruders saw themselves as coming not to Wayne—they habitually referred to the College of Liberal Arts as "Wayne," as if they themselves at Monteith were not Wayne—but to a new venture, Monteith, which they felt to be of greater distinction. For them, the casual bonhomie of Pearson was a periodic irritant; but we think it likely that, without the home-guard attachments and non-abrasiveness of Pearson and Karr, Monteith might have had a more difficult time surviving beyond the span of the original grant. Conversely, many of the social scientists were an irritant not only to the parent institution but to those at Monteith who had some identification with Wayne. Nevertheless, without the newcomers, Monteith would have had less color, less distinctiveness. Like many symbioses, this interdependence was often cursed by each partner, in the way that many people suppose that if they could only go it alone, life would be glorious.

Make No Little Plans?

The tasks that faced the initial recruits to the three Monteith staffs were implicit in some of the assumptions in the Gray Document. It was assumed that average Wayne undergraduates would accept a required program with a carefully designed sequence of courses, not building up to an undergraduate major but to an all round amateur competence in three areas of General Education. Such an assumption would be questionable even in an elite residential college where the majority of students pursue a regular four-year program that is not generally intended to be terminal. Wayne undergraduates, however, are accustomed to gathering credits under the usual system of distribution, where a range of different courses taken in various orders can fulfill the same requirement. Yet it was known before Monteith was opened that the average undergraduate took eleven semesters to get a B.A. At Wayne, people readily transfer without feeling committed, and rarely become fervent alumni. This casualness is illustrated by the practice of taking part-time or nearly full-time jobs, even when these are not absolutely essential financially; college is itself in effect a part-time job.[24]

The original planners of Monteith were more realistic in their attitude toward the vocational aspirations of first-generation students: they were willing to make concessions, for example, to civil engineers, and they did not require that the liberal arts have hegemony, only a substantial share distributed through all four years. Nevertheless, the Gray Document assumed the willingness of potential students to postpone or sidetrack a vocational identity and to enjoy explorations in courses labeled "Man and Society" or "Man and Art." Even the largely upper-middle class students at St. John's College in Annapolis do not universally enjoy such explorations—there is an attrition of close to sixty per cent. To imagine that a student body, many of whom plan their courses to meet a car-pool schedule or a job at a nearby drive-in or department store, would find such courses appealing seems to us an act of rather innocent faith.

The problem of finding faculty who would want to try their hands at teaching such courses raised equally grave questions, which the authors of the Gray Document seem in retrospect to have taken lightly. They knew what sort of faculty they did not want: those who did research that appeared trivial, pedantic, or excessively specialized; and those who cared not at all about teaching and certainly had no interest in helping ordinary undergraduates appreciate

[24] When Wayne, to please the Legislature and to show its economy-mindedness, went on the quarter system in 1963, a good many students robbed it of potential savings by deciding not to drive in and out during the icy winter quarter, but to take a full-time rather than a part-time job and return to school in the more pleasant spring quarter.

Aristotle, Shakespeare, and Galileo. They assumed that they could find faculty members who would ask themselves not what the students could do for them, but what they could do for the students. Beyond that, such hopes called for the recruitment of a faculty with extraordinary evocative power and inventiveness in designing and teaching curricula to bridge the gap between the subcultures of the student body and the subcultures of the faculty.

IV Faculty Recruitment and Academic Careers

From William James to William Arrowsmith, critics have attacked what the former termed the Ph.D. octopus. College presidents have often bemoaned the stranglehold of the graduate schools over undergraduate colleges, believing that they must hire people not trained to do or to value undergraduate teaching but trained instead to do research that most of them will not go on with. There is now a handful of progressive or experimental colleges that, while not explicitly rejecting people with Ph.D.s, are critical of prevailing patterns of academic certification—particularly the widespread belief among faculty members that in general it is better to teach graduates than undergraduates, and better to teach career-oriented and committed students than uncommitted ones.

Both Oakland and Monteith started recruiting at a time when the critique of the graduate schools was much more muted than at present, and when the general drive of American academia emphasized quality more than equality. Not surprisingly, Oakland followed the conventional graduate school channels in recruiting its faculty. Although Monteith was an early entrant to the small group of good liberal arts colleges that pay less attention to the Ph.D., it, too, used the graduate schools as the source of its initial faculty.

We happened to overhear a telephone conversation between a faculty recruiter at Oakland and a potential recruit; afterward the man remarked to us that the candidate was a Columbia man, referring to where the latter had received his Ph.D., not where he had gone to college. No effort was made at Oakland to recruit people who had attended Columbia College, despite the fact that the Columbia College Contemporary Civilization Program, carried to Oakland by a man who had taught in it, played a considerable part in the College's required curriculum. Determined to plan a General Education program, Monteith in recruiting, however, did not focus on discovering faculty members who had attended as undergraduates innovative institutions like Antioch, St. John's (Annapolis), Swarthmore, or Chicago, though graduates of the latter two and of Reed did turn up there.[1] Indeed, no networks of friendship or of sponsorship going back to undergraduate days helped locate people at either Oakland or Monteith.[2]

Perhaps the very diversity and heterogeneity of American undergraduate education make it difficult to consider undergraduate experience as a basis for recruiting, particularly when the charmed circle of graduate schools that turn out most of the research-minded Ph.D.s is so small.[3]

[1] See Chart 1 on pages 62 and 63.

[2] The situation is of course markedly different in the United Kingdom, where a "First" at Oxford matters much more than any later honor or degree. See in this regard A. H. Halsey's account of the central role played by Oxbridge in the British structure of education at all levels. A. H. Halsey, "British Universities."

[3] The American Council on Education report by Allan Cartter indicates that the number of departments doing substantial graduate training known to be reputable varies among fields somewhere between fifteen and fifty. See Cartter, *An Assessment of Quality in Graduate Education.* To be sure, reputation is influenced by a halo effect which operates to raise the level of specific departments in universities that are regarded as distinguished overall, and to lower it in universities that are regarded as less distinguished, but the very fact that good graduate students are attracted to the places that have the better reputations creates a self-confirming effect, as these recruits socialize each other.

Because the major graduate schools are more selective than the average undergraduate college, they provide for a great many Americans a second

An undergraduate college with ambitions to distinction will seek not only to recruit its faculty from the graduate schools that stand high on Cartter's list (most of which are members of the Association of American Universities) but also to develop a combination of academic styles attributed in fact or folklore to particular eminent departments. For example, a new sociology department may want the empirical observation believed to characterize Chicago, the theoretical bent associated with Harvard, the comparative style of Berkeley, and the survey and research techniques characteristic of Michigan. At the same time, the newly minted graduate student will understandably want to know whether the hiring institution will permit him to function as a microbiologist, or a demographer, or a critic of modern poetry in his teaching as well as in his scholarship and research, and whether he will be in a milieu where others of the same persuasion will understand and support him. If the department that seeks him is building a mix, he will want to know whether the "schools" represented are of greater or lesser combativeness or exclusiveness. He will want to find out how his own inclinations may fare, and how widely he will be permitted to roam without being regarded as a trespasser.[4] However, the

---

chance where an elite graduate degree blots out the first degree. Of course, it is also true that it is easier to enter an elite graduate school from an elite undergraduate college, not so much because the name of the college carries weight as because its faculty are more likely to know people at the graduate institution and, as a result, write more effective letters of recommendation. For a systematic study of this process at the Harvard Graduate School of Arts and Sciences, see Humphrey Doermann, "Baccalaureate Origins and Performance of Students in the Harvard Graduate School of Arts and Sciences."

[4] Many critics of academic careerism underestimate the degree to which academicians, like other people, seek stimulating work, supportive colleagues, and responsive audiences. Though the quotations in Theodore Caplow and Reece McGee in *The Academic Marketplace* have the ring of truth and can often be duplicated in our own experience, their tone and that of the book itself overstate the cynicism and opportunism of the more mobile academic men who were the main objects of the study. (For a detailed analysis of many factors in the academic labor market, see David G. Brown, *The Mobile Professors.*) Such data might reflect the prevalence among educated Americans of a new kind of hypocrisy, which pretends to vice and covers up virtue, lest one be thought naïve or priggish. This hypocrisy ends up misleading

Chart 1

PRIOR EDUCATIONAL EXPERIENCE OF
FACULTY AT OAKLAND AND MONTEITH
(Interview Sample Only)

Oakland Faculty

Area	B.A.	M.A., Ph.D.	Recent Teaching
Natural Science			
1.	Seattle University	University of Washington (MSU)	Seattle University, MSU
2.	Berea	MSU	None (industry)
3.	California Institute of Technology	Princeton	MSU
4.	University of Illinois	University of Washington	Haverford
5.	Cornell University	University of Illinois	None
Social Science			
6.	Swarthmore	University of Michigan	Wesleyan
7.	University of Washington	University of Chicago	Chicago Teachers College, MSU
8.	Wayne	University of Illinois	MSU
9.	Pennsylvania State University	MSU	University of Florida
10.	Dartmouth	Harvard	Wesleyan
11.	MSU	MSU	MSU
Humanities			
12.	Georgetown	University of Chicago	University of Chicago
13.	Manhattanville	Columbia, Wayne	None (journalism)
14.	Fresno State	Columbia (M.A. only)	None (journalism, research)
15.	American University	Columbia	University of Alabama, Southern Illinois University
16.	Cornell College	Harvard	Stanford
17.	Belgrade University	Prague	None (social work)
18.	Moscow	Moscow, Hamburg	None (Radio Free Europe)
19.	Yale	Columbia	Vassar, Emory
20.	Skidmore	Brandeis	Brandeis
21.	CCNY	Columbia	Brandeis, Oberlin
22.	Wisconsin State	University of Virginia University of Wisconsin	None
23.	Columbia	Columbia	Columbia
24.	Mount Holyoke	University of Chicago	Wayne
25.	Beloit	None	None (journalism)
26.	Flint Junior College	MSU	MSU
27.	Texas A & M	University of Chicago	MSU
28.	(Not Ascertained)		

Chart 1 (continued)

Monteith Faculty Area	B.A.	M.A., Ph.D.	Recent Teaching
Natural Science			
1.	Wayne	University of Chicago	Wayne
2.	New York University	University of Minnesota	Minnesota, Industry
3.	University of Wisconsin	University of Wisconsin	University of Wisconsin
4.	University of Colorado	University of California	University of Michigan
Social Science			
5.	Wayne	University of Chicago	Merrill-Palmer, Wayne
6.	Manhattanville	University of Chicago	University of Chicago College
7.	Loyola (Chicago)	University of Chicago	Loyola
8.	Queens College	University of Chicago	University of Chicago
9.	Swarthmore	University of Chicago	Michigan State University
10.	DePaul	University of Chicago	None (research)
11.	UCLA, University of Chicago College	University of Chicago	University of Washington
12.	Reed	University of Chicago	University of California (Berkeley), University of Chicago College
13.	Boston University	Boston University	University of Michigan (research)
14.	University of Arizona	University of Chicago	None (research)
15.	Sorbonne (Paris)	University of Chicago	University of Chicago College
16.	San Diego State	University of California (Berkeley)	None
Humanities			
17.	University of Missouri	Yale	Wayne
18.	University of Pennsylvania	Wayne	Wayne
19.	Syracuse University	Syracuse University	Syracuse University
Administration			
20.	University of Wisconsin	University of Michigan	University of Michigan (services)
21.	University of Chicago College	University of Chicago	Wayne
22.	University of Michigan	Wayne	Wayne

attempt to create departmental Noah's arks by bringing together
representatives of different academic breeds was not pursued at
either Oakland or Monteith (though at the former, some thought
was given in the recruitment of the staff for the Western Institutions
course to finding men who could cover the various fields and
epochs of Western European and American history). In considerable measure, the original recruiters were selecting faculty in fields
outside their own domain. In any case, the number of people recruited initially was relatively small, limiting the possibility of developing a plurality of academic emphases. Neither college had enough
lead-time to consider carefully what sorts of faculty might contribute to filling out plans that were still vague. Yet it was this
hastily acquired faculty, once arrived on the scene, who would
take the control out of the hands of the founding fathers. Indeed,
academic freedom in the ordinary sense means that professors set
their own curriculum and judge each others' work as fellow professionals with only limited scrutiny from bureaucratic superiors, student or community clients, or other outside groups.[5]

If we look now at Chart 1, we see that no institution dominates
in the undergraduate training of the faculty. Indeed, no two people
at Oakland had attended the same undergraduate college, and the
twenty-two faculty members at Monteith represented nineteen different colleges. (There were two each from Wayne, Wisconsin, and
Chicago.) At the same time, if we look over the whole list of institutions, it would appear that both new colleges had in fact drawn
faculty who, in more cases than otherwise, had attended selective

---

men as to their own motives, since sounding "realistic" and "tough" is preferable to having obscure and Quixotic motives that might seem "sentimental"
—a kind of intellectual *machismo*. These buried motives might very well be
repressed in an interview with a bright and witty academic colleague. At any
rate, a study done in the middle 1950s is not likely to capture the presently
very evident revolt against careerism.

[5] For an analysis of this definition of academic freedom and its contemporary
lacunae, see Walter Metzger, "Academic Freedom in Delocalized Academic
Institutions." On the problem of getting faculty members to perform assigned
duties such as turning in class schedules or grades, as academic administrators
look at it, see Mark Ingraham, *The Mirror of Brass.*

undergraduate institutions.[6] It is our impression, although we lack the statistical supporting evidence, that the faculties to be found at most commuter colleges would have done their undergraduate work at less distinguished places on the whole. Conversely, the faculties at Oakland and Monteith appear to us to have been drawn from the same orbits that one would find represented in major universities and university colleges. If we are right, it is notable that men and women with "good" backgrounds were willing to come to new commuter colleges when many must have had other choices. It is also worth pondering what tensions might exist for them, given their backgrounds and the gap between these and their prospective student bodies. We are talking about a question of degree, of course, since there will always be some gap of this sort because no faculty is likely to resemble in status and style the general run of students at the college at which it is teaching.

We do not mean to suggest that there is any simple relation between the particular sort of education one has had and one's later outlook. All experience is in some sense vicarious, and an educational reformer just as likely may be someone whose own education seemed to him atrocious as someone whose aim is to give others the benefits he himself enjoyed. Moreover, faculty members may themselves "attend" an institution by teaching there: any college that sets up a genuinely new departure must in part train its own faculty.

We would be inclined to say that, in general, men and women of privileged educational background are more likely to be sympathetic to the poorer students than those who have come up the hard way through non-elite channels: the latter are likely to want to kick down the ladders they have climbed. There are exceptions either way, but it does seem clear that the ex-proletarian is not necessarily a better teacher for new generations of proletarians.

[6] An academic or social snob would not regard all these institutions as elite colleges, but almost all are within the orbit to which guidance counselors in good secondary schools try to direct their students. All were given Selectivity ratings of 60 or above—some were well above 60—in Alexander Astin's rating of 1015 four-year colleges and universities. Cf. Alexander Astin, *Who Goes Where to College?* (The mean score for the institutions is 50, with a standard deviation of 10.)

Thus one could not predict the conflicts Oakland and Monteith would have with their communities or student bodies from the mixture of faculty recruited.

Tensions *within* the institutions seem to us more predictable. For example, not only was the humanities faculty at Oakland numerically dominant at the outset, but eleven of the seventeen men in it came from private universities, with the exception of one who had done graduate work at Virginia and Wisconsin and another whose training had been at Wayne in addition to Columbia. Such men might be expected to have varying degrees of sympathy for commuter students, but not much sympathy for those faculty members at Oakland who had been at Michigan State University (including one who had been at MSU and was recruited from Seattle University, one of the less distinguished of the Jesuit schools). The non-humanities faculty at Oakland were likely to have attended state universities for their graduate work, seven of them in the Midwest and four at MSU. Correspondingly, the tension that developed at Oakland between the dominant humanities staff and the science minority reflects these somewhat different academic and, hence, cultural backgrounds of C. P. Snow's "two cultures."

At Monteith, the intrafaculty division took a different form. Six of the twenty-two faculty there had had prior experience at Wayne, three of whom, including Sidney Karr, had been at Chicago as well. In addition to his old friend, Karr, Donald Pearson brought two administrators and one instructor in humanities with him to Monteith from other parts of Wayne. But this group of people from Wayne were outnumbered from the start by a group from the University of Chicago: twelve faculty members had done graduate work at Chicago; two had degrees as well from the College at Chicago. This clustering occurred mainly in the social sciences: of the twelve members of that staff, ten had done graduate work at Chicago and five had either taught or been students in the College. All ten of the Chicago people on the social science staff had done graduate work during approximately the same period (1952–58); five of them were anthropologists who had known one another before. The recruitment of these close friends gave a degree of momentum to the staff that accentuated the impact of common experiences.[7]

We believe it was an advantage for Monteith that Alice Corrigan had a relatively free hand to recruit an initial cohort of social scientists with whom she felt compatible. Monteith had set out to present the academic disciplines in non-departmental fashion: there were to be no courses labeled Political Science 1 or Physics 1 or History 1. If the staff-taught sequences were to be more than simply additive, with the political scientist coming in to do his stuff for six weeks, followed in turn by the sociologist and the economist, some kind of non-traditional amalgam had to be worked out or borrowed piecemeal from somewhere—at Monteith in the social sciences, from the University of Chicago, which had pioneered in this style of teaching. The other two staffs, smaller at the outset and less cohesive, adopted the same model of a staff organization and joint development of materials. But as we shall see more fully as the story unfolds, there has never been any college-wide unity at Monteith, and perhaps, given the surrounding facilities and protection of Wayne as a whole, it was not necessary. As the humanities were dominant at the outset at Oakland, so with the social sciences at Monteith—and it is rare that a dominant group is loved when its power is only partial.

Academic Orientations and Innovation

Though faculty were not recruited to Oakland or Monteith with explicit concern for their capacity to find new ways for educating commuter students to either academic or high cultural pursuits, both colleges did have to look for faculty willing to help start a new college; they could count on their novelty to legitimate the move for some who would have snubbed offers from the parent universities. Beyond that, the two institutions parted company in what they

[7] In the following chapter we shall see that four of the Chicago recruits in the social sciences, including Alice Corrigan, were not only Catholics but (pre-Conciliar) avant-garde Catholics—an additional source of cohesion among themselves and of potential friction with others.

were looking for. Although Oakland began with divisions rather than departments, it presented itself as valuing academic specialties and young men of promise in a particular field. Twenty-two of the twenty-three teaching faculty in its first year had the Ph.D., and this unusually high proportion was made a symbol of the College's distinction.

Neither Oakland nor Monteith could offer the scenic advantages of California or New England, nor the college-town ambiance of Ann Arbor or Madison; Oakland was in an exurban wasteland, and at the outset could not offer a community to migrant faculty. Why, then, did they come? Many were attracted by, as they said, "a chance to get in on the ground floor." They wanted the freedom to teach their specialties and the power to develop their own programs without the restrictions imposed by academic seniors elsewhere. As Chancellor Varner presented Oakland to them, they would have complete authority to establish their courses. One man told us that every book in his field was one that he himself had ordered for the library, and that he could teach both European intellectual history and American diplomatic history. "Where else could I do that? I'd have to do one or the other." Another man told us, "I had an offer from Michigan, where I'd have been low man on the totem pole. I would be there ages before promotion." At Oakland, he told us he had a free hand. He added, "Here I'm a member of the Faculty Senate and I have a say in things."

Again and again in our interviews, faculty said that they were attracted by the opportunity to build a program different from the conventional one. Yet when we drew them out as to the nature of their proposals, they often expressed only marginal differences from prevailing models—differences, in fact, shared by many young specialists in their branch of the discipline. A young social scientist who had come to Oakland as an assistant professor told us, "I was attracted by the opportunity to get a program going as I liked. . . . I thought I would be able to get an experiment going without limitation." We asked him what he had in mind, and he replied, "I have no specific ideas, but I wanted to do a different thing than had been done elsewhere." Then he went on to tell us about an arrangement of prerequisites for the advanced courses that would make it less necessary for students to repeat earlier work. "The present system is very inefficient. I always have to go back and teach what I have taught in earlier courses."

On the whole, such men saw themselves as engaged in a mopping-up operation against methodological backwardness and fuzzy, unsupported thinking, carrying on the mission of influential mentors from graduate school. Graduate school does more than set a young man or woman on the first step of an academic career. It often accentuates an intradisciplinary mission that may have originated earlier: to become not simply a sociologist, but a sociologist of the Mertonian or Millsian persuasion; not simply an economist, but an economist after the fashion of Samuelson or Friedman; not simply a teacher of English, but a critic-intellectual in the style of Fiedler. Often these agendas are seen in negative terms. Thus, one can be against the older, perhaps less "scientific" and almost certainly less sophisticated definitions of the discipline. Or, one can be battling for recognition of a new subspecialty, at once recondite and sharp, with which to dispel the fog and the vagaries of earlier, now outdated, pioneers.[8] Indeed, the displacement of earlier discoverers by men who build on their efforts can be as cruel in academic life as in the civil rights movement, where new black militants scornfully push aside the older, still dedicated, more law-oriented fighters of the NAACP or the Urban League. We have already seen that at Wayne the lobbyists for the creation of Monteith included men who felt something of this pressure from younger academic sharpshooters.

For well-educated, talented Americans, academic life has had some of the same attractions that small business has for the less educated: the chance to set their own pace and standards of work. Unlike small business, the better colleges have provided protection from control by the client—be they students, students' parents, or

---

[8] While in the natural sciences, as Merton and his Columbia colleagues have documented, struggles over priorities and paradigms are of prime importance, James Watson's autobiographical account, *The Double Helix,* indicates the relevance of issues of style. For a discussion of some of these issues as manifested in sociology, see Robert A. Nisbet, "Sociology and the Academy."

their representatives. But this protection against the client depends
on the existence of a relatively powerful demand for men with
Ph.D.s. While academics have continued to insist almost obses-
sively on tenure, perhaps as a sign that they are appreciated if not
loved, their real protection and assurance have come from their
ability to move.[9] Even the faculty members without the doctorate
could come to Monteith if they had sponsors elsewhere, and Ph.D.s
could come to Oakland with the awareness that, if the hopes proved
false and matters turned out badly, they could seek employment
elsewhere, chalking up to experience the costs of their search for a
better academic home. Indeed, some of the men who were very
happy with their freedom at Oakland or Monteith were later lured
away by attractions comparable to those that had drawn them to
the colleges originally. This happened even though they had begun
with the look of permanence about them: they had bought or built
homes and did not expect to move.[10]

In contrast to Oakland, Monteith with its staff-taught courses and
unconventional programs was less insistent on people with the Ph.D.;
in the first-year staff, eleven of nineteen faculty people had the
doctorate. These differences were not a question of age: both
faculties were young (only half of each faculty was over thirty-
five) and half had not held prior teaching positions other than
serving as teaching assistants at the schools where they had done
their graduate work. Rather, the differences in degree attainment
reflect the different career emphases at the two colleges. Of the eight
non-Ph.D.s at Monteith, six were definitely planning to complete
their theses, while two were indefinite about finishing. Even when

[9] Some recruits to Oakland from elite private universities were a bit apprehensive at the outset about what sort of protections of academic freedom
a state university could provide. The general reputation of Michigan as an
enlightened state and of the University of Michigan as one of the world's
freest helped overcome hesitations; still, faculty members have continued to
watch the administration closely on this issue. In turn, the administration has
had not only to defend academic freedom but, to retain faculty support, to
make amply clear that it was doing so.
[10] Of the original twenty-eight interviewed in 1960 at Oakland, sixteen were
still on the staff in fall 1963. Of the original twenty-two interviewed in 1960
at Monteith, thirteen remained in fall 1963.

faculty were active in research and writing, the staff organization at Monteith—with its emphasis on collective planning—put minimal pressure on the faculty to complete the doctorate. Furthermore, being in a city and with a less conventional program, Monteith began with a large proportion of single and divorced men and women, whereas Oakland was almost entirely populated by family men.

The resultant style of many Monteith faculty was a side effect of the program, a consequence of looking for people who were willing to teach interdisciplinary courses in a non-departmental setting. Consider the problem of recruiting staff for the natural science division at Monteith. Even the most distinguished liberal arts colleges have been hard-pressed to recruit Ph.D.s in mathematics and the sciences (and equally hard-pressed for quite different reasons to recruit them in sociology). For example, Smith, Amherst, and Mount Holyoke have all built multimillion-dollar science centers in the past few years, hoping to entice academically talented scientists to the faculty and to the student body. Yet the very social distinction of these liberal arts colleges has meant that they do not produce many science majors other than premeds; some, like Dartmouth, Wesleyan, and Bowdoin, have moved tentatively and spottily into graduate work, principally as a basis for recruiting faculty. In contrast, Monteith provided scientists with no laboratory facilities and asked them to teach introductory courses that had no concern for coverage and made no effort to bring students to the frontier. Working as part of a staff in teaching a non-specialized and novel interdisciplinary program repelled professionals closely committed to departmental specialization and eager to establish themselves in a field. One faculty member in the College of Liberal Arts at Wayne warned a Monteith teacher, "You are ruining yourself. You are ruining your career by staying here. It can't last more than two years."

Some of the faculty attracted to Monteith would not have been too upset if it had actually fulfilled this prophecy. A few who did not yet have their Ph.D.s were hoping to secure them and then move to a "real" university. They could afford to dally at an institution of ambiguous status because, once their degrees were conferred, their next positions would depend on the status of their graduate school rather than on wherever they had been before getting their doctorates. At the same time, they did not want their teaching to interfere too much with their careers. Howard Rich illustrates these complexities. When we interviewed him at Monteith, he was completing his Ph.D. dissertation at the University of Chicago. He told us he had come to Monteith because he wanted more teaching experience and this was the only ·job available at an adequate salary. He saw the demands from students and the many staff meetings as incursions on his budding professional career; he complained that the students were not good enough for the material and that his specialty was insufficiently represented. Rich was one of the few Monteith faculty members actively involved in research during the first hectic year of the new college, not only on his dissertation but on another project as well. Nevertheless, beneath his denunciations of the non-specialized and overdemanding staff-taught program at Monteith lay a greater idealism and a greater dedication than he admitted. The severity of his criticisms of the materials being employed seemed to us to reflect a buried concern. The fact that he had come to Monteith in part because of a desire for experience as a teacher—a desire that is unusual in many academic men—points to the possibility of his own ambivalence. While he told us that he intended to stay only a year, and while he did get his Ph.D. the following year, he remained a total of three years before going elsewhere. Several years later, with what looked to us like the return of a repressed vocation for teaching, he left a distinguished department for the more hazardous life of a teacher-researcher at Bard College.

Other men, less ambivalent than Howard Rich about the demands of teaching and the busywork of innovation, were willing to put off the demands of a professional career at least for a time. For example, Harold King said that he had been drawn to Monteith (from Berkeley, where he had been a teaching fellow) "because there was a thing going on here—a formation of a new college, a new society, a new culture. . . . I didn't calculate career opportunities as I would if I were asked to go to Wayne." There then appeared in his comments a note we found repeatedly as Monteith faculty told us what they had rejected: "I wasn't prepared to go into the academic rat race of vocations in a top-rate department. . . . I saw those guys sweating blood for tenure at Berkeley, substituting a paper for any long commitment to anything. They were forced to play a game. . . ." King was then thirty, married, and without children. After several years at Monteith, he took a leave of absence in order to complete his Ph.D. (but during the three years that we remained in touch with him, he did not do so).

Another Monteith faculty member, Werner Wald, had taken his Ph.D. in psychology at a university whose department, though of high caliber, was fanatically experimental. As an undergraduate, he had been curious about the relations of psychology to philosophy, anthropology, and law; he said that, as a result of this, he had experienced repeated rebuffs during his pursuit of the Ph.D.[11] He told us that his department chairman had laughed when he asked for a job as a research assistant: "He called me a dabbler, a madman at the periphery." Later he asked his chairman why he was having difficulty getting a teaching job and was told "word had gotten out that I wasn't really a psychologist." The man who told us this is a person of evident ability, and his publications have brought him wide attention in recent years. Observing Werner Wald at staff meetings and in casual conversation, we saw a powerful iconoclasm which no department could easily have contained or redirected. At Monteith, this led to a passionate devotion to the original innovative ideals, and eventually to an embittered depar-

[11] An essay by Joseph Ben-David and Randall Collins describes the development of psychology as a discipline by physiologists who, unable to find chairs in mid-nineteenth-century German universities, gravitated to philosophy to create a new syncretistic field that reflected philosophical problems and physiological methods. Often, reflecting on our interviews, we concluded that much depended on timing and luck (as with so many crucial events of life) as to whether an individual found support as a graduate student for a somewhat idiosyncratic interest or felt rejected and therefore sought new identifications. See Joseph Ben-David and Randall Collins, "Social Factors in the Origins of a New Science: The Case of Psychology."

ture. So far as we know, he has not found a permanent academic abode.

Another faculty member, William Roberts, told us of the tensions and crises that had led him to leave one graduate school for another, where he was described by a colleague as able and interesting, but also "difficult, disturbed, and very much at odds with economics." Roberts came to Monteith when he was told in effect that the university to which he had transferred was too upwardly mobile to take a chance on him. Still another passionate supporter of Monteith, George Green, came there when he felt he could not continue toward a Ph.D. at Wisconsin. He commented, "I don't have a career. Since mine is so much in doubt, this place isn't going to help or hurt me."

While men like Roberts and Wald were unhappily marginal, torn between the kind of work that attracted them and the specialized departmental definitions they met in their early careers, Green and others who shared their disaffection were more insouciant (saying, as one of them did, "I am not ambitious, careerwise"), relatively unhurried and unworried, either about getting their Ph.D.s or about the incremental accumulation of credentials. Yet what these two kinds of irregulars had in common was a certain openness about their careers. They rejected, often with visible ambivalence, the values and rules of a specialized discipline and especially its standards of defining a career. This does not mean that they were not competent scholars. A number achieved repute through writing, research, or action in various fields. Yet however they might define themselves, as philosophers, mathematicians, or anthropologists, they did not visualize their lives with the definiteness and direction that marked the more career-oriented. They were less interested in getting somewhere—hence their stress on the present and their comparative indifference to the future. In some ways, their outlook foreshadowed that of the beats and hippies. The academic department, the graduate school, and the apparatus of a "field" all spelled a definiteness of role and a limitation of audience with which they felt uneasy.

This view has today become so widespread that many students

and critics automatically assume that all the academic disciplines are unchanging enclaves within a closed corporation. But in historical and cross-cultural perspective it seems clear that few disciplines in American academic life are really static. The changing tastes, styles of work, and new knowledge force fluidity in all but the most entrenched. Of course there are differences in the degree to which a field is in flux: biochemistry more so probably than organic chemistry, linguistics probably more so than English literature. In varying degrees, by providing the paradigms laid out by great progenitors, the departments create a floor below which incompetents are rejected, while at the same time the paradigms make possible the very discoveries that will eventually lead to their replacement.[12] Of course, only a few in any discipline will discover a new paradigm, and a good many will find in an existing model a barrier through which they cannot break. The latter may include some who are available (although not in every case willing) to undertake a new pedagogical venture. Innovations outside the disciplines and especially in General Education have found their staffs from among such people. Among them, as we have already suggested, are some who want to transcend their specialties and others who could not make it in a specialty.

For most recruits to Oakland and Monteith, academic life—however broadly or loosely defined—was central to their definitions of themselves. But there were a few who saw themselves as neither outside nor inside the organized academic guilds. For such men and women, academic life served as an available subsidy for extra-academic interests. Thus one of our respondents was a writer. He enjoyed teaching English at Oakland, but said of himself, "I write. This is the central thing for me. Everything else is secondary." He lived at a distance from his colleagues and spoke in terms of what "they" were doing. Similarly, a respondent at Monteith saw his most vital activity in being a consultant to a Detroit industry. Remote from his colleagues, he lived in a suburb and found his friends among businessmen. Another man remained at Monteith in spite of offers from Cornell and Whitman College because he

---

[12] See Thomas S. Kuhn, *The Structure of Scientific Revolutions.*

was attached to his house and neighborhood outside Detroit and did not want to move.

For married women teachers especially, home and family were the crucial foci of life. But their identity was not at stake either in the development of the College or in that of the discipline. This often meant that in their relations to students they could respond directly and personally, without a commitment to uphold professional standards or a need to see in the students' development some sort of testimony to the College's success. Students, of course, sensed the consequences. Thus one of the social scientists at Oakland remarked that students classified faculty as "for or against students." By this he meant "whether or not [faculty members] knock themselves out to give the students the stuff, or communicate the attitude that 'Here is the stuff, you probably won't get it.'" He gave the example of languages. Russian was getting more majors than French, despite the fact that French is an easier language for Americans. "The French faculty are cold to students. The Russian faculty are not. Serge Kortsoff organized the chess club and played six games at once with six students. And of course Grulenko and Fetich are, well, you know, you've met them and you've also met people in French." Grulenko and Fetich were women in their forties, born and raised in Russia. They had held a variety of jobs, but neither teaching nor Russian studies were the causes for which they lived. Toward students, they were warm and accepting, in contrast to the aloofness and distance of colleagues in the other language departments. Indeed, they were critical of those who demeaned students.[13] In supporting students, they were not currying favor or overidentifying with youth (though it may have looked that way to more distant colleagues), for indeed they often made great demands upon their students—but they did this with good cheer and warmth.

[13] We are not implying here that women are invariably maternal and undoctrinaire as teachers! However, it has been our observation that academic women are in general less vain and narcissistic than men. Cf. essays by Alice Rossi, David McClelland, Erik Erikson, and others, in Robert J. Lifton (ed.), *The Woman in America.*

The administrator is also, to a certain extent, outside the normal system of academic careers; he too is marginal. Thus D. B. Varner, the Chancellor who left Michigan State for Oakland, had a lot to lose if Oakland should fail. Long removed from teaching, he would have found it difficult to return to it, nor would it have been psychologically easy for him to return to MSU. Compared to him, many of his faculty would turn out to be as transient as the student body.

We have already noted that there was no one at Monteith comparable to Varner, only a trio of division heads with no more administrative experience among them than a chairmanship. Yet in moving to Monteith, they changed their careers in a fundamental way. One of the senior men who came over from Wayne was in effect seeking a second career after many years in a regular academic department, which he told us he was glad to leave, as it had become less congenial to him of late. Second careers are not necessarily second-best or *faute de mieux* choices; they depend very much on individual talent and the chance element that mediates between the development of an individual and of a field or an institution.[14] The same drive that might lead one man to throw himself into starting a new college might lead another to start a new department in microbiology or the history of science, while still another might fight within a history department for a place for social history, or within an economics department for a place for economic development.

We have observed perhaps fifteen new colleges get started in the years since the Second World War. Indeed we know one man who has been called somewhat romantically the Johnny Appleseed of academia, for he is now on his third new college. Any new product has bugs, but industry has a somewhat easier time than academic institutions in disposing of waste products and poor hires. Most of the new colleges we have watched have had crises of morale and mission, and most also have suffered from more than the usual financial problems. Yet there seem to be people—apparently intelligent, sen-

---

[14] Cf. for general discussion Everett C. Hughes, "Cycles, Turning Points, and Careers," in *Men and Their Work*, pp. 11–22.

sible, and moderate—who are willing to start a new enterprise. Some who join at the outset become in effect cofounders and sometimes discover more of life eaten up in committee meetings than they had expected, while others discover that the students can be cannibals too. Even so, as our story of Oakland and Monteith makes clear, while all new enterprises have a plethora of committee meetings and most encounter unanticipated difficulties, the nature and intensity of their vicissitudes differ markedly.

Monteith, fluid and unspecialized, attracted faculty willing to take chances in terms of professional success in order to pursue their interest in a particular kind of undergraduate teaching. Since the time in 1958 when a few intellectual adventurers went to Monteith, student pressures, faculty guilt, and administrative intervention have led to an increased preoccupation with undergraduate teaching and learning. The Union for Research and Experimentation in Higher Education holds frequent conferences on these matters, and new journals such as *Change* magazine report the debates, the rhetoric, and the rare discoveries that accompany the altered attitude. In a number of places, students are themselves creating courses and looking for faculty who will teach them, or rather, in the current idiom, who will join the students in a common enterprise of learning. The problems of creating a curriculum for commuter students that will neither ignore nor cater to their limitations are hardly better understood now than they were when Oakland and Monteith began. Moreover, the institutional mechanisms for providing career lines for faculty who want to focus on issues of teaching and learning have yet to be devised.

V Academic Styles of Life and the Encounter with Non-Elite Students

The first generations of students at Oakland and Monteith were startled by the frankness and, as it seemed to them, impiety of their faculty. We cannot say with certainty that the shock was greater than it would have been had the students attended the parent universities, but we think that it probably was, because of the small classes and the intensity of impact. At a time when Oakland County was not within easy commuting range of Detroit, the area still included many white families recently arrived from the South, bringing their fundamentalist religion with them; Lutheran and other conservative families were already settled there. Students in the county's high schools took it for granted that schoolteachers were supposed to set a good example, that is, patently to adhere to the common moralities and decencies of genteel middle-class life in 1960. They expected college teachers to do the same. In Detroit, where conservative Catholic parents were beginning to allow their children to attend secular Wayne State University, the high schools were somewhat less provincial; even so, Monteith faculty did not conform to their students' ideas of what was proper. In both colleges, students were unsettled by teachers who took detached and critical, even hostile, attitudes toward institutions that students revered or at least took for granted.

Agnes Green, a member of the English faculty at Oakland, said that her students' high school teachers were "stuffy, overly moral people, and they [the students] are doubly confounded to find a woman as college professor of a very different kind," namely, herself.

I used the expression "Going to hell in a handbasket" in the class. One of the girls had repeated it at home that evening and the parents had been deeply upset that one of the professors should talk that way. The kids were shocked by *Catcher in the Rye,* by frankness, by some of the words that are used. They were shocked when I asked one of them to analyze the scene in which Holden meets the prostitute in his hotel room. . . . All this opens a new kind of world for them —one that the parents find it very difficult to understand.

Mrs. Green is a woman in her forties, well dressed and with an air of intellectual toughness combined with femininity. Coming from an upper-middle class New England family, she attended Mount Holyoke and then got her Ph.D. in English from the University of Chicago. There are certainly not many high school teachers like Mrs. Green, although Oakland County schools may have more of them now. Mrs. Green also puzzled her students by her preoccupation with the excitement of ideas.[1]

Religious Orientations

The first class we visited at Oakland in the fall of 1960, a discussion in the Western Institutions course, helped to clarify for us the discrepancy between the outlooks of students and faculty. That

[1] Perhaps a number of the students might have made somewhat similar discoveries about diversity had they not attended college. Since those who attend and do not attend college tend to be different in other respects, it is hard to separate the impact of college from the impact of other experiences. Most public-opinion poll data make clear that college does have an impact, however much faculty members may doubt this. For one of the few studies that look at people who did not attend college, see John C. McCullers and Walter T. Plant, "Personality and Social Development: Cultural Influences." See further Riesman, "The 'Jacob Report.' " See also the recent study by James W. Trent and Leland L. Medsker, *Beyond High School.*

particular day was devoted to examining Martin Luther's address to the German nobility. The professor, a brilliant medievalist, tried to bring the issues home to the students by suggesting that Luther's hammering of the theses on the church door at Wittenberg was comparable to posting a notice on the bulletin board of the Student Union. It seemed to us that for the Catholics, Lutherans, Presbyterians, fundamentalists, and many other religious groups among Oakland's students, the discussion of Luther could be illuminating, but also difficult and disturbing. Actually, despite his best efforts, the instructor was not able to evoke much reaction. We sensed a certain uneasiness, which, perhaps mistakenly, we attributed in part to the sensitive nature of the topic. Those who did speak were the few upper-middle class students who obviously knew what the Reformation was in a more than cursory way and who were at ease discussing religion or other controversial subjects. Most of the girls were passive, and while the class of twenty or so had been kept small for discussion purposes, it actually ended up being more lecture than discussion.

Afterward we pondered what might have happened if the instructor had departed from his schedule to deal directly with the religious illiteracy of his students, most of whom no doubt thought of themselves as conventionally religious but were actually quite ignorant of the doctrinal themes that separated their particular denominations from others. Had this been done, possibly the students would have gone home that night and raised questions their parents would have found difficult to answer. One Oakland faculty member told us it was hard for the students not to fall into a pose in order to avoid trouble at home:

> In one actual case with one of my kids, he asked why they always say grace every night in the same way; he asked if they really mean it. He is not a smart-alecky kid. He likes his family, but he got thrown out of the house for saying that.

Some faculty members at Oakland and Monteith consciously tried to get students to question their beliefs, feeling perhaps that this was part of the process of liberation and enlightenment. But much more common was the unintended impact on students of the relativism and skeptical manner of the faculty. Many faculty on their first teaching jobs found it difficult to realize the weight their passing comments might have, for they considered themselves to be dealing with impregnable students. Only a few could imagine the kinds of problems with their families that are created for commuter students in the United States by faculty traditions of candor and plain speaking (and by the fact that few commuter colleges can keep their students on campus long enough so that when they return home their parents are apt to be asleep).

There is a good deal of evidence that academic men tend to be dropouts from conventional religion, and the Oakland faculty was no exception.[2] Many Oakland faculty described their own homes as nominally Episcopalian, Congregational, or Methodist, but they possessed little feeling of identification with their parents' denominations. Not a single member of the humanities faculty was affiliated with a church. (One humanities professor told us that he and his wife had "gone on a church kick" for the sake of their eleven-year-old girl, but they balked at signing the Confession of Faith and left the church.) If some students were shocked by faculty irreverence, many faculty members were antagonized by the religious fundamentalism they found in the area and by what they regarded as an excessive puritanism in the local churches, both Protestant and Catholic.[3]

Monteith students found the avant-garde Catholicism of five members of the charter Monteith faculty at least as bewildering as Oakland students found the more characteristic agnosticism of Oak-

[2] Appendix C shows the religious attachments of both faculties. We agree with Zelan's judgment in his paper "Religious Apostasy, Higher Education, and Occupational Choice" that academic values constitute a sort of non-theocratic religion comprising "a self-conception—intellectualism; the career—the academic profession; a political ideology—liberalism."

[3] One of the many signs of dramatic change at Oakland from those early days is the off-campus presence of liberal Catholic and Protestant chaplains who, as in so many other universities, provide an "Opening to the Left"—in the Catholic case, often at odds with the local bishop and diocese. On the liberalism of the campus minister, see Phillip E. Hammond, *The Campus Clergyman*.

land faculty. These Monteith Catholics adhered to the critical and intellectual versions of Catholicism that James W. Trent has spoken of as "the critical devout."[4] For example, Alice Corrigan had grown up in an upper-class Catholic family that "thought of priests as boors," and had attended Manhattanville, going on to become a student and later an instructor at the Sorbonne. She identified herself with French intellectual Catholicism and, before Vatican II, expressed her alienation from the American Church. She said that she preferred theological conversations with Lutherans and Jews, for American Catholics were so awed by priests that they were unable to think or talk freely. Joseph Grady, a seminary dropout who had grown up in Chicago in what he termed "an Irish-type village," discovered Catholic Action via students in Montreal and through his friendship with Simone Bouvet, a French-trained Left Catholic, and Alice Corrigan, who had recruited him and Bouvet to Monteith. Grady, like the others, went out of his way to cultivate friendships with non-Catholics; he studied non-Catholic theologies, and characteristically went so far as to protest providing a Christmas tree for the Student Center. He and his "critical devout" wife frequently wrote on ethical and religious themes for the student mimeographed paper, *Brine*. Some faculty members saw Grady and the four social scientists in the charter group of Monteith faculty as "the Irish Mafia" in terms of their influence on curricular decisions.

But for the students, especially the Catholic students, these avant-garde Catholic faculty presented a threat. They were unlikely to have met before any Catholic with the outlook, at once serious and sardonic, that characterized these men and women. Students from fundamentalist backgrounds, whether Protestant or Catholic, were likely to conclude that their own religious style was neither respectable nor defensible. In intimate class discussions and in more casual out-of-class encounters, Monteith faculty (notably, the social science staff) sought to confront and challenge their students,

[4] James W. Trent, *Catholics in College: Religious Commitment and the Intellectual Life.*

but even if they did not do this directly in terms of religion, they undoubtedly did it by implication.

A companion study to our own indicates that Monteith had a significant impact on the religious attitudes of its students. In a comparison of religious habits and beliefs among students at the University of Illinois and at Monteith, Warren Ramshaw found that Monteith, although a commuter school, produced more change in religious outlook than did the residential University of Illinois. Ramshaw also found that Monteith students showed greater intellectual capacity in defending both belief and non-belief than did students at Illinois, who apparently were less frequently challenged.[5]

Faculty and Community

In both colleges, faculty members tended to see themselves as members of a cosmopolitan world and viewed their local settings at best with indifference, at worst with fear and distaste. Indifference was the characteristic attitude of Monteith faculty toward Detroit, for they had a kind of extraterritorial protection, being encapsulated within the more highly visible parent university. Moreover, since so many Monteith faculty were single or childless, they could live somewhat anonymously in Detroit, not being dependent on the community for its services. The Oakland faculty were more likely to be married and to have families, which meant that, since their wives and children became involved in neighborhood schools and activities, they could not so easily withdraw from their surroundings.[6]

Friendly approaches were often as jarring as hostility; an Oakland professor in the humanities told us that being asked to join Kiwanis "offended my sense of academic decorum"; he added, "It

[5] At Illinois, the outlook of women in particular was seldom affected, perhaps because they remained sheltered in sororities or in specialized fields of study such as education. See Warren C. Ramshaw, "Religious Participation and the Fate of Religious Ideology on a Resident and Non-Resident College Campus: An Exploratory Study."

[6] Appendix C shows the family situations of both faculties.

is probably the snobbishness of the East that the service club is for businessmen and not for professionals." Many Oakland faculty, particularly those who came from private universities, interpreted town-gown polarities in regional terms. One man, for example, declared that he hated "the climate and social personality of Michigan . . . the people in the Midwest have the bad manners of the European lower class plus isolationism and a rigid bigotry. . . ." He liked Midwesterners no better when they hungered after culture, remarking: "Art, music, are nothing, unless they have some social value, like the Flemish exhibit. . . . People were standing around with their backs to the paintings, shouting, 'Look, there's Mabel.'" One does not need to move to Michigan to find such attitudes. It is as much a class as a regional difference, of course; however, many faculty did notice that automobiles dominated the conversation of their students—although again this may not be entirely a Michigan specialty.

In a way that now sounds a bit old-fashioned, a number of Oakland faculty deprecated their students as lower-class hedonists on the make, who could assess their teachers only in terms of the latter's affluence and conformity to patterns of business success. Some had come with high hopes for their students and were disappointed, whereas others did not expect them to have any "concern about more basic values than material comfort or gain." During the Eisenhower era, when the general culture was comparatively complacent, many faculty probably concluded that the students were unredeemable, and doubted their ability to convey to their students what one faculty member termed "a certain aloofness from their culture."

Any evidence of the influence of faculty attitudes on the outlook of students at Oakland and Monteith is deficient because of the great attrition and the little that is known about the students who left. But for those who stayed, there is a good deal of evidence that their cultural attitudes were profoundly altered. Examples will appear in subsequent chapters, but here we might note that the plurality of Oakland students who entered secondary school teaching soon had a reputation in Michigan school systems for being non-conformist innovators. A relatively small proportion at both colleges sought the commercial main chance on graduation.[7]

Faculty could have influence on students whom they saw every day, even in rather formal settings. But when it came to the surrounding civic community, it took longer for Oakland faculty to feel any sense of comfort or accommodation with their neighbors. For example, tensions were exposed when Oakland University staged an international art exhibit. Local people were asked to lend some of their *objets d'art* for the exhibit. Some of the wealthy members of the Oakland Foundation were among the contributors. But the professor of art in charge of the exhibit refused to take most of the proffered items. "It's miserable," he said. "We can't show this in a university." A compromise had to be reached in which he accepted some things but returned others.

National politics provided one more illustration of mutual mistrust. This occurred when, in the fall of 1960, the great majority of Oakland's faculty signed an advertisement in the Pontiac *Press* supporting John Kennedy for the presidency; this did not sit well in Republican Oakland and Macomb counties. Some faculty were apprehensive lest the Chancellor not fully defend them against local monitoring, while the latter felt that the faculty, whom he did defend, had not taken account of the local costs of possible confusion between the institution and the faculty members acting as private citizens. The very visibility of Oakland, which its publicity had helped to create, increased the resonance of any radical opinions; for example, the attack by a faculty member on American policy toward Cuba in 1961 was played up in the local press.

If Oakland had possessed a law school or a medical school or a graduate school of business, and especially if it had recruited part-time practitioner faculty for these, it would have established some ties with local professional societies. (Since the teacher

7 See the discussion of the resentment of American academicians over their supposed lack of status as a demand for the deference that no elite receives in America, in Seymour Martin Lipset, *Political Man*, Chapter 10; and Melvin Seeman, "The Intellectual and the Language of Minorities." Cf. Richard Hofstadter, *Anti-Intellectualism in American Life*, and the review by Riesman.

education program focused on the liberal arts and possessed hardly any faculty of its own, it did not tie Oakland into local school systems—particularly since its graduates went to take jobs all over the state of Michigan.) But such ties were almost impossible for a college with a strong liberal arts emphasis. An Oakland economist told us that he felt that academicians should do applied work such as the consulting he himself did, but his position was not shared, and he stayed at Oakland only briefly. Oakland faculty saw themselves as accidentally located in Oakland County, whereas to many local residents the expectation had been that faculty would provide community services for the benefit of the area and its students. When some of the administrators who had come to Oakland from MSU did their best to pull their weight in local civic organizations, they proved to the faculty only that the administrators were not really legitimate participants in academic culture.

Since Monteith faculty members lived all over Detroit, a few in the semi-slum adjacent to Wayne, it was natural for many of them to make Monteith their center of gravity, the Student Center as well as their crowded, lively, and noisy offices. Not defensive vis-à-vis Detroit or the Middle West, they did not regard their students as emissaries from a vigilante culture, but rather as potential allies with whom they could create their own culture within a more or less Bohemian oasis. Perhaps indeed the marginal characteristics of some Monteith teachers contributed to their viewing students as isolated from any contacts other than those within the College. They did not have their guard up in the Oakland style, where students were sometimes regarded as infiltrators who would lower both academic and cultural standards unless they were resolutely fought off. The very fact that students at Monteith would turn up unannounced at faculty apartments gave faculty a sense of common cause that was lacking especially in the early years of Oakland, when the campus was usually deserted in the late afternoon and evening, and where the faculty's style of suburban family life meant that there were no casual meetings or spontaneous dropping-in by students.

In the early years of Monteith, Wayne was under attack by local

right-wingers for refusing to ban Communist speakers on the campus
(Wayne held to its traditional openness). Yet Monteith faculty
never had the feeling of being surrounded by neighbors who looked
askance at them for their opinions or how they voted.[8] Wayne
has always had strong support from the UAW. Correspondingly,
many Wayne faculty in Liberal Arts and the professional schools
have had close ties to the unions and to other centers of influence
in Michigan. A few members of the Monteith faculty have had such
ties as well. But it took a while for Detroiters to discover the degree
to which Monteith has been a center of radical thought, critical
even of the liberal wing of the Democratic Party. For a Monteith
student from an auto-worker family, it was a surprise to discover
that his social science instructor, although voting for Kennedy, did
not do so for the same reasons the student's parents did. Some
faculty supported Castro; many were deeply cynical about American
party politics in general. Monteith faculty edited *New University
Thought;* Monteith Catholics allied themselves with the local equivalent of worker-priests. Even so, especially in the early years,
Monteith was not clearly distinguished from Wayne, and it has
not been a particular target of backlash.

It would be a mistake to polarize too sharply the differences in
faculty styles and community settings of Oakland and Monteith.
There were squares at Monteith and beats at Oakland from the
beginning. The difference was clearest in the early years when
Oakland faculty were almost uniformly concerned with home and
family, occupied with their academic specialties, and culturally out
of sympathy with what many took to be Midwestern values, whereas
the Monteith faculty—which included men and women who were
more marginal to begin with—were less aggrieved culturally and
more radical politically. Now, with Oakland grown so much larger
than Monteith, its subcultures have become more visible. The increase in students and faculty, accompanied by changing cultural
styles, have led to such diversity of subcultures so that the Monteith we have been describing easily could have been assimilated at

[8] Appendix C shows the 1960 presidential choices of both faculties, which, as
might be expected, were overwhelmingly for the Democratic Party.

Oakland ten years later. We have discovered on our past several visits that some Oakland faculty have now established connections with professional and industrial leaders in nearby Bloomfield Hills and Birmingham, while others are involved in the wider artistic, political, and professional circles of the whole metropolitan area. Oakland began the 1969–70 academic year with a faculty of over two hundred. These men and women no longer feel isolated, but in the everlasting round of committee meetings, student activism, and enlarged community demands, some may look back almost wistfully to a time when the faculty housing subdivision had the quality of an expatriate colony uneasily perched on alien soil.

VI   Academic Ideals and Colleagueship

Every going academic concern develops its own specific atmosphere; even those new institutions that look like many others to the tourist feel unique to the insider. Yet some academic cultures are more idiosyncratic and coherent than others; and it is our sense that Oakland and Monteith developed their very special atmospheres with great rapidity—atmospheres that in turn influenced and reflected the different styles of teaching at the two colleges. As we have noted, this outcome was not the result of conscious recruitment of faculty with definitive ideas as to how they should be grouped (whether into departments or staffs) or how they should teach. Nor was thought given to the sorts of people who might be especially gifted in conveying a demanding academic program to first-generation commuter students. Naturally, the administrators wanted faculty who were interested in teaching undergraduates and who were willing to come to a new and untried place. But once faculty came, it was they who set their stamp on the curriculum and sifted later faculty.

The Negative Identity of the Parent University

Certainly the administrators had not begun with the idea of recruiting faculty whose positive models were the smaller, highly selective private colleges such as Oberlin, Reed, Swarthmore, Antioch, Chicago, and Columbia—and who correspondingly would disdain the parent institution. Yet the initial faculty at both colleges regarded Michigan State and Wayne State as impersonal and cancerously big—with little of the distinction that Berkeley or Michigan musters at the graduate and professional levels. Faculty self-respect depended on being sure that the new institutions would be different from their parents. Oriented to a world of friends, colleagues, and opinion outside of Midwestern public higher education, the newcomers resented any imputation that they were "at Michigan State," or "at Wayne," nor did they want to be thought of as teaching at branches of the parent university.[1] Snobbery toward the parent was facilitated at Oakland by geographical distance, while social distance produced the identical result at Monteith. In retrospect, this polarization seems inevitable. It is doubtful whether Monteith faculty could have brought themselves out of their mutual involvement with curriculum and students in order to cultivate ties with men in Liberal Arts departments, while the Liberal Arts faculty tended in turn to think of Monteith faculty as unscholarly and undisciplined. Oakland faculty would have had to make a considerable effort to make contact with men in their own fields at the East Lansing campus or vice versa.[2]

[1] When the two colleges began, the movement of major universities to establish branches in the metropolitan centers had not yet assumed its present momentum, which for example, has put the University of Wisconsin into Milwaukee, the University of Massachusetts into Boston, the University of Missouri into St. Louis and Kansas City, the University of Illinois into Chicago, Louisiana State into New Orleans, etc. Up to the present time, the "branch" has considerably less status than the parent, much as an older model for the same procedure—UCLA—has, despite its eminence, not been able to overtake and surpass Berkeley. For a discussion of this development, see Riesman, "The Urban University."

[2] As we noted in the previous chapter, Oakland faculty made no effort to cultivate the professional men living or working in Oakland County or other nearby areas.

Some Monteith faculty did develop ties with liberal Catholic and similar groups in Detroit. Later on, Monteith became one of the charter members of a league of mostly small and struggling private colleges: the Union for Research and Experimentation in Higher Education, which includes Shimer, New College (Sarasota), Antioch, Goddard, Nasson, Stephens, Sarah Lawrence,

For the first two years, Oakland's full designation was Michigan State University Oakland (rather than Michigan State University—Oakland, which is more typical of branches). Trucks formerly in use at MSU were put into service at Oakland, and their lettering of MSU was converted to MSUO; but since this additional O was not painted on clearly, students who had absorbed the faculty attitude toward MSU complained. Faculty members, in talking with each other and with us, cracked jokes about the confusion: one instructor in the humanities remarked, "Some people snicker when we make these pronouncements about cultivation of ideas and ideas for their own sake. They think of us as part of a cow college." Sensitivity at Oakland about belonging to an entirely different, highbrow world of, so to speak, hand-crafted *objets d'art,* rather than mass products, brought in its train severity toward students but also an emphasis on teaching in relatively small classes, even when this made greater demands on faculty. This meant in practice that the "Oberlin ideal," when transplanted to Oakland, might involve considerable punitiveness vis-à-vis students, who could not possibly live up to what was expected of them. Moreover, holding on to this ideal would soon also involve making a decision to build dormitories and to recruit students from outside the area. And here admissions personnel, complaining that the name MSUO was a hindrance to recruiting good students beyond commuting range, added their weight to that of the faculty in pushing for total dis-identification with Michigan State. Many of the Ivy League types at Oakland wanted to call the institution "Oakland College," but during the fourth year the Trustees decided to change the name to "Oakland University." This satisfied both those on the faculty who wanted to keep the grade of "university" and the great majority who wanted separation from MSU, displeasing only those aware of the fact that, among elite private institutions, to be a "college" rather than a "university" can be a point of pride.

At Monteith, the desire for separateness was also reflected in the

Loretto Heights, Hofstra's New College, and, in the public sector, Northeastern Illinois State College (formerly Chicago Teachers College North).

use of names. Indeed, after our first several visits to Wayne, we fell into the common practice of referring to the College of Liberal Arts as "Wayne," an implication that Monteith was not, and were admonished for this by the College adviser, Tom Gant, who had worked in the Wayne administration for a number of years before moving to Monteith. He pointed out the obvious fact that Monteith was part of Wayne, saying, "We should really talk of Monteith and of Liberal Arts." But we noticed that even Sidney Karr, whose academic life had been largely at Wayne, did not make this distinction.

Students of gang life have noticed that a name is essential to the development of identity and loyalty. Without the umbrella of a name, Monteith could have been regarded as simply a program at Wayne, one in which some students did their work in General Education, spread out over four years, rather than concentrated in the first two years as in the basic colleges or General Education colleges of some state universities. Indeed, if it had been a program in General Education without a name, the passionate identification with it among the students would have been impossible, and the style of those most ardently identified—called "Monteithy" students —might never have emerged.[3]

A name, in other words, can accumulate elements of mystique, and at Monteith it helped to confer an aura, perhaps particularly on the faculty. The Monteith Program Study survey revealed that Monteith students often viewed their instructors as men with national reputations in their field—a halo effect that may have intimidated some students while encouraging others to dream of themselves as possible candidates for the same career.

[3] The cluster colleges at the University of California at Santa Cruz have developed a considerable loyalty based on a name, so that students will identify themselves when on the campus as members of Cowell College or Merrill College. Raymond College of the University of the Pacific developed a somewhat similar loyalty in its first years. See the discussion by Jerry G. Gaff in his report *Innovations and Consequences: A Study of Raymond College, University of the Pacific;* and for a general discussion of cluster colleges, Warren Bryan Martin, *Alternative to Irrelevance: A Strategy for Reform in High Education,* Chapter 3.

The Relevance of Backgrounds: Social and Academic

By its location in an area of growing population not yet served by an open-door public college, Oakland might theoretically have joined the league of other Michigan state colleges, such as Western Michigan, Eastern Michigan, Central Michigan, or Ferris State College, that in the past served local constituencies.[4] But Oakland had entirely different ambitions, while Monteith College, with its focus on General Education, was modeling itself on the aristocratic value of "learning for its own sake." Indeed, it was also rejecting what we have termed the higher vocationalism of the graduate academic professions, which leads to rewarding an undergraduate who wants to become a physical chemist or a demographer, while paying less attention to those students who propose to go to work or to start families after the baccalaureate.

Yet neither college was staffed with birthright aristocrats. At both Oakland and Monteith, almost two thirds of the faculty were the first generation in their families to attend college; most came from the broad spectrum of the middle class, with the remainder evenly divided between working class and upper class origins.[5] As one might expect, the most upwardly mobile faculty included some of those most dedicated to elite education; thus, nine of the seventeen teachers in the humanities at Oakland were "first generation."[6]

[4] In a recent book, Alden Dunham describes the way in which Western Michigan University has sought to distinguish itself from its regional rivals in the quality of its professional programs and in its rapid march toward doctoral programs. Cf. E. Alden Dunham, *Colleges of the Forgotten Americans: A Profile of State Colleges and Regional Universities.*
[5] Appendix D contains data on the educational and class origins of Oakland and Monteith faculty.
[6] Of course, some men make what might be thought of as a two-generation jump in a single generation and arrive in their own lifetimes at an outlook that resembles the noblesse oblige of the patrician. Some, like the angry young men in the United Kingdom of the 1950s, carry their social class with them into their new careers, identifying with their class of origin. But a great many upwardly mobile academic men regard their work and their success

In varying degrees, college attendance and postgraduate training provide academic men with new "families," new reference groups, which replace their families of origin. Those members of the humanities faculty at Oakland who had attended selective, private liberal arts colleges contributed much of its anti-vocational bias and vehement insistence on excellence. We have already noted the recruitment to Oakland of six men who had been at Columbia University; Mark Williams, the original proponent of the Western Institutions course and later Associate Dean for the Humanities, was one of these. When we asked him what he wanted Oakland to be like, he responded: "Ideally, it would be Columbia College," adding, "Of course, it's so completely different, but I am happy to adjust to it. . . . I'm used to integrated courses and highly prescribed curricula." The students also had to do some adjusting, trying to master the Columbia College volumes and the expectations of the Oakland humanities faculty.[7] Current student complaints to the contrary, Columbia College has been characterized by the devotion of many eminent faculty to teaching undergraduates, as for example, Lionel Trilling and Daniel Bell have done. In that respect, Columbia was a not inappropriate model for Oakland. But in other respects it was misleading, as were other models faculty carried in their heads from Wesleyan, Dartmouth, or Swarthmore. It was not until Sargent Hennessey became Dean of Faculty, after Richard Lane,

---

with profound ambivalence, even with the contempt that often pervades the novels about academic life written by academic men and women. At times, snobbery toward administrators, educationists, and other academic beasts of burden appears to be an attempt to project this self-contempt onto visible and vulnerable others.

[7] Readers of Daniel Bell's book *The Reforming of General Education: The Columbia College Experience and Its National Setting,* are aware that the Columbia College model has not proved viable even where it began, primarily because of the increasing influence of the graduate and professional schools. Daniel Bell recommends a less autonomous undergraduate faculty and a focus on introducing undergraduates to the styles and processes of the various academic disciplines, as against the survey courses, which from the 1920s onward had been the trademark of Columbia College. What will happen to alter the curriculum in the wake of the student rebellion of April and May 1968 is still unclear.

that the elite private college model was seriously called into question
and the search for a new model and a new attitude toward students
began in earnest.

Ivy League models never had complete hegemony even in a
single division at Oakland, let alone throughout the various waves
of faculty recruits. Columbia College was influential for some,
but completely unknown among others. In contrast, as we have
already seen, The College of the University of Chicago was the
decisive model for almost all of the Monteith social scientists. They
had been at Chicago during the 1950s, when The College came
under intensive attack—it had never been popular—from many
of the graduate departments and professional schools of the University; this attack intensified the hostility toward narrow and
pedantic academic professionalism that was widespread in the College under Robert Hutchins' leadership.[8]

Like Anabaptists leaving Germany or Hutterites leaving America,
some of the faculty recruited to Monteith hoped that the Chicago
tradition in General Education might be carried on in its new
setting, no matter how modified and truncated in its place of
origin.[9] The College at Chicago prided itself on never using text-

[8] Beginning in the 1930s, the Chicago College had been innovative in its
chronological staging of higher education, in the emphasis on undergraduate
teaching in contrast to research-oriented work with graduate students, in a
preference for the supposed Great Books, and, among both students and faculty,
the cultivation of both analytic and verbal virtuosity. An impressionistic
vignette of the accomplishments of the social science program during these
years at The College of the University of Chicago appears in Robert Nisbet's
article "Hutchins of Chicago." For another brief account, see Christopher
Jencks and David Riesman, "The Anti-University College," in *The Academic
Revolution,* pp. 493–99.

[9] People and ideas from The College of the University of Chicago have been
influential in other liberal arts settings in addition to Monteith College. One
of the oldest colonial colleges, St. John's at Annapolis (and its new offshoot
at Santa Fe), was reorganized in the 1930s on a Great Books model; there
has been mutual support between St. John's College and The College at
Chicago, and some exchange of faculty. Shimer College in Mt. Carroll. Illinois, founded as a female seminary, became in the 1950s a kind of satellite
campus for The College at Chicago, and its interdisciplinary program resembles that of present-day Monteith in its non-departmentalism and focus
on undergraduate teaching. Another group of Chicago-influenced faculty be-

books and on offering integrated or interdisciplinary staff-taught courses. Presently The College at Chicago is, according to Cass and Birnbaum's *Comparative Guide,* among the most selective in the country, with eighty National Merit Scholars enrolled in 1966–67 and a third of the students scoring about 700 on both the SAT and MAT tests. But transfer of the Chicago model to Monteith, a locale with a very different student body, led one ex-Chicago social scientist to remark on the dangers of this incongruity, "Here we brought our own environment. So much so that we must avoid being God-damned progressive cranks."

Some of the social scientists hoped to introduce still more of that environment by bringing Charles Rhodes, a member of the Examiner's Office from The College at Chicago, to Monteith in March 1960 to investigate the possibility of developing a comparable office there, with perhaps the hope of recruiting Rhodes himself to Monteith. The program of outside Examiners at Chicago had a variety of aims: it helped turn faculty members into dons who coached their students to meet an outside test; it helped insure the integration of courses against the anarchy of individual faculty members; it facilitated accreditation of novel courses at other institutions. But as Rhodes pointed out, the program had offended many of the graduate departments at the University of Chicago because the students who went on lacked the specialized underpinnings that graduate professors, especially natural scientists, demand.

We sat in on the discussion between Rhodes and the Monteith faculty in 1960, and we noticed that the "Chicago crowd" was grouped on either side of Rhodes, while the rest of the Monteith faculty sat around the table at the opposite end. Sidney Karr thought Rhodes's warnings were not especially relevant to the Monteith situation, since a student could pursue both General Education

came the nucleus of the humanities staff at the College of New York State at Oyster Bay, which has since become the State University at Stony Brook. In the present large University Plan, the early Chicago notions have become attenuated. Very likely, there are other places of first and second settlement by Chicago migrants, and it would be an interesting work in intellectual history to trace their impact, as well as to see what remains in The College at Chicago of the ideas that can now be found in more pristine form at Monteith.

at Monteith and specialized education at the College of Liberal Arts: "If he [the student] feels he wants to be a mathematician, he can begin his math in his freshman year and gain his cumulative knowledge without any contradiction or conflict." He estimated that Monteith absorbed only one third of a student's course work. Rhodes responded that at Chicago it had been not only a question of the meshing of programs, but a psychological one of the meshing of attitudes: students coming from The College to an introductory chemistry course resented the fact that chemistry had no general principles or theories and therefore regarded the material as dull. They would often drop out after a semester or two, or transfer to another department. They found the specialist graduate teachers unstimulating in contrast to the exciting and intellectually bold teachers they had had in discussion sections in The College. Harold King, a Chicago-trained anthropologist, picked up this theme and responded to Karr by saying that students going through the program at Monteith would also be antagonistic to the specialized disciplines they would encounter in other areas of Wayne.

Still drawing on Chicago experience, King pondered whether Monteith graduates would be sufficiently conformist to stay with it, if hired by industry. If they went into professions, would they conform to the codes of their professions? Would they be viewed as queer, offbeat, "nuts"? (This last term was introduced by one of the Chicago people and then used by many in the discussion as a shorthand description of the non-conforming person.) Karr objected to this and insisted that skilled people would always be needed. King and Wald (another social scientist) replied that most of Monteith's students could not aspire beyond middle management jobs. Here, they maintained, "the nut will not be cherished." One member of the natural science staff drew on his experience with industrial organizations to support King and Wald, saying that the speeches about a need for generalists were only the businessman's "window dressing."

Throughout this discussion, the mathematician Sidney Karr was focusing on content and saw no contradiction between the Monteith General Education courses and the program of a math major from the freshman year onward. His judgment turned out to be correct for those whose primary identifications were not in Monteith but somewhere else at Wayne, either in a preprofessional program or in a liberal arts department, who could bridge the two worlds by accepting the Monteith one, so to speak, on its cognitive surface. However, those who became more exclusively identified with the Monteith world, and particularly with the social science staff, were going to find themselves facing the conflicts Rhodes had described and that King and Wald foresaw.

Tom Gant, the head adviser, had all along maintained that the "way-out" Monteith program would be disorienting for many entering students, and foreign to their parents, who expected Monteith to provide their children with immediately usable vocational skills. While agreeing with King and Robinson that Monteith might unfit students for the world of ordinary work, Gant was making a criticism of the direction in which the College was headed. For King and Wald, the most fervent of ideological missionaries, this was a criticism of the world and not of Monteith.

King and Wald and others like them at Monteith were not seeking to prove a point against the world by creating career dropouts at Monteith; they were not seeking to mobilize students as a new underclass who might make the revolution. Rather, they were scholarly men of high intelligence who may well have underestimated the degree to which commuter students from less privileged backgrounds could retain the option of joining the upper-middle class even when their undergraduate years did not succeed in compensating for earlier lack of preparation. Students who have known what it is to learn easily, work hard, and persist in the face of obstacles, have a number of second chances to regain academic and professional footing, after even a prolonged moratorium. Second chances for first-generation students from mediocre high schools are less easy to come by, or even to be aware of. One of the problems of mass higher education arises from a kind of subtle elitism by which the moratorium of the well-endowed is indiscriminately brought into institutions for the upwardly mobile—thus ironically preserving the class structure and its meritocratic defenses.[10]

(In grasping the impact of the intellectual ferment of Monteith on first-generation students, we have again and again to emphasize that these students had the easy alternative of opting out of Monteith and transferring to Liberal Arts or to another undergraduate college at Wayne—and many did so.)

The dangers to which King and Robinson had pointed arose in those aspects of the Monteith program in which faculty members sought to influence more than the cognitive style of the students and, in some cases, to de-emphasize formal learning. We shall see that there was great variation in this respect, even among the more personalistically oriented social scientists; in the other divisions, the kind of straightforward instruction that Sidney Karr represented was more prevalent. In such orbits, students could manage without feeling that their values had been upset: they were asked to harness their old aspirations and values to the new context without a radical readjustment.

At Oakland in the early years, faculty members were not much concerned lest the students be unfitted for the world outside—if they made it through Oakland, they would be well prepared. The trouble was that so few could make it. Like many selective colleges until very recently, Oakland was tougher than most of the occupational world, whose standards for a "passing grade" are usually lower.

Two Academic Atmospheres

Oakland's atmosphere was like that of a hotel or apartment house whose guests or tenants are expected to be polite but not particularly neighborly, while Monteith was more like a family,

[10] When one of us was in Japan in 1961, there was an outcry when it was discovered that a schoolmaster in Hokkaido beat his students if they did not work hard. The Japanese, on the whole, are soft on children, especially boys. The headmaster responded to the criticism by saying that his school was not located in Tokyo, that it did not have the best teachers or students from professional and intellectual families; his students could compete only if they were forced to work to overcome these handicaps.

where the privacy of office and classroom hardly existed.[11] Monteith, of course, did not have its own campus but had to create its style of life amid the chaotic non-campus of sprawling Wayne. Classes were and still are held in the same buildings as other Wayne classes, but the faculty and administration offices were (and remain) located around the neighborhood in old-fashioned, barely converted houses, where the common bathrooms preserve the sense of family life. When we first visited Monteith, one building housed the administrative offices, the natural science staff, and the Student Center, a combination that produced an interesting mélange of noise and movement, with students coming and going and the phonograph constantly blaring. The natural science faculty often fled from the noise. Two blocks away, in what was known as "the gray building," the same sense of stir and bustle was generated by the crowded conditions under which the social science staff worked. The two floors of the house were devoted to offices, and the foyer had been turned into a secretarial office, where the secretaries, young and colorful enough to pass for students, did not act as forbidding presences. People moved across the small corridor into each other's offices and into the secretarial office and, whether offices were private or shared, they were rarely locked. Indeed, office doors were usually kept open, and instructors sometimes complained that colleagues borrowed books without permission and took staff dictaphones without returning them.

In the spring of 1960 the social scientists and natural scientists moved into a former apartment house next to the Student Center. Still later, when the students, on their own initiative, moved the Center to another house, what had been the Student Center was converted into offices for the humanities staff and the administration. But even under these less crowded conditions, when for the first time each instructor had his own office with a sign on the door, the open-door policy remained. Later, staff coffee rooms be-

[11] Another analogy can be taken from Michael Young and Peter Willmott's *Family and Kinship in East London;* in the suburbs, people "keep themselves to themselves," as against the three-generational noisy coziness of the slums.

came the loci for group meetings, still without inhibiting movement in and out of people's offices.

Even when the Monteith Student Center had its own building, several of the faculty made a point of spending a good deal of time there and were critical of others on the faculty who did not. There was also much concern about whether faculty should encourage students to call them by their first names; especially in the social sciences, a number were explicit in using students' first names and encouraging students to reciprocate. In dress, too, many manifested a similar informality, hoping in this way to reduce barriers vis-à-vis colleagues and students. One Monteith social scientist told us how much he resented the fact—how old-fashioned it seems now; this was 1960!—that "professors support their status by their dress and demeanor," while students "have too much respect for authority anyway." This man could have "passed" as a student, and he felt that this freed his students to argue with him. Typical of Monteith was the anecdote of a young professor who was ordered out of a projection booth by a camera operator who could not believe that this man who needed a shave, wore a short-sleeved shirt and no tie, could be a faculty member. Even the three staff chairmen dressed in ways that departed from standard middle-class norms.

Understandably, members of the student "family" sometimes overstepped the limits of familiarity. An illustration of this was an incident that occurred during one of our interviews with a social scientist, a woman who spent a good deal of time at the Student Center. While we were talking in an isolated corner of the Center basement, a student happened to enter the cloakroom, in which we were sitting. He stood behind her. She asked him if he wanted anything, and he said, "No, I am just listening, or is this a—do you mind?" She said, "Yes, I think I do mind." He left. After he left, she said, "At first we wanted communication so badly that we just couldn't talk this way at all to students. Now we feel that we have reached a point at which we can do this."

At Oakland, the more restrained atmosphere was supported by the architecture and layout. The three two-story, motel-modern, and architecturally uninteresting buildings erected during the first two years were planned for growth, and in 1959, with only freshmen on hand, they had an empty look. Fewer than six hundred student commuters could almost be lost in facilities built for many more. Most of the faculty had offices in North Foundation Hall, which also contained a temporary (and often nearly empty) library, science labs and classrooms, administrative offices, and two large lecture rooms. A Student Center connected by a walkway held cafeteria, lounge, and bookstore facilities, and there was another classroom building.[12] Most faculty offices were located on one side of North Foundation Hall, with twenty-four identical cubicles spaced along two corridors. Each instructor had his own office, and usually the door was locked or closed. The doors were solid with glass transoms above, so that—quite contrary to the Monteith open-door policy—it was not always possible to know whether anyone was inside; one had to knock, and could not wander in casually.[13]

During that first year at Oakland, it was unusual to find a faculty member in his office except by appointment. At the outset, when the library was unsatisfactory and rudimentary, serious scholars were inclined to do their "own" work at home and to keep on their office bookshelves mostly texts and materials connected with class activities. This tendency was heightened by the fact that the faculty dining room at the Student Center did not develop until much later.

[12] New buildings have been continuously added, but always with the spacious layout reminiscent of some of the new university parks in England or the landscaped expansiveness of MSU, Illinois, or Indiana.

[13] Although the Educational Facilities Laboratory has studied the relation between spatial and social arrangements, we know of no systematic study of the relation between layout, secretarial barriers, and faculty-faculty and faculty-student contacts. The multiplication of faculty secretaries with the rising level of grants, amenities, and busy-ness may be an unnoticed element in the growth of feelings of impersonality of which both faculty and students complain. A teaching assistant may find that he cannot confer privately with students because he shares his office with several of his fellow T.A.s; a few years later, he may have his secretary sharing his office with him; not much later still, access to him may be barred by a protective, or simply an officious, secretary. For general discussion, see Martin Trow, "The Campus as a Context for Learning: Notes on Education and Architecture."

Indeed, no "infrastructure" surrounded Oakland—at that time not even a gas station, let alone a coffeehouse or off-campus bookstore—as casual meeting places for faculty and students. Students took off for home when their car pool left or when their own classes were over, whichever occurred earlier. Even now, when the new greatly expanded library building is the most striking and beautiful on campus, it is still not an adequate research library for many men in the social sciences and the humanities.

The paucity of meeting places also kept faculty at Oakland from seeing as much of each other as they might have done had there been a greater provision of amenity. This was especially true of the physicists and chemists, who were a bit isolated from other faculty in an end of North Foundation Hall, accessible through a separate entrance and adjacent to the laboratory in which the science instructors taught. This very arrangement, however, facilitated contacts between science students and faculty, especially when in the third year the creation of a Science Building some three hundred yards from the Center enabled many faculty to bring their own lunches and to rely on the Science Building's coffee table. Indeed, the casual meritocracy common among natural scientists makes such arrangements frequent even where there is a faculty club, and comradeship between faculty and students in the natural sciences may be one element in the "two cultures" division on the university campus.[14]

The Structure of Academic Work

The mealtime colleagueships and intense discussions among faculty at Oakland did not upset the boundaries faculty members have

[14] Does this way of stating the "two cultures" division imply that the scientists should have made the effort to come to North Foundation Hall while the rest of the faculty needed to make no effort to come to the Science Building? Certainly C. P. Snow's own essay remarked on the greater willingness of scientists to seek to understand the humanities than the other way around, something one can notice in many curricula and in most academic conversations. As the institutionally stronger power, it may indeed be necessary for the scientists to come more than halfway if the gap is to be bridged even partially.

traditionally kept around their courses and the physical space of their classrooms. Despite the close linguistic relation between the words "college" and "colleague," college teaching is usually neither supervised nor observed by peer or superior.[15] It may even be that one element in the contempt of university-trained college teachers for those they refer to as "educationists" and toward those whom the latter train lies precisely in the fact that schoolteachers do practice-teaching and are observed and evaluated on the job.[16]

We had been warned at Oakland that we would not be able to observe classes. In part this warning may have reflected the norm of privacy, but it also reflected, as did that norm, a certain antagonism to intrusive social scientists, which was expressed by several faculty members when we first described the study we were planning. But in practice, the antagonism—common enough among people in the humanities and to a lesser degree in the natural sciences —evaporated. Later, some Oakland faculty did occasionally visit each other's classes. Discussion about teaching and curriculum was passionate and intense in the early years.[17]

[15] Graduate-student teaching assistants who are in most cases very loosely supervised are a partial exception. See, however, the description of efforts to reform this casualness at the University of Utah in Charles H. Monson, Jr., "Teaching Assistants: The Forgotten Faculty."

[16] Some junior and community colleges are in this respect more like high schools than they are like liberal arts colleges. Their instructors often have come from high schools; their deans and presidents may have doctorates from places like Teachers College, Columbia; the textbooks they use, the methods they employ, and the grades they give may be supervised—as happens occasionally also in non-elite four-year colleges, but usually with less direct intervention. At several junior colleges we have visited, male faculty have been instructed not to wear beards and females not to wear their hair long, a deference to community attitudes that reflects local control of what is often regarded as the thirteenth and fourteenth grades.

[17] A professor in humanities at Berkeley told us some years ago that when he asked a colleague for the latter's course outline, this was interpreted as meaning that he could not be a serious researcher. At a different state university, a professor in the social sciences told us that camaraderie among his colleagues depended on an absolute taboo on talking political science, so much so that when he had asked his predecessor to tell him what he did in the course he was to take over, he was told that it was entirely up to him and that it was nobody else's business.

Somewhat later, when Oakland students began to publish quite careful evalu-

At Monteith many of the boundaries that were the norm at Oakland were absent or residual. Faculty bookshelves contained other books in addition to course-related materials, suggesting the relative lack of separation between work and home, teaching and scholarship, personal and collegial life. Moreover, as we have seen, all three of the required major sequences at Monteith are taught by a staff jointly; while advanced tutorial seminars could in principle be taught individually, a number, especially in the social sciences, in fact have been taught collegially. In accordance with the original design, the Senior Colloquium was taught the first time around by three instructors, one from each staff; as we shall see, this interstaff collaboration broke down. The important point is that no one could teach at Monteith without taking part in one of the three required sequences, and nothing prevented several men from teaching from time to time in more than one division.

As among the Israeli kibbutzim, the degree of collectivization varied; the social scientists, as one might expect, exhibited the greatest degree of participatory democracy. At the outset, the first version of the first year's social science sequence was planned by the so-called "secret six" from the University of Chicago clustered around Alice Corrigan, but subsequent parts of the five-quarter sequence were planned by committees within the staff. The first terms of the natural science and humanities sequences were planned by Sidney Karr and Donald Pearson respectively, in subsequent terms by staff committees. Future plans, as well as the problems of the course then being taught, were constantly under discussion by the full staff. In all three divisions it was never expected that the courses would be planned with any finality, and modifications were frequently being introduced or contemplated.

The original Gray Document had described a staff structure in which a master (experienced) teacher would preside over a staff of younger disciples. In such a structure the norm of private property usually prevails, and the relation between the professor and staff is

---

ations of courses, the majority of faculty who had never been in anyone else's classroom naturally became privy to student opinion beyond what hearsay and faculty conversation had already furnished.

analogous to that of the owner of a small business and his employees. If the employer is respected, the employees may carry out his mandate as best they can; if not, they may do their best to sabotage and undermine him with the customers—an attitude not uncommon among teaching assistants in places like Berkeley, Harvard, and Columbia. However, such a model was never implemented at Monteith. The interplay between specialists on a particular subject and the remainder of the staff preserved a high degree of equality; for example, though a specialist might be someone of lesser rank and personal stature, his expertise would still be drawn upon without any notice of such distinctions. The expert could never hide behind the walls of his trained specialty, nor could he have other forms of privacy. For instance, some of the early social science readings described the composition and interaction within small groups. One of the psychologists had developed a series of sociometric exercises for the students to use in connection with the readings. Anthropologists, sociologists, and others on the staff criticized this exercise, despite the supposed expertise of the psychologist. On another occasion, the same man had developed a system for evaluating the field observations of students, but this attempt was also attacked by the staff.

Beyond expertise, the distinction between staff chairmen and the rest of the staff made for some limited hierarchy, and informal leaders and factions emerged. Yet the fundamental pattern of staff equality never became distorted to the point where a course could be called the property of even a leading clique, let alone a single person. In any such collective enterprise, those who care deeply are likely to carry more weight than those who care less; they may leave their mark on a course through a particular reading or a particular approach to the materials. This happened at Monteith, yet the courses did not become pastiches of unintegrated bits and pieces. In the natural science sequence, history of science, philosophy of science, and specific scientific disciplines were all drawn within an historical framework. In all the sequences, the norm of integration and the group decision process tended to mute the development of subareas under the dominance of specific disciplines, and hence of specific individuals.

Some fields, or rather the people in them, lend themselves more readily to integration than others. It was probably no accident that the social science faculty at Monteith found it difficult to introduce economics into the program. At the outset, an effort was made to include a section on price theory; this proved to be an undigested lump. Later, economics entered through the door of economic development—that paradoxical field that has refreshed economics by forcing it to deal with "backward" countries. Similarly, the harder branches of psychology, such as experimental and general psychology, were not included. These areas have reached such finesse that their devotees find it frustrating to mix with softer academic breeds. The Monteith brand of psychology tended to be social-psychological, reflecting the interactionist school at the University of Chicago and especially the intellectual tradition of Everett Hughes in sociology and Robert Redfield in anthropology. Political science came in through the door of political sociology and not as it would have been taught by a disciple of Leo Strauss or Charles McElwain. Of course, even under this system, a particular instructor could in his own classes emphasize some readings and approaches and underplay others, but the common lectures and examinations put severe limits on the degree of discretion that could operate.[18]

Needless to say, closeness can become claustrophobic for some people, and a number of faculty left Monteith because of the pressure of demands for involvement with fellow staff members. In our own visits to Monteith, we noticed that a great deal of the daily shop talk was concerned with staff meetings and staff problems. Often our interviews evoked complex descriptions of the respondent's

[18] Some administrators and faculty and a great many students regard departmental specialization as an evil, reflecting the bad faith, inertia, or obscurantism of academicians. But anyone who observed the effort that went into the creation and further development of the courses at Monteith knows better: viable interdisciplinary courses that are not merely additive can be built only with imagination, erudition, and endurance—and then they have a short half-life. Cf. David Riesman, "Some Problems of a Course in 'Culture and Personality.'"

version of the motives and moods of his fellow staff members. A difficult reading assignment might be criticized as an effort to show off one's profundity, or be supported as revealing one's faith in the capacity of ordinary students to absorb extraordinary literature. (The students themselves were often aware in a general way of these struggles.) For some faculty, the egalitarian structure of the joint course and the mutual stimulation of working together on it were the great contributions of Monteith to their development. As one faculty member said, "I don't think of the staff as a job group performing a task. It is an intellectual community. When I taught at Wisconsin, I just simply talked *to* them [the students]. I didn't get ideas. I wouldn't like joint courses unless they had this characteristic of being an intellectual community." For others, however, these activities seemed to drain off creative energies into matters of small consequence: "We have a diverse staff with diverse ideals and a diverse course. Communication is no good. We have no committee system. We spend hours and hours and hours at things. People resent this. The more efficient an organization is, the less meetings it has."

In this environment, almost every question of procedure and course content was forced through a sieve of discussion. Arguing about materials and their accessibility for students exposed the intellectual craftsmanship of faculty to one another, but these skills were on more direct display in the lectures given twice a week to the entire group of students taking the core courses. Faculty rotated lectures; all faculty attended the lectures, presumably to enable everyone to draw on this material in the small class discussions. Since lectures were held in a large auditorium, instructors from other staffs and administrators occasionally attended also.[19] After the lectures, people would ask: Did so-and-so deliver a good lecture yesterday? Is he improving? How was his delivery? His organization?

[19] Thus, the head of guidance, Tom Gant, went to most of the social science lectures. During one of our visits in the second year, we attended a natural science lecture, and several social scientists were also there; afterward, they told us that they thought the lecture was inept and badly organized. A natural science staff member judged it equally severely.

It would be said of someone that he was not at his best in front of a large audience, or of another that he spoke to the cognoscenti, particularly his faculty peers, and not to the general level of students. As time went on, this kind of hashing over the lecture became formalized; in the third year, panels of faculty discussed each lecture at the following session and encouraged students to ask questions from the floor.

These efforts to create an improvisational atmosphere in the lecture halls were only partially successful, in part perhaps because the auditoriums were like those at most universities—very large, with elevated lecterns and platforms. Even for small classes and discussion sections, Monteith depended on Wayne classrooms, which were conventional and rarely included seminar tables; but it was possible to move the furniture about so as to provide a makeshift circle, and Monteith faculty and students usually did so. This accommodation to an informal style, however, went far beyond the alteration of the classrooms. Here are examples of the general style from notes made on one of our early visits:

I found Ken Roberts, Howard Rich, and George Green having lunch at a nearby restaurant. I knew that Green and Harold King were giving a class together at one o'clock. Joseph Grady and Rich also had some relationship to the class but I wasn't sure what it was. We talked about this at lunch. This is the first term in the social science sequence for those students who entered Monteith "out of phase," at the beginning of the spring term. They are taking two terms of natural science in one. . . . The social science staff has devised a special course for this situation. Green, Rich, and Roberts spoke of it with enthusiasm. They see it as a loosely constructed thing in which they attempt to sensitize students to imaginative observation. They do not use social science materials. Instead, they have been reading and discussing novels. At present they are reading and discussing C. P. Snow's novel *The Search.*

As happens at Monteith, Ken Roberts, who is not one of the instructors in this specific class, decided that he would also go to the one o'clock class. I had already asked Green and King for their permission to attend. Ken did not ask them if he could attend. He announced quite casually that he would also go. There was nothing strained about the announcement.

Roberts sat in the front of the class, in the first row of seats. He turned his chair around so that he faced the rest of the class. Green and King (the "real" instructors for this class) sat in different parts of the room, and many students had pulled their chairs around in order to make conversation easier. Harold King's wife, Jane, a biologist, came in and sat next to him. Jane announced that she had come to defend Snow, as she had heard that he was being maligned. A good deal of the discussion involved a defense of and attack on Snow's portrayal of the procedures of science. As the discussion continued, Ken Roberts came to dominate the discussion. He drew a diagram on the board of scientific methods in one of the social sciences. Others of the faculty and Jane King participated in the discussion of this typology. The class accepted this free-for-all and Roberts' role in it with little visible anxiety about who was the teacher. (When students participated, they directed remarks at the most pertinent faculty member.) Harold King did try to play the role of leader, to bring the discussion back to the business of the Snow novel and other books discussed in the past. While students entered the discussion, it became more and more a colloquium among the faculty with Ken Roberts at the center. At one stage I [Gusfield] was even drawn into it, so difficult was it to tell who had ownership or control of the class. During the discussion one of the students wanted to know who I was and asked me for my opinion on the topic under discussion. . . .

The class ended at two o'clock. At 3:30, Howard Rich, who had not been there, met us in the social science office and said: "I hear the one o'clock didn't go off well," and proceeded to render a fairly accurate account of the class. "The one last week didn't either," he added.

During our interviews with faculty, we followed the procedure of asking them if we might "sit in" on a class at some future time. . . . Sometimes, as in this case, we were unable to do this until just before the class met. Today, finding that I had an open hour between 1:00 and 2:00 P.M. I decided to try to observe one of Ken

Roberts' classes. Not being able to reach him that morning I decided to get to his classroom early and meet him at the door.

I had lunch with Werner Wald, two other Monteith staff members, and the Shelbys. (This latter couple were in town for a possible job at Monteith.) I was anxious about the time, not wanting to walk into Roberts' class "cold." I mentioned this to the luncheon group, and Wald said he thought it a good idea if the Shelbys attended both his and Ken's classes. He also thought that he would like to go to Ken's class. This made four of us.

I told them which classroom was scheduled for Roberts' one o'clock. Werner Wald said he was pretty sure that Ken would have moved the class to someplace else, most likely the Student Center. Wald was right. We walked in several minutes late. Despite my reluctance, he insisted that this was all right, and the four of us marched into the room where Roberts and nine students were holding a discussion to the background of noise from a phonograph in the next room. Several other students came in later.

We did not enter into the discussion until the last fifteen minutes, when Wald began to try to turn the discussion into a new channel. What had been largely a dialogue between Ken Roberts and an articulate student became a three-cornered argument and then a dialogue between Roberts and Wald. The discussion had been focused on a movie the students had seen earlier, presenting life in Hobohemia. Werner was trying to push the discussion into a comparison of subcultures while Ken had treated it as a problem of defining deviance. In exasperation, Ken said, "You want to jack this discussion up to the fifth level. I want to bring it down to Howard Street [the San Francisco main stem]. I will throw you out of *my* class." Even this did not stop Wald. (Although Roberts did not seem especially angry at the time, he brought up the matter two days later at a party and spoke with bitterness about Werner Wald's "breaking up" his class.)

This section had only nine students officially registered, but more were present. In fact, students were encouraged to shop around, and some attended more than one section in the same course. Occasionally instructors would simply shift a class over to a room in the Student Center (the Wayne campus does not have many tree-shaded lawns where outdoor classes can be held). There was little emphasis on punctuality, and no one seemed disturbed by people coming in late or leaving early. In the modern idiom, Monteith hung loose.

In the early years, Oakland was far more antiseptic, and even its staff-taught courses had little of the family flavor of Monteith. In the Western Institutions course, while the materials and examinations were common for all the sections, each instructor met his class four times a week and there were no shared lectures. As already indicated, the readings were those originally prepared for Columbia College, but an instructor with literary, philosophical, or historical interests could within the limits of the examination emphasize these materials differentially without feeling pressure from his peers. Some staff members tended to regard the course as "belonging" to its chairman, Mark Williams, the Columbia-trained historian, and thus to absolve themselves of full responsibility. As one historian told us, "I don't like the fact that the readings are assigned by other people"; he continued, "I'm not much interested in some of them, and the kids don't get much out of them. Mark [Williams] has included a lot of Kant and Hegel, for example." As soon as he decently could, this man pulled out of the Western Institutions course and concentrated on "his own" history courses. Correspondingly, there were no joint lectures in which a total group of students was exposed to different teachers, nor did colleagues ask to attend classes given by other professors. The students themselves tended to be more docile than some of the "Monteithy" types, and unlike the latter, were not encouraged to shop around among the various sections of the required University Courses.

Oakland's more formal and structured pattern of faculty-student relations provided a comforting base for many entering students at the very moment when they were emancipating themselves from family and non-college friends. Shaken in many of their preconceptions, they could at least hang onto the belief in some authority and the feeling that there was someone in charge. But unlike

Monteith, where students had the option of transferring to other programs at Wayne, those Oakland students who could not stand the culture shock or make the grade had only the option of dropping out.

VII Teaching Styles and the Polarities of Work and Play

Some observers, including students and faculty, have seen colleges as "total institutions," analogous to mental hospitals, factories, jails, and armies. Such language tends to collapse into a single model a variety of encounters between students and academic institutions. In a classic study, Willard Waller described the high school as an arena in which teachers and students battled for control in the classroom and over the requirements for promotion or graduation. Waller saw both teachers and students as victimized by the struggle,[1] while contemporary writers on the subject have tended to see only the students as the victims.[2]

Hyperbolic language about such victimization can shape a student's actual experience of education. A student's sense of injustice can move him to expend most of his energies trying to outwit his exploiters, either by Good Soldier Schweik tactics or by more direct action. Affluent students in good colleges can afford to use their

[1] See *The Sociology of Teaching*.
[2] Discussing Berkeley, Nathan Glazer notices the way in which undergraduates in apparently benign American universities have been able to persuade themselves and many others that these institutions are repressive and authoritarian rather than permeable and loose. See Glazer, "'Student Power' in Berkeley."

college years in tacit or open combat with the institution. Such students sometimes realize the power they have over their teachers; they are aware that they are a resource, and they may become accustomed to having adults take them seriously. Most of the students at Oakland and Monteith were not so privileged. It did not occur to them, any more than it occurs to most students, that they held in their own hands the relative success of the two educational experiments. Some at Monteith did become aware of the faculty's dependence on them, especially the social science faculty. At Oakland, where the faculty relied more on colleagues than on students for a sense of worth, the students had somewhat less power; but they could always wound individual faculty members by selective inattention. The majority of faculty members at both colleges had come because of some interest in teaching undergraduates. Lacking graduate students and only rarely involved in outside consulting, they were not casual about how the students would react.

Work Versus Play

What surprised the faculty at both institutions in the early months was the seriousness of these commuter students about their academic obligations. They were not collegiate; they did not goof off; they seemed to want to do what was expected of them, if only they could find out what it was. At Monteith about a month before the term began in 1959, the natural science and social science staffs sent a joint letter—later referred to as "the Plato letter"—to all the incoming students. In it, they stressed the unity of learning, and the need for students to read materials prior to discussion. A section of a Platonic dialogue was assigned for the first day of class, and most of the students had read the assignment by the time the first class convened. At Oakland, the faculty were even more astonished by how hard their students worked. There was no well-established student culture with which instructors were obliged to bargain, no shop stewards among upperclassmen from whom freshmen could learn what they might get away with. They came with expectations based on what had happened to them in high school,[3] but any nascent high school type resistance to faculty demands crumbled after the first grading period.

The very good student from a college-educated family may subordinate himself to faculty demands because these hold intrinsic interest for him or because he considers it important to demonstrate his adequacy to relevant others or to himself. The middle class in general, however, is aware of how to get its way vis-à-vis bureaucratic and other obstacles, and the sophisticated student recognizes that instructors may not be as tough as they seem, or that they may be setting high standards merely as initial bargaining points. Some of the faculty had come to these new colleges because they disliked teaching such students. One Monteith social scientist said of his well-coached University of Chicago students that he was tired of the "smart alec who gets in his carefully phrased sentences three times each meeting," and who wants to be "noticed for his cleverness and for having read something extra." Another Monteith social scientist felt that his Chicago students needed him less than those he hoped to find at Monteith; at Chicago he saw his students as learning some of the great ideas from him, but no values or more personal things, which he hoped he could convey to less privileged students. Similarly, two social scientists who migrated to Oakland from Wesleyan, one of the richest of the selective colleges, did not think the students they had left behind would suffer without them; they hoped to find a less homogeneous student body in a commuter school, one to which they would be able to make a greater contribution.

But students who are the first in their families to attend college are not necessarily easier to teach because of their ignorance of what goes on in "halls of learning." They often have a difficult time identifying with faculty members and, hence, either learning from them or seeing ways of getting around them. This can lead to sullen-

---

[3] This was true not only in terms of academic work, but also in social life. There was no real break. Many students returned to their high schools during the lunch hour when lunchroom facilities were not yet adequate; many continued to date high school friends.

ness and apathy. It took most Oakland and Monteith students quite a while to learn how to deal with the faculty when it became evident that the tricks used in high school did not work.[4]

We have seen that the great majority of faculty members attracted to Oakland came with their guard up against the dangers for academic standards of Big Ten collegiate rivalry and the kind of high school youth culture vividly described by James Coleman.[5] It took a while before the faculty discovered a more subtle enemy in the disciplined, industrious attitudes of a student body that was anxious about its immediate postcollege occupational future. We ourselves became aware of this double-take of the Oakland faculty, especially in the humanities, on one of our early visits. In an attempt to lend vividness and excitement to materials currently being read in the required course in Western Institutions, the faculty had arranged for a showing of the Laurence Olivier film, *Henry V*. To the faculty's dismay, the students attended the film as they would have attended a lecture, with dutifulness rather than delight. Anxiously, they set out to grasp what they were expected to get out of it. As became evident from the poor attendance at voluntary cultural events held later at the college, the great majority would not have gone to *Henry V* if it had not been required, but would have attended to their required reading, to their part-time jobs,[6] to their families (with whom they lived), or to the

---

[4] One encounters considerable romanticism about the relative poverty of students in state colleges in contrast to elite private colleges. The latter can afford to recruit much poorer students by scholarships that pay subsistence as well as tuition, whereas most residential state colleges, though they have negligible tuition for in-state students, can only rarely offer scholarships to cover all college costs.

[5] James S. Coleman, *The Adolescent Society*.

[6] Like Monteith students, many Oakland students were faced with the necessity of working. Some could have managed, with loans and summer work, to devote full time to being students. But in the milieu from which they came, this would not have made sense either to them or to their families. Unsure of the future and, in the case of the girls, fearing a negative dowry, there would have been anxiety about taking a loan even when in reality it could easily have been paid off at low rates of interest (and in inflated dollars). Parents could understand when their son had to drive over to the college for chemistry

bursts of relaxation they considered were owed them. What the faculty really wanted was cultural transformation, and while the students' obedient ingestion of materials was an improvement over Philistine hedonism, it was nevertheless a deep disappointment. The faculty often spoke of "learning for its own sake" and usually found that such a notion was strange to naïve students concerned with getting on in college and the world.

Perhaps the faculty themselves were naïve for not realizing how difficult it would be for the students to make a two-generation jump in a single generation. It was especially difficult because, as we shall see in the following chapter, the grading pattern required the students to attend to these unmistakable signals concerning performance at the expense of the more subtle signals about cultivation and enjoyment that some faculty were also sending out.[7] Some faculty soon caught on to the problems they faced. An Oakland historian observed, "It's kind of hard to have an Ivy League institution without an Ivy League student body. This faculty doesn't know how to teach the students to play." The historian was not speaking about the fact that many of the Oakland faculty were themselves first-generation scholars who would have had a hard time teaching themselves to play, men who had learned to make a living through ideas rather than regarding ideas as the breath of life itself.[8] But it is an open question whether a faculty more playful in intellectual style would have done a better job, given the Oak-

on Monday, Wednesday, and Friday at 10:00 A.M., and they could understand when he had to take an examination. But if he were returning in the evening only for art cinema or a discussion of Vietnam, he might as well stay home, help fix the roof, or join the family in watching television.

[7] Becker, Geer, and Hughes, in *Making the Grade: The Academic Side of College Life*, discuss at length the interpretation made by students of faculty nonchalance about grades. Just as the rich man (or the hopelessly poor one) can afford to be nonchalant about money, so faculty can afford to ignore grades, which still remain the currency of the system that students face.

[8] See Richard Hofstadter, *Anti-Intellectualism in American Life*. Arthur Miller, writing about repertory theater, has spoken of the difficulty of learning how to play "in the defensive, cautious, psychological position" based on the need to have aesthetic innovations pay off in success.

land student body. We are inclined to think that such a faculty would have confronted the hard-working, anxious Oakland students with models even more difficult to emulate, and in some ways perhaps more patronizing.

Oakland proceeded to build dormitories and to attract "better" students from a wider catch-basin. These academically better-prepared students also tended to be more socially adept, and Oakland's boot-camp atmosphere relaxed somewhat. But even then, no large cadre of faculty devoted itself to encouraging intellectual and aesthetic playfulness—these qualities crept in later and interstitially.

In contrast, many of the most influential Monteith faculty in the social sciences encouraged their students to explore questions and to play with ideas in the context of a curriculum that remained quite demanding: Monteith had announced that there were to be no texts and no spoon-feeding, and all three divisions exposed students to intricate readings, required many papers, and in the social sciences, several original research projects. Yet Monteith's looser style allowed many students to be chronically unprepared for their discussion sections and to goof off without serious penalty. Faculty members who had supposed that "proletarian" students would be hungry and eager for learning found that they did not fit this ideal but were rather like unmotivated and mediocre students elsewhere. A humanities instructor said to us:

> . . . I have had three classes today and very few people have read the material. One class has seventeen students. Nine attended, and of these only three had read the assignment. . . . The last class, however, was different. Everybody had read it and they talked about it quite well. Generally, though, the discussions are poor. They just don't work. At Syracuse they didn't work either. Syracuse was the Miami of the North. The students came from fairly wealthy homes —they had made it—why should they work? I felt when I came here they would be much more committed to their work here. It's not so. The only difference between these kids and the ones at Syracuse is that the ones here are not as well dressed.

Didactic and Evocative Classroom Styles

In visiting classes at the two colleges and asking faculty members what they thought characterized a good class or good teaching, our concern was with the efforts made to bridge the gaps between students and teachers, and between students and students. We were interested in the questions that haunt us in our own teaching, namely, how to deal with diversity? For whom should one teach? It is our impression from visiting classes in a number of institutions that faculty members tend to gear their teaching somewhere above the median of class ability and quickness of grasp; sometimes they may gear it to the top two or three students and only rarely to the slowest or least attentive. As our examples will indicate, classes at Monteith were often quite small—a dozen students or less. Oakland had a less favorable faculty-student ratio and larger sections, averaging around twenty (although upper-division courses were smaller). Both colleges took the advising and counseling function very seriously, insisting that much of it be done by faculty themselves and not farmed out to ancillary, para-academic people. In such face-to-face settings, faculty members could gear what they said to a specific student without having to orchestrate messages to a diverse group.

Our attendance at classes was in no way systematic, often being guided by the accident of whom we were having lunch with or what class was available at a particular hour. But in our interviews with faculty in the second year of both colleges, we asked all of them about teaching, about what they considered a good class and a bad class, a good student and a bad student, and so on. We asked several teachers in mathematics at Oakland what made them feel they had done a good job of teaching. One mathematician explained, "Everyone distrusted mathematics when we began and dared me to get them to like it. Now they are interested. They are reading and getting together. There is a difference between active and passive students though. . . . The active student must be part of the process. . . . A good teacher is going to create this atmosphere." One of his colleagues said, "A good day is when I feel I've had difficult concepts and have gotten them across."

Within each college there were, of course, enormous differences in style and attitude among faculty, but on the whole, Oakland faculty tended to emphasize didactic teaching, while Monteith put more emphasis on evocative teaching. A didactic teacher takes for granted his greater knowledge and authority, and invites students into the materials in terms set by him. The class is a production in which the instructor is the producer, the director, and the writer, while the students are the actors under his direction and also the ultimate audience. At the very least, what is asked of them is that they "get the material"; but the effort also may be to help them become active and go off on their own. In the classes we came to call evocative, the instructor was less concerned with covering ground or conveying ideas than with getting the students to connect what they were reading with their own experience, even at the cost of a certain fuzziness of outline. The invitation to learning was put into the students' own hands; they were allowed to help write the script or even to rewrite it. (Of course, such a class could fail miserably, conveying neither information, nor mood, nor competence.)

A good example of the didactic style was a psychology class we visited at Oakland. The topic was "Research on Small Groups." It was larger than most classes we saw: some thirty or thirty-five students sat in rows of separate metal or plastic armchairs. (The seats were movable, and could have been arranged in circular seminar fashion, and were so arranged on another occasion in a section of the Western Institutions course.) The class began promptly on the hour. The instructor, having mimeographed a number of sociometric matrices and put them on the blackboard, proceeded to show how Robert F. Bales had derived his typology of small groups from the same data. Moving about the room, or standing, or sometimes sitting on the desk, he managed to convey a great deal of his own excitement about the elegance and clarity of Bales's ideas. He lectured without a break for questions or comments; the students paid attention, most of them taking notes.

About two minutes before the end of the fifty-minute hour, many of the students began to put away their books. The lecture was well organized as well as highly successful in communicating the lecturer's excitement and pleasure in the subject. So far as we could tell, the students were diligent, although there was no way of gauging their involvement in the material.

Less overtly didactic was a social science discussion section at Monteith in which small groups was also the topic. In a classroom used by the College of Education, six young men and three young women were entertaining themselves by reading the children's literature on the bookshelves while awaiting the instructor, who was ten minutes late for his nine o'clock class. Some wooden tables were arranged to form a U pattern, with the girls sitting on one side and the boys on the other. Upon arrival, the instructor stood at the open end of the U, remaining there during the entire period, sometimes walking to the blackboard and sometimes standing at the table.

He began the class by quoting from the syllabus. After reading a quotation proposing that the next logical step after studying "relations" was to study "small groups," he asked, "Why is the study of small groups the next logical step?" Variations on this question constituted the content of the period. He wrote on the blackboard the terms describing the major topics studied during this term in the social science sequence: "relation," "small groups," "socialization," "differentiation," "pattern." "What we want to do is get the logical connection between 'relations' and 'small groups'!" He proceeded by asking questions and soliciting answers until he received an answer he regarded as satisfactory. Students also volunteered, and he called on them, or at times ignored them. He managed to draw out the point that moving from relations to small groups was a decrease in depth and an increase in extensiveness.

The participation of the class grew, and most of the students volunteered as the hour went on. The instructor's questions set up tensions of finding the "right" answer, tensions that were dissipated when he moved on to the next point. Several times a student interrupted to make suggestions, but the instructor did not encourage him. This same student, at another time, proposed a logical but false solution to a problem; the instructor shrugged his shoulders, said "Maybe," and passed on to others in his quest for the answer he wanted. Occasionally a dialogue would start up among the students. The instructor sat back and listened, then returned to the point at issue before interaction among the students went too far. Five minutes before the hour's close, the instructor himself began to answer the major questions with which he had opened. Then he stated the original question again and read the answer from the syllabus, explaining each term as he went along.

If we compare these two classes, it might seem on the surface that the Monteith class was less didactic than the Oakland one, and perhaps it was. Many students might well have felt that they took a more active part when they raised their voices than when they were silent. But such an assumption neglects both the vicarious participation that is possible in a lecture and the overcontrolled activism of a discussion where the prime task of the student is to fill in the blanks on a diagram already given. One could say that in the second classroom both students and teacher were subordinate to the syllabus, but the responsibility for the proper outcome remained almost entirely in the hands of the instructor, who saw the task as getting the students to understand the syllabus, to "cover ground," or to get across a certain content.

In another social science class at Monteith, the instructor was less concerned with content. This class also took place in a classroom borrowed from Wayne, too large for the five men and six women who were taking it. Here, the students clustered together at one end of a U-shaped arrangement of tables. The instructor sat close to the students. The effect was of a small group huddling together in the corner of a large room. The class began with a question from one of the men, asked just before the bell rang. Erving Goffman's article "On Face-Work" had been assigned in the week's reading, and the student wanted to know if the article related to the concept of "patterns." The instructor responded to this as a prelude. Then he began the class by asking the group, "What impressed you most in this section?" One of the women responded, "The article on the dyad." (She was referring to an essay by Georg Simmel on numbers and social groups, which was also in the assignment.) A male student then commented, "We knew these things ourselves, but we never realized them before." A middle-aged woman asked if the article on the dyad was sociology or philosophy, and the instructor said, "Let's defer the question until we find out more about the idea of 'relation.' "

The concept of relation occupied much of the subsequent discussion. The middle-aged woman talked of this in the light of her personal experiences. An exchange developed between her and a girl sitting next to her, who disagreed with her conclusions. The exchange became heated, but the instructor did not interfere. He then asked if a relation ends when a person dies. He mentioned a tribe in which the death of a relative is followed by the adoption of a child to replace the relative. The older woman compared this to the Jewish custom of naming a child after a dead person. One of the students responded to this, as did the instructor.

Only when this topic seemed to have exhausted itself did the instructor move on to something else. "What did you think of Orwell's essay 'Shooting an Elephant'?" This elicited a few reactions, and the instructor asked if anyone could use the article to explain how a person might be led to an action violating his own ethical norms. The irrepressible older woman said that one might be put into a position of feeling obligated to comply with another's demands. A boy entered the discussion in very general terms, using the word "relation" pretentiously in an apparent effort to impress the instructor. The instructor did not respond but sought instead to get the others to talk about their own lives as a way of illustrating his questions about the Orwell essay. He asked whether any of them had ever felt themselves in a situation where, as in "Shooting an Elephant," there was only one thing to do in the light of the expectations of others.

By now, half the class time had elapsed and most of the eleven students had participated. The instructor tried in different ways to escape the domination of the middle-aged woman, sometimes ignoring her and sometimes encouraging others to speak in order to shut her out of the discussion. In the remaining time, the discussion turned to dyadic and triadic relations, and students drew on their own relationships with friends and relatives for illustrations. After the bell had rung, the instructor suggested they write a paper on face-work and dating behavior. Someone asked if it could be a personal experience, and the instructor said it could.

However chaotic this class may have seemed to those accustomed to more structured situations, the instructor was in charge at all times. What he rewarded was never the correct answer, nor did he actually propose "correct" answers, but rather the effort by students to draw on personal observation and to gain a new purchase on it through the reading and discussion. Using terms uncoupled with experience was not rewarded. In considerable measure, what happened was not in the script. For one thing, the older, talkative woman could be only barely kept in control; she was indeed meeting the payroll of personal experience—only too much of it. (In one of the classes we visited at Oakland, just such an older woman, neither innocent nor docile, was of immense help in breaking the ice in a rather frozen discussion.) At the same time, the class was not permissive or "student centered" in the way those terms are often used, for the instructor was not seeking experience alone and uninterpreted, nor was he allowing students to assault or invade one another under the guise of candor or therapy. We could see that he already must have gone a long way toward reducing the barriers of age and rank between the students and himself. His aim appeared to be the use of the class to evoke the experience related to the materials.

This is what we mean by an evocative class, and as we have already suggested, a climate of evocativeness was consciously sought at Monteith. While it might seem that classes in the more "social" social sciences or in some of the humanities would lend themselves more readily to this, we visited a class in the natural sciences that exhibited a similar style.

This was a class scheduled for 8:00 A.M. with about half a dozen students. On the morning we visited, the instructor arrived a few minutes late, but the students had already begun asking each other questions about the material. The instructor came in and sat down at the head of the table; after the students had handed in their outlines (their reading had concerned the historical development of atomic theory), he began the discussion by asking what had led the chemists Davies and Berzelius to propose a dualistic theory of matter. How did one of the experiments bearing on the idea of elements support the received theory as against new theory? In the state of the science at that time, molecules were thought to repel, while atoms must attract to make up a molecule. The discussion proceeded in question-and-answer fashion in an attempt to develop possible explanations or theories for the facts that were known at that time.

The instructor at one point referred to an experiment reported in their readings where, with electrodes and water, there was a separation of water into hydrogen at one pole and oxygen at the other. The problem then became one of developing a theory that would resolve the problem of repulsion and attraction. One of the girls made a suggestion, which the instructor restated and then diagrammed on the board. Another student criticized this. The instructor agreed with the criticism and pointed out the grounds for his view. Then the girl tried to defend her original idea against the criticism. The instructor rejected this, explaining in detail why he did so. Then he gave a hint as to how the problem had been solved historically, saying that her ideas were indeed on the right track. One had to think in terms of a "mechanical" answer (by which he meant an answer in terms of what atoms were thought to look like). Two members of the class volunteered their own ideas, and the same girl now proposed an ingenious model of molecules in which the atoms were arranged as on a color wheel. At one point her model of complementary colors or atoms became complex, and the instructor said she had lost him. She went to the board and made a diagram of it. The instructor then added a new condition to the discussion to see if she could integrate it into her model. One of the boys asked if the model really did explain the facts of the experiment and those known at the time. Much discussion focused on the girl's model and its potential usefulness, and another student sought to add to the model. Most of the class entered in.

At this point the instructor pointed out what was unclear in the model and what it failed to take account of, as well as indicating the reasons why it would have been rejected in the historical period under consideration. A boy then suggested a new model. As the hour drew to a close, the instructor himself suggested still another model and pointed out how the girl's model had come close to meeting the problem.

In this class, as compared with the one just described in the social sciences, the emphasis was somewhat more on readings, which were to be understood, than on experiences, which could be shared. Even so, the instructor was not especially concerned with eliciting the correct answer; what he rewarded in students was the contribution of something interesting, whether or not it was correct. That is, the materials were a means to draw out the class, to involve it in problem-solving. To be sure, in dealing with the history of science, the instructor could count on less knowledge than did the social science instructor talking about dyads and human relations. But he did his best to erase differences of age and knowledge so that the students would feel free to talk and make mistakes.[9]

Another class we visited, in the humanities sequence, taught by a gifted musician, was devoted to the question of how to look at paintings. The instructor passed examples of great variety around the room, then put them up on the board and asked students for their impressions, hoping to free them of their awe of Art and

[9] We would certainly grant that there are many subjects that cannot be handled in a particularly evocative way: elementary language training, for example. We recall visiting a class in ancient Chinese history at a progressive girls' college where the mandate for the instructor was to be wholly non-directive and permissive, and where only discussion, and not lecturing, was approved. Yet some reading of a textbook in English hardly gave the students enough to talk about; to begin their careers by playing at being Arnold Toynbee was not sensible, and the instructor in fact conducted a brief lecture disguised as a discussion.

get them to see in an active way. He provided information casually and often interestingly, but his main effort was evocative. In still another humanities class, dealing with *Oedipus Rex,* the instructor sought to get the students to understand that the moral conflicts of the play were embedded in a social context not entirely alien to contemporary America.

As suggested by these examples, the Monteith faculty could treat the same syllabus materials in a great variety of ways. While they were all preparing students for a common examination, there were many loopholes which allowed individuation of sections. Especially in the social sciences, students were permitted to take examinations over again to erase previous failures, or to take Incompletes: all the staffs preferred examinations that were not "merely" factual. All opposed what they regarded as premature specialization, and the ideology of the College led the faculty to oppose didactic teaching as perhaps suitable for the development of "technicians" but not conducive to meeting the kinds of intellectual and personal issues that could prepare a student for advanced professional goals or for a satisfying life.

When ideology went against the grain of a professor's temperament and character, he might feel caught in a dilemma. One Monteith anthropologist was aware of his tendency "to kill discussion," adding that if students "direct their comments to each other, *I* get lost." He added that he was "pretty authoritarian." Another man told us of a class that became "polarized into a student-against-faculty situation . . . the students began to get the idea that they shouldn't participate, that, like high school, they should play it cool."[10]

But even teachers who made a specialty of evocativeness were not always successful. In one Monteith class we observed, the

---

[10] One perhaps unanticipated side effect of a premium on evocative teaching may be to diminish the willingness and hence the ability of students to learn from didactic mentors. Such mentors may seem authoritarian rather than authoritative. Paralleling our work is the research of Joseph Axelrod of the Center for Research and Development in Higher Education at Berkeley on styles of teaching, which distinguishes between "student-centered" teachers who are cognitively oriented and those who are more affectively oriented. See his *Model-Building for Undergraduate Colleges.*

section leader, an anthropologist who wore a loose tie and no jacket, sat on the edge of the desk swinging his legs, using four-letter words (before they had become part of the vernacular), and telling the students how rough and tough he had been as a boy. For some students, this was an invitation to learning, when many other teachers they had encountered had seemed too remote. But for others it was confusing because, after all, the instructor had a Ph.D. and, despite his hipster argot, was erudite and widely traveled. He may have turned off the diligent and conscientious and those seeking through attendance at college to escape the culture of the street; perhaps some may even have seen him as subtly condescending. So, too, such an instructor may make a tacit alliance with the men in the class against the women, who may be "cooled out" to the point of becoming frozen. When confronting more than a handful of students, a teacher can hardly help sacrificing the requirements of some of his constituents to those of others, and even the most tactful and alert may not always recognize what the different needs are.

It was characteristic of Monteith that we could talk to the instructors after class about just these questions. Monteith faculty were often aware that, by seeking to reduce formality, they could stifle students who wanted to maintain their distance. Yet especially among the social scientists, the ideal was a classroom in which the teacher was at most first among equals, following the line of the students' own interests as they brought these in from outside the readings, and seeking as outcomes insight and involvement rather than skill or finesse. As one Monteith anthropologist said, a good class was one where "the instructor becomes a part of the group." Sitting in on such a classroom, the observer might suppose that no demands were being made on the students, but this would overlook the demand that evocative instructors made on their students to adopt a certain style of intellectual-emotional involvement. Indeed, the insistent encouragement to become an intellectual, critical of received patterns and ideas, was often extended by charismatic instructors who underestimated their impact, seeing themselves only as members of the peer group. Few students came to either

Oakland or Monteith with the idea that they might themselves become academicians—a schoolteacher, perhaps, for that was a familiar role, or an engineer, or a member of some vaguely defined, respectable, white collar job. However, both colleges in their first years did convert a number of students to the academic life, and many of these students told us in interviews that it was an instructor they regarded as evocative who furnished the original inspiration. Such conversions are not automatic testimony to the quality of teaching, and we cannot be sure that these students would not have followed the same path at any other undergraduate college. But we think it unlikely that they would have overcome elsewhere their resistance to the very idea of an active relation to such material. Perhaps even more dramatic are the instances of students, both white and black, who entered Monteith with only the most tenuous hold on the idea of finishing college, but later became convinced, almost in spite of themselves, that it was manageable for the likes of them. In opening up their own emotional lives to students, faculty members made it possible for some students to identify with teachers in a way they had learned to avoid in the more didactic setting of the high school.

College Teaching: Adult-Forming and Youth-Prolonging

On the whole, the Oakland faculty asked of its students a rapid putting away of childish things. As we shall see in more detail in Chapter X, some were so tough on students as to threaten not only them but the institution itself. The result was to put some students off and to put others away altogether. But some students were invited to join the adults, to enter the particular subdiscipline of the faculty member and the intramural debates within the field. The didactic style sets limits on what is asked of students; when they perform competently, they can join the club. Oakland provided a home away from home for students of this sort, whose seriousness could make contact with the residual Puritanism of the farmers and working class people in Oakland County, even while it pulled a student away from his parents in occupational, political, and cultural terms. Yet, there were some Oakland faculty, especially in the humanities but also in the social sciences and counseling services, who saw in such victories the high price that had been paid in driving underground any independent student culture, any hope of fostering playfulness, if not of an intellectual then at least of a collegiate sort. If one could not evoke in these students excitement about a problem in calculus or about an Elizabethan drama, even if one could obtain a certain level of proficiency, was it worth the effort?

One can also regard playfulness not as frivolous, but as actually containing a latent purposiveness in the opportunity it provides to cultivate expressiveness and solidarity in the face of growing merito-cratic pressures.[11] It is perhaps more accurate to say that some college teachers provide a model of youthful adulthood—adulthood without tears—while others present a more sober model which does not pretend or aim to extend the stage of youth. Certainly Oakland today presents a great diversity of adult models, as well as a more diversified student body. Indeed, growing affluence and hedonism have invaded the "poor but honest" social strata whose college-bound children had come to Oakland at the outset, and on that campus now one can find the characteristic tacit alliance between the radical and the non-conformist who seek to reduce institutional power on behalf of societal reform, and a large collegiate faction who want looser dormitory hours and a more relaxed curriculum.

As we have seen, in contrast to the original Oakland faculty, many Monteith instructors were somewhat less eager to induct their students into a particular specialty, preferring to protect them against what they regarded as premature, dehydrating adult demands. Some sought to link their students with a humanistic, rational outlook on the world, holding up an alternative style of adulthood

[11] See Talcott Parsons and Winston White, "The Link Between Character and Society," pp. 89–135. See, for a contrasting view, Bennett Berger, "On the Youthfulness of Youth Cultures." For still another view, see Herbert Marcuse, *One-Dimensional Man: Studies in the Ideology of Advanced Industrial Society*, especially Chapter Three, on "Repressive Desublimation."

rather than prolonging adolescence. Others, by the example they themselves set, tended to discourage their students from entering a specialized adult career; they were in effect asking them to join another kind of subculture, that of the Bohemians or the intellectuals.[12]

Monteith has changed less—and anticipated current styles more—than Oakland. In some ways, it could afford to be more experimental vis-à-vis its students, since they always had the option of transferring to the College of Liberal Arts or other undergraduate colleges at Wayne. Yet when it succeeds in holding onto students it is far from resolving all the problems created by this very success. A minority of students conclude that, to become an intellectual, it is enough to take on the styles of faculty models and talk the lingo of the avant-garde—the grander the better. Here the rejection of departmentalism by many of the Monteith faculty, especially in the social science division, tends to emphasize the intellectual at the expense of the academic. However, in the contemporary student idiom, with its emphasis on feeling, anti-academic attitudes can readily become anti-intellectual ones as well. While at the outset some Monteith faculty idealistically assumed that their undergraduate students could reach their own level even though lacking similar preparation, today the faculty are well aware of the dilemmas in-

---

[12] For a description of one Monteith subculture of this sort, see Susan Flax, " 'Everybody Has to Do His Own Thing': Life-Styles of College Youth." Some of these students appeared to us to fit the style of moratorium described by Joseph Adelson:

> . . . the student who seems untouched and untouchable is in a state of limbo . . . waiting for the proper time to commit himself. He does not feel ready to find a personal identity. . . . He is not really waiting for the right model to come along; he is waiting for something to happen inside of him. Then he will make his move.

Joseph Adelson, "The Teacher as a Model," in Nevitt Sanford (ed.), *The American College*, pp. 396–417, especially pp. 407–14. See also Wilbert McKeachie, "Procedures and Techniques of Teaching," *The American College*, pp. 312–64, and Joseph Katz, "Personality and Interpersonal Relations in the College Classroom," *The American College*, pp. 365–95; also Joseph Katz and associates, *No Time for Youth: Growth and Constraint in College Students*, especially Part Two.

volved in such expectations. Like the Oakland faculty, although
with less sharpness, they have been troubled and divided by the
definition of appropriate level or of standards to expect of their
students.

VIII Conflicts over Academic Standards and Curriculum at Oakland

Max Weber saw the educational system as torn between the "specialized type of man" and the older type of "cultivated man,"[1] a dichotomy that translates easily into Sir Charles Snow's depiction of the two cultures—of the British literati and of the men engaged in the sciences and technology. Snow considered the latter group genuinely humane, broad in its sympathies, oriented toward the future of mankind, and concerned with the welfare of the great mass of the unlettered. He saw the literati as conducting a snobbish, rear-guard attack on the contemporary world, an attack influential not only in intellectual and academic circles, but also in government and economic life.[2]

There are Ivy League colleges and other enclaves in the United States where somewhat comparable divisions persist, although with far less support outside the academy. What is involved here is not just the conventional resentment of men in the less affluent humanities vis-à-vis natural or social scientists, who until recently have appeared to be better supported; more important is a certain attitude toward cultural and academic exclusiveness and toward students

[1] See *From Max Weber: Essays in Sociology.*
[2] C. P. Snow's lectures are now republished with added remarks as *The Two Cultures: And a Second Look.*

who are not refined and seem not to seek refinement. At urban (but non-urbane) Wayne State University, such polarities have had narrow scope, and the divisions at Monteith between the social science faculty and the other two staffs, which are described in Chapters IX and XI, have sources other than cultural snobbishness. At Oakland, however, C. P. Snow's distinction is of some relevance in understanding early strains. It is true that in some respects the faculty have been more united across the disciplines than divided between them: faculty members in the humanities and in the natural sciences have seen each other as allies in the defense of high academic standards against student ineptness, sloppiness, and lack of craftsmanship; and they could jointly defend the purity of their several academic callings against the demand that they prepare their students for such professions of relatively low prestige as school teaching, accounting, social work, and other local civil service. But C. P. Snow's distinction does help to clarify the fact that the Oakland humanities faculty has been troubled by student barbarism or lack of cultivation, while the mathematicians and natural scientists have been more prepared to accept students who can do the work, even if they lack intellectual elegance. Likewise, while the "two cultures" have tended to be in agreement in wanting to gear the curriculum to the one fifth or so of the students headed for graduate and professional schools, the faculty in the humanities have been perhaps even more allergic to working with students planning to be businessmen or government employees. Lacking the taste for social as well as academic exclusiveness, the natural scientists have been slightly more willing to tolerate students heading for "applied" callings.[3]

What has made the battles so intense at Oakland is the fact that they occurred within the context of a unified academic program. In most state universities and in many private ones, collisions among faculty members with widely different expectations are muted by

[3] Aside from the one fifth of its students who continue in graduate or professional schools, Oakland has sent a little more than one third of its students into (mostly secondary) education, while the remainder have gone into industry and government service. See placement data in Appendix F-4.

the division of the campus into different colleges. At the University of Michigan, for example, the College of Literature, Science, and the Arts, and the College of Engineering are highly selective; Education, Pharmacy, Business Administration, and Nursing are less so. Since each college in such a system is relatively autonomous, it can protect its students from more stringent standards elsewhere by recruiting, for instance, captive psychologists to teach students of education and captive economists to teach students of business administration.[4]

Faculty Assumptions About the Students and Their Effects on Grading

The relation between higher academic culture and grades may be at best oblique, at worst contradictory. Grades serve not only to sort and certify students but, more symbolically, to sort and certify faculty vis-à-vis one another. Undoubtedly, many faculty members would prefer that grading transactions, just as decisions about salary or honorarium, be kept under the table, so that matters of seemingly greater moment could be communicated to students. Yet inevitably the shorthand of the grade symbolizes to

[4] The "service" faculty in a technological institution may adjust to what the students regard as their main chance by making minimal demands, grading softly, and seeking gratitude rather than awe. Cf. the discussion on marginal humanities and social science teachers in a technological institute by Eugene S. Uyeki, "The Service Teacher in Professional Education." See also the pattern in which academic rigor and prestige are associated at a state-supported institute of technology, so that the industrial management program recruits the leftovers who cannot make it in the hard sciences or in aeronautical or electrical engineering. Cf. Nahum Medalia, "Choice of College Major by Contest Mobility." Refusing in the small collegial atmosphere of its early years to create service courses, Oakland faculty sometimes managed to work out arrangements of a more ingenious and less invidious sort. For example, the small faculty in Business Administration occasionally sent their economists to attend mathematics classes that the business administration students had to take, in order to help persuade the instructors to make adjustments for the ways in which these particular students could best be helped to learn math—which were not to "water down" the program but to increase its suitability for a particular cadre of students.

the student not only how he should organize his time but how he defines his sense of adequacy. To the faculty member himself, the grades he gives are representations of how he stands in the cross pressures between loyalty to his field and loyalty to colleagues in the institution; of the different echelons of students whom he teaches or hopes to teach; and of the degree of his self-confidence about his judgment over the fates of others, in this case his students.[5]

The charter faculty who came to Oakland, dominated numerically and ideologically by men in the humanities, wanted to act as if they were teaching at a private, highly selective liberal arts college and focus on students good enough to sponsor to graduate school. But some faculty members and, of course, administrators wanted from the outset to make room at Oakland for undergraduate professional training as well. Conflict over the shape of Oakland centered on two issues: the stringency of grading, and the share of curriculum given over to General Education for students who also had preprofessional requirements to meet. In the controversy over grading, there were some differences along the lines of C. P. Snow's two cultures; in the controversy over curriculum, the line-up was quite different.

We will turn first to the issue of grading. The discrepancy between faculty demands for academic standards and student expectations concerning the rewards to be given for hard work was flagrantly revealed at the end of the first-term grading period in the fall of 1959–60. National newspaper publicity as well as campus talk declared that seventy per cent of the entering class had failed in one or more courses, and in the post-Sputnik climate Oakland's Spartan severity and fealty to academic excellence were acclaimed. As usually happens, the legend was more dramatic than the actual facts: of the 570 students in the entering class, 35.8% (204) received a failing grade in at least one course, and a similar proportion of the grades overall in the first term were either D or F. But even

[5] In many respects the analysis in *Making the Grade: The Academic Side of College Life,* by Howard S. Becker, Blanche Geer, and Everett Hughes, of how students make the grade provides a counterpoint to our treatment of how teachers give grades.

at the level of reality rather than legend, the pattern of grades must be seen as severe in comparison with otherwise similar academic institutions.[6] The low grades actually given and the even lower grades believed to be given during the first year stamped Oakland with an image of harshness and boot-camp discipline in terms of which faculty members and students assessed each other then and in later years. Indeed, ten years later, the grading crisis of that first year helps provide the Oakland campus with its sense of uniqueness, even among faculty members who would now recall its severity with some embarrassment. In the first term of the first year, as we shall see, grading was most severe in the proverbially "male" subjects of mathematics, chemistry, and economics. (Political science and French were not far behind.)

These grading standards rested on an easy meritocracy which allowed faculty members to distinguish the capable from the inept with quantitative assurance. One physicist put it this way:

> It's very easy to grade a student. Someone who can read a book and take an exam. We had one who got 235 out of 240 points on the exam.

Eliminating those who could not make the grade was a way of improving the breed. Comparing his present students to those he had taught earlier at the University of Illinois, a chemist said:

> They are about the same as at Illinois. In a place that takes all students, you get a pretty random sample. Unless you do something to get better students, this will happen. . . . You've got to recruit them, just as you would recruit a good football team. There have been a lot of questions about failure. We flunked thirty-eight per cent during the first term. They deserved it. We will damn well do it again! That's how we will get better students.

There is nothing inherently sadistic in such a comment; it is like a sports coach who drives his players hard. In fact, the natural scien-

[6] See the discussion in Chapter IX of grading patterns at Monteith and at two Big Ten universities compared to Oakland's grades.

tists at Oakland had endless patience and were not in the least standoffish toward those students who survived their screening. Their genuine interest in teaching was demonstrated by their taking jobs in a new college without a graduate school. One physicist, for example, said that he hoped Oakland would be able to follow the model of Miami University in Ohio and send on the best chemists to get Ph.D.s at leading graduate schools. Like many academicians elsewhere, such men focused on securing majors in their own fields; as one physicist said,

> We have twelve [majors] now. The standard way of recruitment of physicists in college is through the seduction of engineers. I've seduced twenty-five per cent of the engineers here. . . . That's my measure of success.[7]

With rare exceptions, the natural scientists at Oakland felt no need to carry the message of their calling to non-scientists—or even to scientists in fields other than their own. When we asked these scientists how they felt about an undergraduate General Education in science that did not aim to convey the procedures of any particular science, they rejected the idea, declaring that it would be poor preparation for future courses in science and that, without extensive laboratory work, the outcome could only be frivolous. There was little sympathy for the idea of what might be termed the humanities of science as part of everyone's General Education.

The relative indifference of Oakland scientists toward a lay audience has to be seen in the context of the post-Sputnik and post-World War II era. After the Second World War, reflecting the successes of the Manhattan Project and the work of the Office of Scientific Research and Development, agencies such as the Office of Naval Research and the Atomic Energy Commission supported scientific research and the training of scientists because they believed

[7] The School of Engineering at Oakland did not begin to retain its own recruits in significant numbers until, with the academic year 1968–69, it introduced an engineering course in the very first year alongside the University-wide courses, as a way of creating morale and professional cohesion among the cadre.

that active work in the sciences was essential for national well-being.[8] Indeed, while the connection between a tinkerer like Edison and a scientist like Willard Gibbs may be quite tangential, the bounteous spinoffs from technology have helped to support the more esoteric branches in the less rapidly applied fields of science. Populist prejudices against science and scientists go back a long way in the American imagination, but on the whole there has been little hostility toward science in popular culture. It is true that the high school boy who hangs around the garage, local airport, or foundry and then registers at a commuter college with the vague idea of becoming an engineer is no ready candidate for the attractions of topology or solid-state physics. But if he is rejected by his science teachers, he is not likely to develop a strong hostility toward science or its practitioners. Until very recently, the only opposition to science appeared to lie in fundamentalist out-groups hostile to vivisection or to the teaching of evolution, and in some humanities faculty who resented the neglect of their own styles of work and the apparent overemphasis on science.

Correspondingly, the students themselves had little external support for mounting a sustained opposition to the grading standards or teaching methods of the natural scientists and mathematicians at Oakland. Because they taught students without fear or favor and gave equal opportunity to everyone to show his stuff, the scientists were not put on the defensive even when a majority of their students failed the first examinations. Had the natural scientists been less self-confident, they might not have relied on the implicit maxim that the stupid will always be with us; they might then have

[8] Contemporaneous with Oakland's planning was the beginning of a movement of scientific evangelism among those who agreed with C. P. Snow that science was too important to be left to scientists and that it must become the property of all educated men. Physicists like Zacharias, educators and mathematicians like Biberman and Kemeny, and many biologists worked to establish curricula for secondary schools and non-elite colleges that would allow students to discover the excitement of science. Ironically, the relative success of this development in the 1960s has coincided with a wave of anti-scientific animus among the most talented students in the better colleges, who see the success of technology as a corruption of science itself and as a cause of war, pollution, and other evils; among these are some students whose search for existential meaning tends to reject all quantitative work.

struggled with the possibility that some of their students could be introduced to science on a slower gradient or an altogether different one. At the time, given the posture that the Oakland faculty took, such concerns might have seemed only an effort at science without sweat.

In Oakland's third year, a General Education course in Science and Society (similar to one of the required Monteith natural science terms) was offered, which gave some of the highest grades of any course; it was the precursor of a number of courses at Oakland on the social impact of science, dealing with such topics as environmental pollution, nutrition, the underdeveloped world, and other applied issues. But such courses were too few and came too late to redeem science for many Oakland students who fell by the wayside or barely struggled through the obstacle course.

While for the natural scientists and mathematicians, stupidity and indolence were the enemies, for many faculty members in the humanities and social sciences, the arch evils were vocationalism and mass culture. Richard Lane declared:

> Students—we don't get through to them. I will talk to them— like Mill's St. Andrew's Inaugural Address—and I can see them sitting there curling their lips and saying to themselves, "Just give us our degrees and let us get out, and we can get a good job."

The very prevalence of good jobs, he said, made it more difficult to "get through to enough students to change them." Then, turning to defend Oakland students against his own strictures, he stated:

> If I had to choose between teaching these kids and teaching white-shoe Yalies and the *nouveaux riches,* I'd certainly take these. Sure, you get bright students in those places, but it's an atmosphere of gentleman's C. We have no such thing around here.[9]

[9] Lane was speaking here of a collegiate atmosphere long past; at present it is the white-shoe Yalies (wearing sneakers or sandals and blue jeans) who have rejected the gentleman's C, if not the alienated or activist's C, and who are less concerned with well-paying jobs than the first-generation Oakland students were.

Even so, several faculty members remarked wistfully, "If only we had some bright Jewish students!" Many believed that Oakland would not improve until it could recruit out-of-state students. An Oakland social scientist felt that the students were being wounded by this attitude. She herself believed that many faculty members were insensitive to the actual improvement of their students: "Even their English has improved over the last two years." In the first months of Oakland's second year, the Dean of Students, who had moved over from Michigan State, submitted his resignation; as one instructor described matters,

> Like several others who are in administrative positions, [the Dean of Students] had come out of a high school setting. He was a former assistant principal. He tended to take a more permissive attitude toward the students in their academic work. The faculty took the general attitude that they gave out the material and the knowledge and the student either got it or he didn't. If he didn't, that was too bad. The Dean of Students felt that there had to be more adjustment of the academic material to the nature of the students they had.

First-term failures were later erased as a special concession for students who could improve their grades by taking the courses over again. But the initial faculty rejection set a tone that outlasted such dilutions of meritocracy. In the first several years, there was a joke among students that there were no seniors at Oakland, and it did not look as if there were ever going to be any. On our first visits, the faculty in the supposedly softer fields, such as education and sociology, assured us that they were as tough and flunked as many students as their colleagues in other fields.

During all these battles, some students were quite aware that they had become pawns in an academic war. They soon came to define faculty as being "for" or "against" them. These student attitudes were mobilized in the third year of Oakland, when several faculty members were informed that their contracts would not be renewed for the following year. One of these men, an assistant professor of English, informed his class that he was being fired.

Some students protested and called local and metropolitan newspapers. As one of them explained, the instructor "was considered by these [protesting] students as a teacher who would do a great deal for students, spend a good deal of time with them, and had a certain respect for them." He himself explained his dismissal as the result of disagreements with colleagues over ways of teaching literature. He saw himself as concerned with bringing students closer to the affective nature of a work of art, as against an overly formal approach to literature which he felt too remote to be grasped by Oakland students. Correspondingly, the students interpreted his dismissal as a way of maintaining the intellectual distance of the faculty and its rejection of the great majority who could not reach the short ladders the faculty held out to them.

The charter class dramatically dropped away, so that by 1963, the normal senior year, 240 of the initial student body of 570 were still in residence, of whom forty-six were not yet seniors. Whereas in 1959 there were three men to every two women, by 1961 there were slightly fewer men than women. Despite the initial focus on Sputnik, only in its first year did Oakland have the look of a small Purdue or Carnegie Tech; since then, the proportions of students in various programs have been similar to those at most state universities.

The Grading Crises

At the opening of Oakland, in the fall of 1959, the only courses offered were necessarily elementary ones, chiefly the University Courses.[10] The charter faculty brought with them the grading standards they had learned as students or as teachers in more selective colleges. So far as we are aware, no discussion occurred in the faculty meetings of the first term concerning standards of

[10] Since there were no two-year community colleges in the Oakland area at the time, Oakland could not begin by accepting upper-division transfers as well as freshman students. In any case, as we noted in Chapter II, it began sparely and could not have afforded the larger ratio of faculty to students that upper-division courses entail. In contrast, Monteith began with a certain amount of "overstaffing" of this sort.

grading; the norms of privacy prevailed, and each faculty member was on his own with only the most flimsy and accidental feedback from his colleagues. Grades varied among the nine courses offered in that initial term from eighty-nine per cent C and higher grades given in sociology to a class of 111 students to the forty per cent of such grades given in chemistry to a class of 181 students (Table 1).

Table 1

Grade Distributions in Oakland Courses, Fall 1959

	Grades					
Course	A-C	D	F	None	Incomplete	N
English	69%	14%	11%	6%	—	523
Economics	45	3	42	10	—	78
Western Institutions	72	13	8	6	1	542
Political Science	52	21	22	5	—	128
Sociology	89	6	2	3	—	111
French	54	13	13	20	—	165
Russian	67	7	12	13	1	111
Chemistry	40	13	43	4	—	181
Mathematics	46	7	44	3	—	137
Mean percentage over all courses	63	12	17	7	—	1976

Sociology, English, Western Institutions, and Russian were decidedly easier than French, political science, mathematics, economics, and chemistry. The two major courses required of all students were Western Institutions and English. These two courses provided more than half the total grades and accounted for about forty per cent of the D and F grades. The three toughest courses were the introductory courses in what are generally considered "hard" disciplines—mathematics, economics, and chemistry. While they provided approximately twenty per cent of all the grades, they accounted for more than a third of the Ds and Fs. In these more or less quantitative areas, faculty find it easier to apply pure meritocratic standards. Students, knowing this, were nevertheless forced into some of these areas by the General Education program. But they also had trouble in generally "softer" or "gut" areas, illustrated in the relatively low proportions of adequate grades given in two traditionally easier courses—French and political science. Over forty per cent of the grades given here were less than adequate.

By fall 1960, the faculty and the students had reacted to the crisis of failing grades (Table 2). In every case but one (mathematics), those courses that had given fifty-five per cent or less A, B, and C grades increased their proportion of such grades, while those that had given more than fifty-five per cent decreased their proportion. In other words, the tough courses got easier and the easy courses got tougher. Although sociology in 1960 gave fewer adequate grades than in 1959 (a drop from eighty-nine to seventy-one per cent), it still remained the most indulgent course at the college.

What seems to have been at work on the faculty in the first few years was a form of the famous "autokinetic phenomenon": in a situation where there were no clear standards at the outset, the faculty over time began to converge on grading norms that reflected university-wide practices. The faculty adjusted to a perceived standard of judgment that avoided the implication of being either too soft *or* too hard. Examining the distribution of grades for the elementary courses at Oakland over the five-year period from fall 1959 to fall 1963, we see a pattern of increasing uniformity among the elementary courses.

The deviation from the average grade computed for all elementary courses in each year declined from 1959, when the average deviation was 13.3 per cent, to 1963, when the average was 6.3 per cent. This meant a continuation of the pattern that began in 1960—that is, the soft graders becoming more severe and the tough graders becoming softer. The two major language courses of the first year, French and Russian, moved in the later years toward each other, with Russian giving more low grades and French giving more high ones. Even social psychology and sociology, whose instructors the students regarded as "for" them, were moving toward a more severe norm; by 1963, the sociology faculty were among the lowest graders at Oakland.

The effects of severe grading were self-generative. One of the

Table 2

Percentage of A-C Grades in Elementary Courses, Fall 1959-Fall 1963, Oakland

Course	1959	1960	1961	1962	1963
English	69%	57%	72%	77%	62%
Economics	45	59	63	77	59
Western Institutions	72	62	62	72	62
Art	—	77	80	78	72
Music	—	64	69	75	76
Political Science	52	67	79	64	60
Social Psychology	—	88	91	86	75
Sociology	89	71	81	73	58
French	55	66	70	68	63
German	—	54	51	60	54
Russian	68	62	61	52	56
Spanish	—	59	58	75	68
Chemistry	40	46	48	61	63
Physics	—	30*	47	72	73
Mathematics	46	42	52	54	51
Science & Society	—	—	75	72	70
Mean percentage, all courses	63%	63%	72%	76%	70%
Average deviation from mean percentage	13.3%	10.0%	10.9%	7.4%	6.3%

*The grade return in Physics for fall 1960 is misleading. Unlike Freshman Chemistry, the Introduction to Physics was a sophomore course, requiring calculus. It was taken by forty-nine students under a system allowing them to take the examination when they felt ready. Consequently, many who received an Incomplete for the fall term later did complete the course: by summer 1961, only 14.5% of the original forty-nine had not completed the course with an adequate grade.

senior professors pointed out that in his department, which had been one of the highest graders, the average had fallen sharply in 1963; in four sections, the grades had ranged from an average of less than C to slightly less than B—. When he described these patterns to an instructor who had given fairly high grades, the instructor's response was, "Damn it, I could have given more Ds!"

Many instructors seem to have assumed that they could go on blithely giving Ds in order to sustain the faculty's sense of probity, even while the Oakland administration set about (as we shall see in detail in Chapter X) to build dormitories and to recruit a student body that might have a better chance of meeting faculty expectations. At the same time, the administration, working through the divisional and, later, the department chairmen, sought to make faculty aware that their severe attitudes toward students as manifested in grading were endangering the viability of the very ambitions that had brought them to Oakland. If they wanted better students, they had to treat the ones they actually had with some delicacy. Otherwise, the admissions counselors in the high schools who had steered some of their best students to Oakland only to see them defeated or even failed out, would refuse to send on any more students. Moreover, they had to realize that if they wanted a bigger library, more equipment and more specialized colleagues, realistic assessments of students were essential. Administrators armed department chairmen with statistics on the high attrition even among students with excellent test scores, and with scatter charts showing the wide disparity of grades given in different sections of the same course. Faculty members came to realize that selectivity in admissions would come only gradually, and that high attrition and inadequate enrollments were not the road to it.[11] By 1962, Oakland's grades were higher than they had been in the previous three fall terms. Three quarters of all grades given in that year were A, B, or C; in the required University Courses, the percentage was seventy-seven.[12] This equilibrium, however, proved unstable: in 1963, the proportion of adequate grades fell to seventy per cent, and while this was above the sixty-three per cent of the first two years, it was

[11] For a fuller discussion of the problems public institutions face in raising admissions standards, see "Admissions Requirements in the Public and Private Sectors," in Christopher Jencks and David Riesman, *The Academic Revolution,* pp. 279–86.

[12] Given the rising aptitude of the students and their willingness to work hard if not always effectively, grades probably did not rise as much as ability did: one might call this the iron law of grades, which is at work in many universities in which aptitude scores rise faster than grades. In some highly selective institutions there was the tendency (until the draft made it difficult) for highly talented students to drop out. Cf. Erik Wright, "A Psycho-Social Study of Student Leaves of Absence." A contrasting tendency in some institutions very recently is a rise in grades, often reflecting neither higher student aptitudes nor increased student effort. Such a rise reflects faculty permissiveness and the more intimate settings in which, as we shall show in Chapter X, students fare better in terms of grades when they are known personally to the faculty.

nevertheless a visible reversal of the pattern that had come to prevail.[13] At the end of the autumn 1963 term, a hundred students were flunked out for poor grades, of whom forty were first-term freshmen; an additional forty freshmen were warned that they ought to leave. (These had been carrying less than the normal load and consequently could not be dropped. Twenty-five of them nevertheless did leave.)

Among those dropped were ten valedictorians from local high schools, whom the Admissions Office had made great efforts to recruit. One guidance counselor in a good high school told the Admissions people that he would never send another student to Oakland. Of course, not all the high schools in the state are good, and some of the casualties reflected inflated high school rankings. For example, one student who had been sixteenth in a high school class of fifty-nine had a Verbal score that placed her in the third percentile of the college students of the nation. When the Dean of Students pointed this out to her parents, they reported it back to the high school, and the discrepancy between the work of the Oakland Admissions Office and the work of the Oakland faculty was highlighted.[14]

We have seen that many students "adapted" by leaving Oakland; a few transferred their curricula. The attrition was much heavier among males and among students in the Engineering and Business Administration curricula, so that the charter class, which had begun in 1959 with fifty-five per cent of its males in these two fields, two years later showed twenty-six per cent in the same fields—

[13] Adequate grades in the required University Courses dropped between 1962 and 1963 from seventy-seven per cent to sixty-seven per cent.

[14] If a college has tremendous holding power for its students, it can give low grades to valedictorians even from good high schools and get away with it. The College of the University of Chicago is a somewhat idiosyncratic case. Its grades are very low, certainly lower than many colleges with comparable student bodies; thus, work and talent that produce a C at Chicago would produce a B at Princeton or Harvard. This is one reason a number of students drop out, transferring to places where the same effort will get them better grades, or less effort equal grades, with no poorer chance for graduate school. For data on attrition at the University of Chicago, see William Spady, "Peer Integration and Academic Success: The Dropout Process Among Chicago Freshmen."

but these were percentages of a group of male students that had dropped from 326 to 86 people.[15]

Student reactions among those who clung to Oakland rather than dropping out are illustrated by conversations with two seniors, Jim Brook and Roy Emerson. Jim Brook comes from a small town a dozen miles from Oakland. He entered the Business Administration program, but when he found the calculus courses over his head, transferred to Secondary Education. He told us of a physical sciences instructor who had steered him away from his own course into a biology course, on the ground that physics would be too difficult for him. He resented this professor less than he did some instructors in history who had no time for students and pitched their expectations on too exalted a plane. Roy Emerson commuted thirty miles each way from East Detroit. He had chosen Oakland because he could get into it, since his high school record shut him out of many other schools to which he had aspired. Although his aptitude examinations had shown him proficient in mathematics and science, he got D grades in chemistry. His best grades were in history, and he transferred into that subject and also decided to prepare for secondary school teaching. He, too, felt humiliated by some of the humanities faculty, though, like many students, he made exceptions for the teachers of Russian. Both seniors complained, as many did, that instructors would tell students that everything would be all right if they only worked hard, and then would "clobber" them in the examination. Roy Emerson gave the example of his former economics instructor, who was always very friendly with students but shortchanged them on grades. The assumptions these students made—that grades should directly reflect hard work, that a friendly professor should also be lenient in grading—demonstrate how little they understood the norms of an elite college, norms that make clear to the entering freshman that there may be little relation between grades and hard work, or between faculty friendliness and severity of demands.

Instances of faculty hauteur were also undeniable. One teacher

[15] See Appendix E.

gave his students a spelling test, because he claimed they did not know how to spell. No doubt they did not, but this hardly endeared him to them. Another instructor asked such questions as "How deep was Walden Pond?" It was principally in the required Western Institutions and freshman English courses, where faculty were dealing with captive audiences, that such reactions arose; in these courses, students often made efforts that loomed large to them but did not impress their teachers.

By the time students got into their majors, both the fact of their survival and the faculty's recognition of the implications their actions had on students' acceptance into graduate school led to much higher grades. Most faculty members wanted majors and were willing to pay for them in somewhat softer currency. They were also aware that, since Oakland was unknown, graduate schools could not know that its credits were being certified by exigent standards; thus, some effort was made to adapt the grades for majors to the national economy of grades. Many of the students who survived took pride in Oakland's superiority to large state universities. They said that Oakland was a place where the professors did the teaching and not the teaching assistants, where classes were small, where the quality of education was high. One Literature major told us, "Here we read seven books, while at Michigan they read only four." This was from a survivor. In the winter of 1963–64, it became apparent that there were not enough students surviving, because each professor retained the power to set standards and in this way to express dissatisfaction with students. Indeed, at a meeting called by the administration to consider the problem of grading, the faculty insisted with a high degree of unanimity that the only answer was to get better students: it would be impossible to lower standards.

By this time, there had developed at Oakland a kind of infrastructure of ancillary personnel and some faculty, who sought to protect students against what they felt to be excessive demands. These *de facto* shop stewards, some in the Dean of Students' office and in the counseling and personnel services, advised students on how to study and how to shop around for courses that would be less taxing. They encouraged those students they thought could make it, counseled out those they thought could not. In a more systematic way than before, the administration set out to call the faculty's attention to the consequences for their students of a failing grade. The Dean of the University assembled data on aptitude scores of students at other public four-year colleges throughout the United States, which showed that Oakland's students were probably exceeded in quality only by students at Harpur College of the State University of New York at Binghamton, by the University of California at Riverside, and in Michigan by the University of Michigan itself. A series of meetings was held between department chairmen and the associate deans of all divisions to drive this finding home and to make clear to faculty that their gate-keeping role gave them enormous power over student careers. Some instructors were shown data about the scatter of their grades in comparison with the performance of their students in other courses, which raised at least the possibility that they had been arbitrary. Some individuals regarded this as persuasion toward leniency and hence an effort to destroy what they considered valuable in Oakland. Such was the case in the Sociology Department, where two faculty members, new to Oakland in 1963, had been responsible for the sudden drop in sociology grades by fifteen per cent (English and economics had dropped equally sharply). These men justified their grades in terms of the low quality of the students, and both left voluntarily that same year. And while, in making replacements, department members and administrators could ask prospective recruits about their grading only in the most gingerly fashion, they tried to make attitudes toward students a factor in their recruiting.

A number of structural changes, singly small but in total significant, accompanied what might be seen as a propaganda blitz on the subject of grades. The method of computing grades was slightly changed from letter grades to numerical scores so as to provide greater differentiation. Students were given the option of dropping a course any time up to nine weeks after the sixteen-week term began—three weeks longer than the earlier time limit. The midterm grade could thus act as a signal for the student; it also worked as a control on the instructor, who would find it more difficult to fail students if he allowed them to think they were doing adequately, and thus not exercise the drop option. This policy led faculty to do more intensive counseling of students, and to counsel them out of their courses if it looked as if they could not bring their grades up.

Simultaneously, curricular changes helped allay faculty fears that their own courses, or their sections of a large course, could be regarded as "guts," while their colleagues could maintain the difficulty and profundity of their own small seminars. The new plan specified that students would take at least one large lecture course in the first year—probably no more than one—and one supposedly tough seminar. In the large section courses, each instructor was given greater control over his own course program to heighten his sense of personal responsibility when it came to failing students. A typical faculty load would thus include a large course and a seminar, so that no faculty member would feel that his particular specialty was carrying the onus of indulgence.

The cumulative result almost overdid it. By the fall of 1964, the failures in the University Courses dropped from seven to two per cent, and the average grade rose from 2.04 to 2.74. The new team in the Sociology Department gave eighty-seven per cent adequate grades, as against fifty-eight per cent the preceding year. Overall, failing grades were cut by more than half. Not everything changed, of course. Language and science courses did not. But obstacles in non-required courses could be got around by formal and informal counseling. On our most recent visit (1968), we were told by one administrator that perhaps the grades were getting a bit too high, with a B— becoming the modal grade. He said he did not dare complain about this lest the faculty in a stampede reverse its relative leniency on the assumption that now they could afford to. (We trust that by the time our book is published, what we say here will not destabilize the uneasy equilibrium over grading!)

The Conflict over Curriculum

Battles over grading had a kind of guerrilla quality, now quiescent, now intense, with occasional single engagements between a particularly astringent faculty member and his departmental colleagues or members of the administration. In contrast, conflicts over curriculum were more strategic, more theatrical and highly charged. Recruiting of faculty for Oakland by Dean Richard Lane began within the context of a General Education requirement that extended over four years and constituted close to fifty per cent of the program of any student; it followed that the first faculty would be mainly in the humanities, including English, Western Institutions, and foreign languages. Of the twenty-three teaching members in the first year, seventeen were of junior rank and fifteen taught in the humanities. To the fifteen humanities faculty of the first year, the following year's additions brought in more tenured men, but the preponderance in the humanities continued: there were fourteen professors on tenure, of whom half were in the humanities. In the tradition of some elite colleges, the Academic Senate was open to all ranks, and faculty committees were drawn from junior and senior faculty alike.

As originally planned, Oakland's program for preparing schoolteachers focused on the liberal arts, with a minimum of courses in education; but by the middle of the second year, when half of Oakland's students were planning careers in education, a preponderant faction in the humanities was not willing to grant even that minimum. Students planning to major in one of the liberal arts and sciences would have no problem with the rigid General Education requirement, which would dovetail readily with an academic major, but those in Education, Business Administration, or Engineering would have great difficulty meeting the General Education requirement and preprofessional ones as well. The issues were joined in January 1961, with the report of an all-College Committee on Instruction, which recommended by a three-to-two majority that the Western Institutions, Rhetoric, and Literature courses be retained, along with a foreign language, but that students be given some choice among social sciences, art, and music, rather than continuing the same requirements for students in all programs. This proposal had the approval of a social scientist, an educator, and a natural scientist.

The Committee minority, a historian and a professor of English (with the support of Dean Lane as a non-voting Committee member) wrote a minority report, which not only declared that the existence of the same set of required University Courses was what distinguished Oakland "from most state-supported schools," but responded to the problems raised by the Education Department by proposing a longer undergraduate program than four years: ". . . Without wishing to intrude upon the sacred precincts of departmental majors, the minority suggests that attention be directed there, as well as to the UC prescriptions. Outside the magically closed circle of eight semesters, it suggests that attention should be given to the radical suggestion that the circle be enlarged (in certain professional cases) to nine—the latter number is, after all, more consistent in mystical tradition." The minority asked for an additional semester course in English literature to be required of all students. This demand has to be seen in the context of a language requirement that then stood at four courses (sixteen semester credits) for all students except majors in mathematics, the natural sciences, and Engineering Science. There was also a state requirement of political science for all students. A student who wished to earn a teaching certificate as well as an Oakland B.A. would not be able to graduate until January of a fifth year, and would ordinarily have to wait until the following September for a place in the school system.[16]

The humanities lobby was saying in effect that anyone so low as to major in education would have to pay the price by an additional term in a true college. One of the faculty in Education remarked that Harvard could afford to insist on a five-year course

[16] In fact, Oakland is now on a trimester system, with April the principal commencement, followed by a short spring session—as well as a rapidly growing summer school for visitors and graduate students.

for the Master of Arts in Teaching, but that Oakland would lose all its students in education if it imposed the same requirement—and then just for the B.A.[17]

On February 25, 1961, there was a memorable meeting of the Academic Senate that came to be known as "Black Saturday." In a wild six-and-one-half hour discussion, with the Chancellor chairing the meeting and often challenged on points of order, the junior faculty in the humanities pushed for the minority's proposal. One man proposed that at the end of a student's college career he be examined to see whether he had developed the kinds of attitudes expected of the liberally educated man.

Leadership of this battle was in the hands of what came to be called the Wild Ideas Committee—actually, the Developmental Programs Committee, which was composed of a mathematician, a teacher of English, and Tom Fraser, who in his administrative capacity was permitted to attend Senate meetings. One of us sat in on a luncheon meeting of the Committee at which the representative of the English Department proposed increasing the English requirement, and the mathematician insisted that, since the faculty should be solely responsible for the curriculum, the Educational Policy Committee should not allow administrators to vote. The unremitting attack on "Middle-Western Philistinism" which underlay the attitudes of this group was suggested when, after passing the motion to deny administrators the vote, someone remarked that a lot had been accomplished at Oakland in a year and a half, and the mathematician responded: "Yes, we stink already."

The extra semester of English did go through on Black Saturday, even though members of most other disciplines opposed the requirement. At a second Senate meeting, in late May, a proposal to exempt teaching interns from one of the requirements in Western Civilization, art, or music was defeated. Since many of the students

[17] Both Juilliard and the Mannes College of Music in New York have inaugurated five-year programs to combine a liberal arts B.A. with a professional curriculum in music; a student who just wants a certificate in music can get it at the end of four years. In principle, a five-year B.A. in education or other fields can be justified, but it was not an innovation that Oakland could inaugurate and hope to find paying customers.

in education had trouble with the four-course language requirement and had to spend a great deal of time on foreign languages, it still seemed impossible to prepare teachers in a regulation four-year period. The Senate meetings had become so polarized that, as one respondent put it, the Chancellor "had to take some things into his own hands, or else we would have anarchy." The day after the May meeting, Varner issued a statement pointing out the need to have a bulletin ready for prospective students and, "since the Academic Senate as currently constituted is obviously unable to resolve these kinds of questions without an extraordinary invest- ment of time and energy," he was appointing a committee to decide on curricular matters for the balance of the year. The committee would include all faculty on tenure, the head librarian, and several administrators.

Earlier, as we have already noted, the Chancellor had appointed Sargent Hennessy as Dean of the University, to take Richard Lane's place as Dean of the Faculty (the change of title was indicative of an increased administrative authority), and he had appointed as- sociate deans in Social Science, Science, and Humanities, thus es- tablishing further links between the administration and the faculty, rather than the strict separation that some of the charter faculty had regarded as essential in a college governed entirely by faculty. Two years later, the nucleus of the "Wild Ideas" group, including the effervescent Tom Fraser, had left for jobs elsewhere. By then, the era of dominance by the humanities was over, although the influence of the early years still shapes recruitment of both faculty and students.

In these same years, there were struggles over the requirements in languages, including English, which have continued to the pres- ent. The English Department itself could not sustain its victory on Black Saturday, and the three-semester freshman English program was voted out. At present, "freshman exploratories" are supposed to take the place of all freshman English, although obviously the faculty teaching them differ considerably in the degree to which they take seriously the all-University requirement that they teach their students how to write. The four-course requirement in foreign

language was also under pressure, in the face of the argument that
a one-year language requirement was worthless and would not develop even minimal skill or fluency. Nevertheless, the language
requirement for students in education was reduced in 1962–63
from four courses to three, and two years later to two semesters for
students in education and the sciences. In discussing these settlements, the Associate Dean of the Humanities, who had led the
fight against relaxation of the two-year requirement, admitted that
the one-year compromise was pedagogically worthless. He defended
it nonetheless, more as a symbol of embattled high culture than
in realistic instrumental terms:

> Actually, the language requirement is symbolic. The kids aren't
> prepared for it. We have to argue for the principle. This place has
> been advertised as a liberal arts college. One of the indices of a liberal
> arts college is language. . . .[18]

In theory, Oakland could have followed a different course from the
very beginning by establishing an Honors Program or even a full
Honors College as a way of differentiating between the more adept
students who could be held to the strictest standards and be groomed
for graduate and professional schools, and the majority with whom
a more peaceful coexistence could be established. By grouping the
ablest students together for the presumably more distinguished
faculty, Oakland would have made life easier for those on the
lower tracks without slowing down the faster ones. It would then
have met the payroll of the community college simultaneously
with that of the elite college. But such a division among students
would have entailed a division among faculty which would have
been inconceivable at Oakland. While Oakland was never so non-
hierarchical as Monteith, it was sufficiently egalitarian for most

[18] In the spring of 1968, linguistics was introduced as a two-semester option
for students to whom a two-semester language requirement remained the
only hurdle for graduation. Thus nine years after its founding, a student
can attend Oakland and receive his B.A. without a foreign language. This
crumbling of the barrier appears to be nationwide as language requirements
come under attack from students.

faculty members to feel that they should share and share alike whatever resources the student body provided. Of course, few would have volunteered to teach only the less adept; more significantly, many faculty members believed that they had to serve as mentors for their students if the latter were ever to be in a position to choose among a variety of upper-middle class careers and styles of life. An avowedly two-class system would have been seen as a departure from the original aspiration to carry all students a considerable distance toward higher academic culture.

IX Conflicts over Academic Standards and Personalism at Monteith

In a controversial paper, "Undergraduate Achievement and Institutional 'Excellence,'" Alexander W. Astin argues that it hardly matters where one attends college, since the impact of college is principally a reflection of the aptitudes with which the freshmen arrive.[1] Astin's effort was to assess what might be termed "value added" by the college experience, but many technical and substantive problems remain unsolved.[2] We agree with Astin's implication that it is wrong to assess colleges, as is generally the case, in terms of the quality of students they attract rather than in terms of what they do with those they get.

But the problem remains as to how the faculty should distribute its efforts: should it concentrate on those students who are most promising and responsive, treating the rest in a perfunctory way; or should it have a more egalitarian dedication in order to spread efforts more or less evenly throughout the spectrum of student

[1] See also Joe L. Spaeth, "The Allocation of College Graduates to Graduate and Professional Schools."
[2] Thus Astin himself points out that colleges with high dropout rates may have better records in terms of seniors because of those who are not there to graduate, while colleges that encourage more students to stay through to the end may look worse when all seniors are averaged out in comparison with entering classes.

aptitude—or indeed should it concentrate on those who are the most deprived and therefore the most in need of help? Such questions of distributive justice are not unique to educational institutions, but reappear in incomes policy, in the distribution of health services, and in the distribution of resources between the rich and the developing countries. Even in an affluent society, there are never enough resources, of money or of talent, to go around. Many have hoped that these seemingly inherent limitations could be overcome by television or programmed instruction or other ways of saving scarce human resources, but so far these enterprises have not been notably less expensive in talent and money than the more conventional methods of teaching. Many devotees of compensatory education would argue that education should make up for deprivations in life-chances, if necessary at the sacrifice of students who are further along in motivation and aptitude. In a society already—if unevenly—egalitarian in spirit, however, such a policy may run the risk of truncating high academic and intellectual culture for the sake of perhaps imperceptible advances elsewhere. Conversely, the faculty members' temptation to devote themselves only to potential disciples not only may fail to unearth talent even in those specialized areas, but limits the possibility of discovering new ways of assisting the intellectual development of the less fortunate.

We presently have a complex and largely hidden system of rationing. An able but not outstandingly brilliant or well-organized student at a highly selective undergraduate college has the benefit of being surrounded by stimulating fellow students, but faculty reactions to him (in the feedback of grades, in rejection for honors seminars, etc.) may convince him that his hope of becoming a scientist or musician or writer was juvenile foolishness; had he attended a less stratospheric institution, he might have emerged with his self-confidence unimpaired, and even enhanced.[3] Of course, there are institutions so benighted that even an energetic student would

[3] For general discussion, see James A. Davis, "The Campus as a Frog Pond: An Application of the Theory of Relative Deprivation to Career Decisions of College Men."

find it difficult to discover stimulation or support. In the large state and private universities with heterogeneous student bodies, a good deal depends on luck: some students will never have a stimulating experience, while the very fact that such experience must be sought for and does not come automatically gives other students the opportunity to come alive, as it were, on their own power. Most such institutions, as we have already remarked, build their elite functions on a mass base, using the tuition or other support provided by large undergraduate bodies to feed upper-division and postgraduate and professional work of high and often esoteric quality.

A purely undergraduate college, without departmental majors or other such protograduate potential, Monteith was at war with this characteristic division of faculty effort. It was also at war with itself as to which students "deserved" faculty attention and how these should be responded to; even with an "average" student body, some will, of course, be more average than others, some more rewarding than others. In our interviews and in our analysis of grading policy, we sought to determine what the often implicit judgments were, who "these students" were thought to be by faculty, and what the faculty division of effort was between classroom teaching and less formal relations with students.

In any human setting, people can choose to emphasize what is similar or what divides them. Looked at from afar, the divisions within the Monteith faculty might seem negligible. Thus, the natural scientists at Monteith took on a coloration in comparison with natural scientists at Oakland and many other places that was closer to the norms of the Monteith social scientists. Their eagerness to teach non-specialists marked them off sharply from their colleagues of more meritocratic cast elsewhere. But within the Monteith context, their differences from the social scientists along this axis loomed large and became the stuff of combat and controversy.[4] In the account that follows, we focus only on the conflicts over

[4] Cf. Leonard Goodwin, "The Academic World and the Business World: A Comparison of Occupational Goals," which shows the similarity in values among academics in the "two cultures" in contrast with men in science and engineering outside the academy.

pedagogic goals between the natural scientists and the social scientists; since the humanities course was the last to be staffed, and since the polarity had already arisen between the natural and the social scientists when they arrived, the humanities faculty tended to choose sides in alliance with the natural scientists.

Being the most coherent and the largest body at the outset, the social scientists set a tone from which the other staffs then diverged. It was a tone of personalistic relations with a minority of "Monteithy" students, while for the most part ignoring the majority, who remained invisible. The natural scientists, in contrast, concentrated on the middling students in a less individualistic way. The economy of effort of the social scientists tended to be casual, centering on those students who showed up outside of classes and especially on those who hung around the Student Center. Such casualness was defensible on more than sentimental grounds, since responding warmly and humanely to those students who happened to turn up could in the long run have a greater impact than a more abstractly just effort to hunt up those students whose needs were as great or greater; in any case, any given faculty member could not reach or respond to the great majority of students. The natural scientists, however, could not conduct themselves in such a fashion, and, being more systematic and less casual, they altered the curriculum to meet the needs of the great majority of students, rather than expend their efforts on a few who could be carried through an unchanged curriculum; they kept all students at something of a distance rather than bringing a few within the charmed circle.

Seeing this, we must at once qualify our comments to observe that we are speaking only of tendencies: within each staff there were faculty members of contrary disposition, though such stereotyping understandably arose at Monteith itself. Furthermore, from a college-wide point of view, one could argue that the cumulative tendencies of the natural science and social science staffs provided a useful division of temperamental labor, and that any college might consciously decide to recruit faculty along lines of such differences of response to students, while seeking to prevent the hegemony of any one type of response.

Given the different value judgments placed on these different types of response, we can appreciate the fact that differences in teaching style and in preference for one as against another student audience were handled at Monteith by a kind of competitive rather than co-operative coexistence among the divisions. Indeed, when it came time to give the required interdivisional Senior Colloquium in 1962–63, when the charter class was in its final year, the social science and natural science staffs collided, found that they could not agree on topics and procedures, and parted again to provide separate colloquia. By then, the different styles represented by the social scientists and the rest of the College had had ample opportunity to manifest themselves. The Gray Document described the Senior Colloquium as the "capstone of the formal general education program," forcing the three staffs into a direct working contact. Grading-policy was naturally one source of disagreement; casualness as opposed to orderliness concerning when and where classes should be held was another. The Colloquium Committee ended in an impasse, which was "resolved" in the way that many colleges resolve tensions among several disciplines, by giving each its turn sequentially: the Colloquium was split into separate courses, to be taught in one term by the social scientists and in the other term by the natural scientists (with the humanities staff working primarily with the latter).

Characteristically, students associated with the social scientists regarded the other staffs as the "enemy camp." These "Monteithy" students included both an early beat or hippie contingent and a cadre of the sort that would emerge in later years on many campuses as the activists, oriented toward extramural issues and student power within the universities. The social science-oriented students were ahead of their time in eventually forming a kind of "free university"—their own Colloquium—which met in various apartments near the campus.

The natural scientists were elated by what they regarded as one of their few victories over the social scientists. In retrospect this seems paradoxical, since theirs was a victory only in the sense that the splitting of the Colloquium prevented them from being subsumed under the moral hegemony and style that the social scientists represented. The demand for a unified Colloquium was taken as a demand for maintaining that dominance—so much so that after the split one natural scientist said that this was the first battle their side had won, "and we will win others. We are not going to be polite any more. We are going to fight for certain values."

Yet such a victory was also a defeat. Another natural scientist during the same contentious year declared:

> The biggest problem is that the various divisions have not been able to get together. We have two entirely different conceptions of the relations between students and faculty, the nature of independent study, the nature of General Education and how a college should be organized. We are really not one college. We're at least two, and maybe three.

Contrasting Educational Ideologies

Some of the social scientists were quite explicit in believing that their mission was far more inclusive than the "merely" academic. One man saw himself as engaged in a "process of acculturation," where he was, in effect, "asking students to come over to our [i.e., the faculty's] world." Some social scientists rejected this model, and the natural scientists were quite put off by it. But both staffs were alike in wanting students to acquire new perspectives and not simply random information. However, in defining themselves as different from what they regarded as the too permissive and sentimental social scientists, the natural scientists would sometimes state their own case in exaggerated polarities. One stressed his division's concern with standards, objective criteria, and "authoritarian-directed teaching." Another expressed the differences in these terms:

> The "free and easy" approach stresses personal values, loose unstructured relationships, introspective work, less criticism. Education is seen as a personalized process, with students involved in the structuring of course materials. My side stresses objective criteria, some standards, materials to be learned, and analysis.

Similarly, the social scientists sometimes expressed themselves in ways that downgraded concern with factual or historical knowledge:

> The natural scientists want to turn out people who know about things, rather than people who know things. We don't necessarily care if students learn a great deal. The things we try to teach them we want them to know of their own experience.

None of this means that the natural sciences course was intrinsically more difficult and demanding, nor does it mean that the social scientists were not serious about their teaching. Rather, the differences had to do with the aspects of students with which the faculty were preoccupied. When we asked faculty members what they hoped to accomplish with students, or what qualities they looked for in them, the natural scientists tended to emphasize what is still the prevailing academic ethos, stating that they were most concerned with developing the minds of their students, by which they meant giving the students a sense of the rational authority of science in place of superstition and irrational authority. This looks like a large order, but it was often modestly put: "Students should understand natural sciences. They should have insights into nature, not just what an individual said."

In contrast, the social scientists wanted to engage students' feelings more intensely. They often said that students should be "shook up"; as one declared: "We should clobber them, lead them to examine their beliefs, understand their backgrounds, involve them as whole persons."

In involving themselves with students, the social scientists entered the latter's world, asking them where they had come from and where they were headed. The insistence was not that they head in any particular direction, but that they engage themselves with faculty. This personalistic outlook led the social scientists to accuse the natural scientists of being "cold," "rigid," and "harsh." The ideological premise for such judgments is conveyed by the following quotations from the social science faculty:

Monteith was like a social movement. If we weren't going to transform society, we were certainly going to do something to transform
the students.

We have a commitment beyond the intellectual. Knowledge is
not like bricks you transport from one person to another. You have
to put it in a meaningful context, meet students' assumptions, understand their world view. You have to involve the whole person, not
just the mind.

At least the first of these quotations suggests a certain ironical
detachment from the earlier missionary outlook. The differences
that eventually developed within the social science staff anticipated
those we see currently between activists and hippies. Some social
science faculty members emphasized the importance of social criticism and activism; their mode was "doing." Others emphasized the
quest of the individual for identity and meaning; their mode was
"being." One of the activist faculty saw Monteith as "a model for
academic guerrilla fighters." Other social scientists were somewhat
less polemical, though nevertheless critical of American values:

I'm a missionary and I'll admit that—I think the problem of
alienation and unhappiness in this society is just overwhelming—and
that's what I think I'm doing at Monteith, what a lot of people think
they're doing at Monteith, because I don't know how you can
separate education from that. Knowledge for what? To play gentle-
men? I don't educate anybody for that. I may help to educate people
so maybe they can dig their way out of the hole a little bit.

Understandably, this kind of education meant that the more missionary-minded faculty members were constantly involved with
students outside of class; Harold King, one of the leaders of this
affectively related wing of the social science staff, explained:

. . . They [the students] came to my house. We went for picnics.
We've had coffee. I went to their parties. We had informal seminars.
I can't think of a facet of life that I haven't had contact with
students.

In an elite residential college, where some young faculty may live in the dormitories, such a non-academic closeness has long been an occasional if not a common practice. In small denominational colleges also, some faculty members may want to influence student character and to share a religious and existential quest with them. Today the radical student movement has brought into being intentional communities that include undergraduates, graduate students, and younger faculty. Furthermore, in many community colleges there is a handful of faculty, concentrated here and there in a drama department, or in anthropology or clinical psychology, who in their intense involvement with students as individuals are rather like some athletic coaches. What has distinguished Monteith is that this sort of faculty involvement with the non-academic lives of their students has been the norm for a large proportion, and this has put the more aloof faculty on the defensive. So visible was this pattern that one sociologist who spent much time with students outside of class denied that she saw students "socially" because she saw them *only* at the Student Center and did not have them come to her home; she needed, she said, the privacy of her home because she saw students all day long on campus.

In general, this particular boundary between campus and home delineates that cadre on the social science staff that did not subordinate questions of curriculum to questions of personal relations; of those on the staff who preferred to have students call them by their last names, all were in this group. They were well aware of the affective modes of learning and, like the other social scientists, saw themselves as inducting students into a kind of style of life, but they differed from the others in not seeing themselves as qualified or responsible for the students' idiosyncratic quest for identity. They were willing while on campus to talk endlessly with students, and they could be counted on by students for help and advice in collective activities such as Student Government and the student newspaper. At times they felt gratified that other faculty in their division preferred one-to-one relations and intense personal involvement with students, since they regarded this as a useful division of labor that allowed them to pursue their own more reserved style. But at other times they protested against a therapeutic definition of education. For them, warmth and intimacy were too much for faculty to give. They feared a certain loss of academic discipline and standards. They also feared the dangers of manipulation and seductiveness among faculty members who made special efforts to elicit the non-academic problems of their students.[5] Some had been involved in this kind of intimacy and wanted to withdraw from it:

> We gave a one-credit course. We faculty really talked to each other, and provided a model for the students. It turned out to be a group therapy session and was getting pretty dangerous. The second time we taught it, we didn't want to invest ourselves so much.

There were also students who recoiled. One of them said that he felt the faculty interfered with things he regarded as personal: "Perhaps they were being kind or concerned, but I didn't want them to be." Another student described two kinds of teachers:

> Some are really concerned with upgrading learning. . . . The other type . . . tries to be a buddy, tries to interact with the students on a personal level . . . they are too involved with the student body.

A number of the social science faculty members who were intensely involved with the emotional lives of their students were charismatic people, and they and their student allies were dramatically visible to members of the other staffs, particularly at the Student Center. Hence it is understandable that the natural science faculty (and some of the humanities staff as well) tended to see *all* the social scientists as sharing a similar style, allowing students to get away with too much, indeed spoiling them.

The way faculty members phrased their judgment of the students

[5] Joseph Adelson describes such teachers as narcissistic in their concern with keeping students' attention focused on them and in their wish to be loved apart from their role as teacher. See Adelson, "The Teacher as a Model," in Nevitt Sanford (ed.), *The American College*, pp. 396–417. Indeed, one faculty member saw himself as influencing students through his personality: "The students and faculty become cronies, people who love you because you're you, not because you do certain things."

anticipated much discussion that goes on today about campus dissent and disruption. Some natural scientists regarded the students as demanding or exploitative or as insolent and disrespectful—although by the standards of 1969 they would hardly seem so. Except in instances of cheating, where social scientists, as we shall see, were severe, they described the same behavior that troubled the natural scientists in an idiom that was more sympathetic and nurturant: vulnerable, rootless, alienated, displaced, etc.

Some of these social scientists had come, as one of them put it, in the hope of finding "unwashed idealists" from the "militant working class." The natural scientists did not see students in terms of a type, whether of social backgrounds, degree of alienation, or mental health. Since they were not looking for converts or concentrating on the students who particularly sought them out, they preferred to direct their attention to the students whom they regarded as typical—those who needed (and usually wanted) more direction:

> We are directed toward the students who need more structure . . . let the others find alternatives. . . . We've gone a little too fast for the mass of students. Since this is a mass, not an honors college, this has to be taken into account.

Some of the social scientists, on the other hand, unwilling to recognize that many students were upset by too much ambiguity and looseness in the curriculum, felt that those who were not performing well needed support through personal attention and nurturance.[6]

6 In an unpublished longitudinal study of the effectiveness of different therapists at the Judge Baker Clinic in Boston, David Ricks has described a tendency of some ineffective therapists to provide a great deal of attention and nurturance when the patient was presenting material about his illness, his difficulties, his rages, and so on, while being less attentive to indications of contemporary health and competence. More effective therapists tended to provide more structure, to make more demands, and to be simply less interested in accounts of earlier difficulties. In lesser degree it may well be that faculty members' effectiveness vis-à-vis various types of students could be analyzed in a comparable way. (David F. Ricks, "Helpful and Harmful Intervention in Schizophrenic Development.")

These differences in the kinds of relationships between students and faculty that were deemed appropriate reflected different sources of personal legitimation for the faculty. In general, social scientists felt legitimated by what they were, natural scientists by what they knew. The latter had no doubts about their subject matter, though they might have doubts about their ability to get it across. Although sometimes regarded as stuffy and authoritarian by student acolytes of the social scientists, they were in fact relaxed and informal in their manners, and as we saw in Chapter VII, they were capable of evocative teaching. Nevertheless, they insisted that they were teachers, not peers:

> Teachers do know more. We have to keep our distance. If you just regard this college as a group of people who are out together on a berry-picking expedition, there comes a time when you have a case of conscience. . . . How can you evaluate the students? You can be friendly, you can fraternize, you can do all the things that are conducive to a less formal relationship without going all the way.

A mathematician said that he wanted to dignify and dramatize his classes; he was willing to talk with students over beer, but that was a "bull session," as he put it, not a class, for which both students and teachers should be prepared to behave in given ways.

Few natural scientists had the kind of contact with students that many said they wanted when they first came to Monteith. They kept open office hours and urged students to telephone them if they had problems. But the Student Center was definitely not their turf, though at the outset they had their offices in the same decrepit house. When we visited the Center, it offered a preview of the hippie world: guitars and loud music; odd and informal dress; an atmosphere not only disorderly but positively hostile to order; an alternation of mood between frenzy and lassitude. Social scientists felt that the faculty were obligated to mix with students at the Center, but the natural scientists were often repelled by the atmosphere; in any case, they did not consider it their job to go there. They were willing to go to the Student Center for a purpose, to a meeting or a lecture, but simply to hang around for unscheduled contacts was not their métier.

We have already touched on the informality that prevailed among the social scientists in their way of dropping in and out of each other's classes and in their evocative styles of teaching. Indeed, some of the social science staff tended to reject all formal classroom work and to consider their real teaching as going on, as one man put it, in "shooting the breeze, going out for coffee; that's where I put my eggs." Long before the first "free university" was set up, this group of social scientists proposed the abolition of grades, examinations, and formal courses.

In most colleges, the number of required classroom or contact hours a week is seen as a fundamental part of the teaching bargain. Teachers know that there must be a certain leeway beyond the contract for consultations with students and for other matters. The social scientists at Monteith tended, as one of them put it, to "break the contract" by going even further beyond it. A clear indicator is the difference in the number of non-required electives taught in each division. By the spring of 1962, fourteen out of a total of nineteen eligible faculty members in social sciences had taught 737 student credit hours of special courses and tutorials. In the natural sciences, four out of a total of sixteen eligible faculty members had taught fifty-one student credit hours in special courses. With these differences in mind, the social scientists saw the other staffs as not carrying their load:

> The other two staffs don't give a damn about the students. They leave at three o'clock and never turn up at student functions, while we knock ourselves out. My colleagues don't pay any attention to this at all, which means that this staff has furnished what you might think of as the extras—the academic extras in the extra courses, and the non-academic extras. . . . Meanwhile, lots of kids are not being touched at all. . . .

The natural scientists countered these criticisms by accusing the social scientists of unnecessarily proliferating special courses; by these means, they thought, the social scientists were attempting to attract student disciples and to avoid the drudgery of spending most of their time teaching required courses.[7]

Faculty Responses to Plagiarism and Cheating

Extending themselves toward the students as they did, the social scientists were all the more crushed when the students responded as students, not as allies or peers, in an incident that took place at the end of the College's first year. The night before the final examination in social science, several faculty members took the exam over to the Student Center to mimeograph it and innocently left the stencil in the mimeograph room. Later in the evening, three or four students broke in, stole the exam, and passed out copies among their friends. Word of the theft got around quickly among other students, who then complained to the faculty. The staff reacted quickly, and by inspired sleuthing tracked down the main culprits. Within a few hours, an ad hoc committee of students and faculty expelled those who had stolen the exam and sentenced those who had been given copies to an Incomplete in the social science course, to be made up the following year.

Memories of this episode were still potent four years later when

[7] In recent years, undergraduates in many colleges have been given the option of proposing Independent Study projects to faculty members in place of regular courses. Faculty members who take these on get no reduction of regular course loads. If they are conscientious and responsive to students, and perhaps if they also become known for personalistic grading, they may discover that they are carrying a great many such projects, while many of their colleagues are carrying none. One of us was present at a heated argument at one of the new colleges of the University of California at Santa Cruz concerning a growing tendency of faculty members to find student-initiated projects unworkable: some faculty members said that this was because their colleagues had become unresponsive, though others contended that the students were exploiting Independent Study to avoid formal courses while plunging into grandiose half-baked attempts. These were faculty members who saw themselves not only as teachers of undergraduates but also as research scholars and as deeply committed to developing a new institution. It is just such controversies over the uneven load of student traffic that Monteith experienced almost from the outset.

one social scientist sadly remarked, "There are those who felt that
here it would be different, that relations between students and
faculty wouldn't lead to cheating." The natural scientists, who had
never had a honeymoon that students could destroy by cheating,
were inclined to believe that the social scientists had been too severe.
One mathematician with whom we spoke in 1962 described the
disciplinary committee that dealt with the cheating incident as a
"Kangaroo court, an inquisition."

Plagiarism was and continues to be an issue at Monteith, and one
which makes the social scientists bitter at the exploitation of relations
of trust:

> Yes, she can drink with us. Yes, she can horse around. But damn
> it all! It doesn't matter half as much if you're treating the kid
> shabbily. But where the kid has this much access, it's downright
> horrible.

Another instructor who was proud of treating his students as equals
plaintively asked one who had plagiarized, "Why did you do it to
me?" Plainly, personalism cut both ways, and faculty members whose
aim was to convey not so much curricular content as a certain kind
of style and outlook, felt that the very purpose of the College was
threatened by cheating.

The natural scientists were matter-of-fact about cheating; for them
plagiarism was a common vice[8] from which students had to be
weaned: they were still only scholars in embryo. As one natural
scientist said:

> The social science people say if you can't depend on a person's
> integrity, there's nothing left. In natural science, we say the student
> was stupid not to put in quotations. For the social scientists, students
> are intellectuals. For me, they are students.

[8] On the actual extent of student cheating, see the study by W. J. Bowers,
Dishonesty and Its Control in College, especially Chapter 4. Fifty per cent of
undergraduates at ninety-nine representative colleges and universities nationwide say that they have engaged in one of four forms of cheating (copying
from another student, plagiarizing, turning in papers done by other students,
using crib sheets during an exam); the percentage goes up at large institutions.

The Co-optation of Student Culture by the Social Scientists

It would be naïve to expect that sociologists, anthropologists, or psychologists would apply to their own teaching and collegial life the empiricism they often employ in research. (Psychiatrists do not always master in their own personal affairs the wisdom they can apply to the affairs of their patients.) By beginning a formidable Program Study simultaneously with the College itself, Monteith had hoped to be able to feed back into its procedures a better understanding of who the students were and of what was happening to them. But the social scientists' frequent statements about the students rarely reflected an empirical assessment of the entire student body, but rather their associations in activities that often had little relationship to examinations, papers, and other academic routines. These students were "the Monteithers," not the invisible students who looked like the others at Wayne. They served, as students often do for faculty, much as a front organization serves a revolutionary cadre, not only to mitigate the latter's extremism in the eyes of innocent fellow travelers, but also to delude the hard core about the nature of the outside population.[9] One or two of the social scientists were troubled by giving attention to this minority, but most were not, even though they recognized that, as one of them said, they were going to miss a lot of people by spending time with students on a one-to-one basis.

The natural scientists, predictably, had that bit of distributive skepticism from the beginning. Some tended to reject the Student Center types, seeing them as the political allies of the social science staff; some rejected them as a small, noisy group of troublemakers. As we have seen, they preferred to direct their attention to the students whom they regarded as more typical—those who needed (and usually wanted) more direction, who if left on their own "would take the opportunity to just do nothing."

[9] This interpretation of the two-way significance of front organizations came to our attention through Hannah Arendt's discussion in *The Origins of Totalitarianism.*

From one perspective, the natural scientists' assessment of the general run of Monteith students was correct. A student whose observations jibed with ours noted that about ten per cent of the student body were fully involved in the College community, while an additional ten per cent used the Student Center with some regularity. Most students, following the Wayne pattern, worked at non-academic jobs as much as twenty hours a week; like other first-generation commuter students, they did not feel that going to college was a full-time job. Talking about a report from the Monteith Program Study on the extent of students' outside employment, one instructor said, "It came like a wet towel in our faces." Outside employment, as well as family and non-college friends, were the competition against which the faculty struggled to draw students into what they saw as more valuable orbits.

From another perspective, the social scientists' concentration on a minority meant that they managed to reach some students who in the ordinary commuter setting or even in the large residential state university would have had little opportunity or invitation to enter into an intellectual community of any sort. Indeed, here we can compare Oakland, where confrontation with faculty left students in isolation at the outset but eventually led to the development of a non-academic student culture well defended from the faculty.[10] But at Monteith the faculty had helped to create a student culture that was the carrier of faculty values. With the encouragement of the social scientists, some students soon became involved in such political and social issues as nuclear disarmament and civil rights, issues completely absent at Oakland in its early years. The *Monteith Journal,* the occasional mimeographed student weekly, became a vehicle not only for social criticism but for examination of College policies; in its offbeat poetry, short stories, and cartoons,

[10] On the general problem of student autonomy vis-à-vis faculty, see Everett C. Hughes, Howard Becker, and Blanche Geer, "Student Culture and Academic Effort," in Nevitt Sanford (ed.), *The American College,* pp. 515–30. Everett C. Hughes describes a medical school where the faculty, identified with research medicine, are not seen as potential models by even the most hardworking students who envisage careers as practitioners; see Everett C. Hughes, "Stress and Strain in Professional Education."

it now seems a precursor of the underground papers. As involvement became more intense, some of the students working on the *Journal* and other irregular vehicles began to find quarters in the tenements and decaying houses surrounding the Wayne campus, thus providing the fragments of a residential student population.

Even though only a minority of the students at Monteith became in any sense "Monteithers," these students had other friends in the student body, and this network extended the scope of the potential community. We know from interviews conducted with the charter class that not quite one quarter of them were involved in student activities in their first year. Yet as seniors, eighty-six per cent said that they had at least one close friend among their classmates. Even those students who were not part of the social science "Monteither" orbit felt strong attachments to the faculty. Astonishingly, over sixty per cent of the fourth-year students mentioned social science faculty members as "meaning something" to them and as "friends." The students who identified more with the natural science and humanities faculty members did not attempt to counter the influence of the social science cadre, which continued to run the extracurricular life of the College. What was at work here was the characteristic division between an activist minority, which has legitimation from equally active faculty, and the "silent majority," as it has come to be called in the late 1960s, who are rarely organized, whose ties with charismatic faculty are less strong, and who often lack the kind of self-confidence that leads the activists to put themselves forward as spokesmen or influentials. Furthermore, the so-called silent majority was not crowded or cramped by the activists; its members were not locked out or intimidated; there was just nothing they especially wanted that the activists denied them.

Grading in the Two Divisions

The social science faculty as a whole tended to be "softer" graders and, as it looked to the other staffs, more arbitrary ones. There was the suspicion that the social scientists bought popularity with students by indulgent grading. Although the percentage of adequate

Table 3

Grade Distributions* in Natural Science 131 and
Social Science 131, Fall 1959-Fall 1962, Monteith

	1959		1960		1961		1962	
	NS	SS	NS	SS	NS	SS	NS	SS
A	16%	15%	13%	16%	15%	20%	13%	15%
B	30 ⟩79%	35 ⟩90%	22 ⟩66%	41 ⟩91%	27 ⟩73%	39 ⟩91%	26 ⟩76%	43 ⟩87%
C	33	40	31	34	31	32	37	29
D	14	8	20	7	15	6	14	10
E	7	2	14	2	12	3	10	3
	100%	100%	100%	100%	100%	100%	100%	100%
N	247	292	307	327	228	290	214	251

*The distributions exclude *all* Incompletes in natural science courses, whether or not grades were later assigned. Incompletes who made up work and were assigned grades by spring 1962 are included in the social science distribution. This is done to give the most conservative estimate, since Incompletes had generally lower grades than students who completed their courses on time. Thus, low grades are somewhat underestimated in natural sciences and overestimated in social sciences. The actual proportions of Incompletes given as final grades in the two courses from 1959 to 1962 were as follows:

1959		1960		1961		1962	
NS	SS	NS	SS	NS	SS	NS	SS
2%	7%	5%	12%	3%	9%	4%	5%

grades (A–C) given to approximately the same group of students in the first course of the social science and natural science sequences was higher in social sciences in every year from 1959 to 1962, there was little difference at the very top: social scientists and natural scientists gave about the same proportion of As (Table 3). It was in the middle ranges—Bs and Cs—that the social scientists were more indulgent. Thus it is clear that both divisions reserved an A for special performance, while the social scientists gave Bs and Cs to students who would have been graded lower in the natural sciences.[11]

[11] This statement rests on the assumption that the amount of work required in the two courses was about the same. We know that the social scientists were more inviting, but this does not mean that their material was. A large group of students found many parts of the social science course baffling and demanding; many indeed preferred the natural sciences. The indulgence

An anthropologist described the social science currency quite explicitly:

> I trust my judgment of what's happening to the students. I make a judgment as to the level and symbolic universe a student lives in. An A has to be first-rate under any circumstances. But I'll give a B if I know his symbolic universe is more limited than most entering students'.

However average a B was for Monteith social scientists, it signified good performance in the larger academic world and elsewhere. This meant that Monteith social scientists relied much more on grades used as rewards than as punishments. Students should be "intrinsically motivated to work," as the social scientists phrased it; if the students were not, the threat of poor grades would not help. If grades had to be given at all, the promise of moderately good grades might act as a spur to students. This policy ran the risk, as one student pointed out, of letting some students "get away with murder and not do anything, but this is a lesser evil than failing many in order to maintain standards."

Social scientists went out of their way to insure students' success. When students did not complete an assignment, they would try to

---

of the social scientists did not extend to the work they required. If anything, they asked students to do more reading and to write more papers than did the natural scientists.

Another explanation for the differences might be expected to derive from differential student aptitudes. Although the same group of students is being compared in each year, they may have been stronger in the abilities required by social science than by natural science. One measure is provided by student performance on Wayne State University tests of Verbal and Quantitative Ability. On the assumption that Quantitative Ability would be in greater demand in the natural sciences, the lower grades in natural sciences might be a result of students' poorer quantitative aptitudes. This might have been the case in 1959, where the average Monteith score on Verbal Ability was considerably higher than the Quantitative score. However, in 1960 and 1961, the Quantitative score had almost caught up with Verbal Ability, and by 1962, it outranked Verbal Ability. Yet the proportion of Ds and Es in natural science was slightly higher in 1962 than in 1959. The grade distributions obviously reflect student abilities to some extent, but not in any simple way.

avoid giving a poor grade by assigning Incompletes (the footnote to Table 3 shows that, in every year, social scientists gave a higher proportion of Incompletes than natural scientists). Some social science instructors would not only encourage students to take Incompletes when they had gotten a C or lower, but told them they could write an additional paper as a substitute for one that had received a poor grade.

Many of the natural scientists were equally eager to help, but felt that they worked within narrower limits. They were aware of the contrast with the social scientists, but thought that they could not do otherwise. Speaking of 1960, when a third of the students received D or E grades in a natural science course, one of the natural scientists admitted:

> Our faculty tends to be much harsher. . . . We had limits below which we would not go even if it was our responsibility. . . . We would be only too happy to have failed fewer. In fact, we gave a special exam and tried to tutor them. But we set our sights too low and we felt we couldn't go any lower. It was hard to flunk so many students. I *know* faculty in other divisions would not have done so.

Monteith and Oakland Compared

Such a view, though at odds with the dominant Montieth ethos, was the norm at Oakland. Chart 2 shows the proportions of D and F grades given at Monteith and Oakland in science, social science, and humanities courses in 1960. A much higher proportion of Ds and Fs were assigned in Oakland's chemistry and mathematics courses than in natural science courses at Monteith. In the Oakland humanities courses (English and Western Institutions) most comparable to Monteith's, the Oakland faculty was also less lenient than the humanities division at Monteith. In social science, only the social psychology course at Oakland was softer than Monteith social science courses.

Compared to other institutions with similar student bodies (Chart 2 also presents the proportion of D and F grades given in elemen-

Chart 2

Proportion of D and F Grades in Elementary Courses at University of Illinois, Purdue University, Monteith College, and Oakland University in 1960

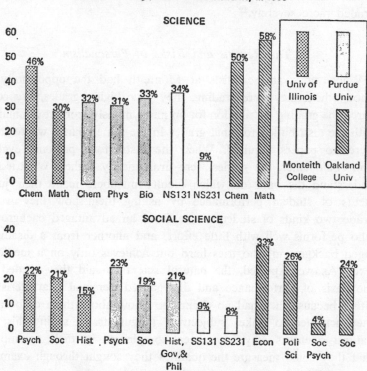

SCIENCE

Univ of Illinois   Purdue Univ

Monteith College   Oakland Univ

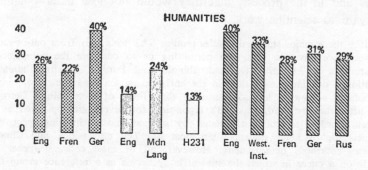

tary courses at the University of Illinois and Purdue University in
1960), Monteith gave fewer failing grades in all divisions than the
various departments at Illinois and Purdue, and, conversely, most
of the Oakland departments, particularly mathematics and English,
graded more severely.[12]

The Returns and Risks of Personalism

Whenever social scientists at Monteith had the opportunity to
know whom they were grading, they gave higher grades. We compared the grading distribution for an anonymously scored examination
with the distribution for final grades in the same course, where there
were no papers required. When the instructors' personal evaluation could enter, the grades were dramatically higher. We tried to
understand the basis on which faculty members made their judgments of student performance by asking them how they would
grade two kinds of students: one from an advantaged background
who performs well with little effort, and another from a disadvan-
taged background who tries hard but achieves only on a mediocre
level. As we expected, the natural scientists said they graded on
the basis of performance and disregarded personal characteristics,
either because they had no chance to know about them or because
they hesitated to make "subjective" judgments. In saying this, the
natural scientists may have been complacent in their assumption
that they could measure the qualities they sought through examinations and in the process, that they would not lose other qualities
relevant to scientific work.

[12] Since these major state universities require SAT tests only from out-of-state
students, we have no firm data permitting us to compare the competence
of students at Monteith, Oakland, Illinois, and Purdue. We have already
mentioned our impression that, in the early years, Oakland drew from high
schools of somewhat less sophistication than those of metropolitan Detroit,
but after the first year, Oakland's reputation for severe grading acted as a
screen. Purdue, a school dominated by science and engineering, probably
attracts slightly abler students than most Big Ten universities, and Illinois
has an enormous heterogeneity. However, all or most colleges appear to
grade on a curve in which the student body serves as a reference group for
itself; correspondingly, indulgence or severity of grading reflects faculty aspirations more than the capabilities of the students.

Conversely, the social scientists may have been naïve in saying, as they did, that they graded students higher if they worked hard— naïve, that is, in believing that they could always tell whether a student had worked hard. It was because they felt confident that they could gauge the personal qualities of students that the social scientists felt justified in taking these into account. One man stated explicitly that he did not give good grades to students who were bright but unmotivated:

> . . . If I have a student who I think is very, very bright and intellectually acute and turns in a performance that is very, very bright and very intellectually acute and he didn't do any work on it, then my attitude is . . . I don't necessarily believe in giving grades for native brightness or cultural attainments.

Another faculty member declared openly, "I play favorites. I don't have the same standards for everyone. If I think somebody's got some stuff, I let him get by. . . ." Another social scientist said that he gave higher grades to students who were involved in the course, whether they were bright or not, and graded down students who were clever but who did not "sit around and worry about what I say."

As we have seen, social scientists were more likely to see students outside the classroom; these contacts provided them with information they used in their evaluations. One student explained to us, when we asked him about his instructors' standards for performance, that faculty members were sometimes most excited not when a student performed well in academic terms, but when "something significant happened to him."[13]

[13] This sliding scale was reflected in the kinds of students from the charter class nominated by social scientists for various graduate-school fellowships. The students chosen were not always the top academic performers from their class, but they stood out in certain personal values and qualities. Compared to their classmates and to the students nominated by the other divisions, they were higher on religious, social, and political liberalism, flexibility, anti-authoritarianism, social alienation, emotional expressiveness, and tolerance. Students nominated by the natural science and the humanities staffs were high on academic performance and on tests of intellectual interests, but were not the sort who appealed to the social scientists. Indeed, most of the

Students became the major channel of communication among the divisions, whose faculty rarely spoke to one another across the boundaries that separated them. Monteith may have been ahead of its time in putting its natural scientists on the defensive; often in talking with us they sounded embattled. At Oakland, the natural scientists were not defensive, but felt the support of the entire culture for the values of science and technology. But at Monteith, having given up the enclaves of departments and thrown their lot in with a General Education program, the natural scientists were made vulnerable by the comparative leniency of the social scientists. One administrator described the social scientists as

> . . . getting the rest of us trapped into things where students begin to play one person off against another. For example, students say, "*He* doesn't care when I get my paper in. Why does it matter so much to you?" So, then, the instructor in natural sciences or humanities thinks . . . "I have a right as an instructor, or as a member of the department, to establish my own standards, but I feel sort of worked into a corner by the liberty which social science has given to this student. . . ." It points out an inconsistency to a student which . . . , when it serves his purpose, he resents. [He says,] "Why can't the rest of you be like social science?"

Student leaders were often well aware of their power. One of them described to us the way certain social scientists would tell him what was going on, information the students could use to "play off some divisions against other divisions," much as children learn to do with parents and other adults.

Because the natural scientists focused on the average students, it was out of the question for them to attempt to establish a counter-lobby of their own; they lacked the favorites and intimates who could have done this and perhaps the taste for power and intrigue that in the novels of C. P. Snow turns up among natural scientists as well as among men in the humanities. As we shall see in Chapter

---

students nominated by non-social scientists achieved high grades in the social science courses but were passed up by the social scientists when it came time to submit names for fellowships.

XI, when it became clear that students could not meet their original expectations, the natural science instructors geared themselves down to cover the material in the syllabus more slowly, so that students could pass the examinations. Hence, believing that they had already lowered their standards as far as they could, they were outraged when they were regarded by students and other faculty as punitive and uncaring.

Still, the social scientists did not completely bypass the problem of evaluation. Some faculty members wished to abolish grades, feeling that they could evaluate students in a more rounded way from their personal knowledge of them, without having to assign a letter grade. One faculty member deeply engaged with students explained to us that having to grade students might undermine the ties he had established with them and thereby undercut the values he was trying to convey (as the incidents of plagiarism and cheating illustrated). When students are being asked to become self-starters and to work out of internalized curiosity and interest, grading may indeed interfere. Grading may lead students to spread their energies evenly over the material or over those parts of it on which they expect to be examined, refusing to become engaged in any particular work or topic that could open new horizons for them. Grading may also lead students to expend their talents in psyching out the instructor. When an instructor tries to cut through this and asks his students to take risks and tell him their real feelings without fear of consequences, and then the students are graded as if their feelings were worth a C on an absolute scale, rather than relative to their own development, they may well feel that they have been led on, at once exposed and manipulated.

As a way of avoiding the dilemma, some social scientists sought to convince themselves that students were not much interested in grades anyway. One instructor said as much to us in justifying his refusal to discuss "trivial" examination details and grading with his classes. Yet we learned of a rebellion in one of his classes: one day the students decided to remain completely silent during a discussion period, to demonstrate that they were essential actors in a discussion and therefore should be given certain rights—including the right to discuss grades. In a rage, the instructor stalked out, wrongly interpreting the students as wanting to be graded for their performance in discussion. He thought they were demanding to be graded on their conversation, and in this way he avoided recognition of the fact that they were far from indifferent to grades.

Another way in which social scientists avoided the dilemma of evaluation was by redefining their span of control. In the natural science and humanities divisions, once a grade was given, its power was used up. But the social scientists, by allowing many students to take Incompletes and to improve their final grades after a course was over, did not allow the lever of the grade to be, as it were, used up completely at the end of the course. Grades were thereby given a more fluid value, which transcended the boundaries of a particular course or year. Implicit in this use of grades was the ability to stave off resistance and protect the social scientists from disgruntled students and the concessions and curricular change that might have been required.

But this was a game that students could learn to play on their own, and it is not surprising that some of the very students in whom social science faculty had invested so much, occasionally played it against them. Some demanded more attention and intimacy than faculty were prepared to give. Others would not show up at classes, miss deadlines on assignments, or drop out of the College altogether. Often they justified themselves in the same terms they had heard from their teachers: they had gotten involved in a "real intellectual pursuit," had undergone an "identity crisis," questioned the importance of doing meaningless assignments that did not spontaneously interest them. They had been invited by the faculty to turn a critical eye on the world, and some responded to the invitation by perusing the social science staff itself.

The social science faculty was vulnerable to student critique, not only out of the endemic vulnerability of the old to the young in America, but because of the complexity of the educational goals and purposes held by different members of the staff. Many wanted to appear to the students simply as friends, engaged in casual and non-purposive relations. Yet when they became intimate with students, they could be hurt when the latter responded regressively or narcissistically rather than by growth and involvement in the College, its courses, and its extracurricular activities. The Monteith social scientists had rejected the preparation of specialists as a goal, but they also wanted something more intense and fundamental to happen to their students than the mere cultivation of middle class tastes. Seen by their colleagues as lacking "standards," the social scientists in a sense had very high standards—but not the conventional academic ones. At the same time that they denounced the "mere specialist" or "bourgeois," they held up a much more difficult model for average students from non-intellectual backgrounds—that of the free-floating intellectual.[14]

In a selective college that recruits a great many students from academic and professional families, the faculty can simply reinforce an already partially formed intellectualism. But to accomplish the same outcome with students who entered with the more usual aspirations of the upwardly mobile, faculty members were obliged both within and outside the classroom to seek, by force of personality and intense dedication, to pull students away from their conventional aspirations. Social science course work itself was geared in a similar direction: it emphasized Great Ideas more than methodology or procedure, insisting that students read the difficult classics of Durkheim, Weber, and Freud, on whom the faculty had themselves been nourished. As interpreted by the staff, these works legitimated the demands on students.

It is no wonder, then, that some students pulled back and others pushed ahead almost too eagerly. Some of the social scientists, particularly those who were unmarried, energetic, and ever-youthful, continued to find time to respond to students vividly and personally, and often identified with the students more than with the faculty, thereby finding themselves at odds with their less enthusiastic colleagues. However, some of the more abrasive and visibly troubled faculty members eventually departed from Monteith,

[14] For a discussion of the free-floating intellectual, see Karl Mannheim's *Ideology and Utopia,* Chapter V. See also Bennett Berger, "Sociology and the Intellectuals; an Analysis of a Stereotype."

leaving legends behind them. Those who remained, even if initially deeply engrossed by students, have tended to withdraw from intense involvement with students, to devote themselves to other demands and constituencies. The contradictions have been smoothed over, or perhaps only submerged, but the ideology of personalism and of the teacher as guide to the intellectual-affective life remain at the core of Monteith's distinctive character.

X Oakland Transformed

Oakland in 1969 is still a crossroads (rather than a streetcar) college, in an area of rolling country increasingly invaded by subdivisions and crisscrossed by major highways. Several churches have been built at the edge of the campus, and the omnipresent gas stations mark the crossroads; but for bookstores, coffeehouses, art theaters, the campus must suffice unto itself. The parking lots are now crowded with cars, not only in the morning, but throughout the day and into the evening. A handsome library, a science and an engineering building, and an intramural athletic center have been added to the initial three structures. The small dormitories that were the first ones built, housing seventy-five students each, are now overshadowed by six- or seven-story buildings to house an increasing number of students who want to live on campus. The Meadow Brook Music Festival during the summer has the use of an acoustically distinguished band shell at a little distance from the campus. The move into the performing arts, evident also in the year-round presence of the British director John Fernald and his theater company brought from London, are all indications of the distance Oakland has traveled from the early ideal of a small college with a classical liberal arts program for commuters in the immediate vicinity.

Yet the original, more provincial Oakland is still there. While half the freshmen in the fall of 1968 were in residence, two thirds of the upperclassmen were commuters. Oakland's commuting radius now includes students whose families have left Detroit after the inner-city riots of 1967, for whom Oakland now seems a safer bet than other commuting alternatives. Placement Office data indicate the preference of many of the students to remain in the Detroit and nearby suburban area, turning down, for example, offers from school systems in California and other supposedly favored parts of the country. Similarly, these data show that while many students go on to graduate school on the East coast or in the West, a good many others go no farther away than Wayne or Michigan.

A New Student Clientele

The invisible heroes of many campus histories are the admissions men who discovered new student constituencies to replace disappearing ones; Oakland is no exception. Wilson Hall had been Dean of Admissions at Kalamazoo College, probably the best private college in the state of Michigan; in this position he was familiar with Michigan high schools, as well as many in the East. Chancellor Varner brought him to Oakland at a time when the local high schools had concluded, as a result of the catastrophic failures of the first year, that a student of average ability or diligence might very well not succeed at Oakland. And when it was realized that Oakland and Macomb counties could not provide students of sufficient aptitude to meet faculty expectations, the decision was made to build dormitories and to go after students elsewhere in the state, as well as outside. A new highway facilitated recruitment in Detroit itself.

By 1963, Wilson Hall's energy had produced dramatic changes in the composition of the student body.[1] While the first entering

---

[1] State law forbids Michigan personnel from using state funds to support recruitment efforts with out-of-state students. Admission staffs smuggle in such efforts by combining attendance at professional meetings with visits to

class had had only four students from outside the state, and virtually all students came from Oakland and Macomb counties, the entering class of 1963 included sixteen per cent from Royal Oak and Wayne counties, similar percentages from elsewhere in Michigan, and seven per cent from outside the state.[2] Until 1962, when Wilson Hall came on the job, the size of entering classes, both new freshmen and transfers, diminished from 570 in the fall of 1959 to 475 in 1962.[3] During these lean years, Oakland escaped legislative pressure to recruit students of poor quality in order to fill the buildings; this, of course, would have accentuated conflicts within the faculty over standards. In the fall of 1964, the entering class reached 887. After that, upper-division registrations also rose, giving Oakland faculty the chance to teach more majors and also to expand in numbers and diversity.

There was a steady rise in the aptitude of Oakland students.[4] By 1963, the lowest scores had dropped off sharply, a trend continuing, with fluctuations, at least until 1966. Ten per cent of the entering freshmen were achieving test scores equivalent to the average entrants at the highest-quality liberal arts colleges, and the average Oakland entrants scored above 500 on both verbal and mathematical ability.[5] Although the average mathematical score was higher than the verbal in every year, the sharpest improvement was in verbal ability: from 1959 to 1963, the verbal

---

nearby high schools. This often restricts recruitment to schools in and around such major cities as New York or Washington, which are locations for national meetings.

[2] This is quite a respectable percentage for a state university. Many noted ones (Minnesota, Massachusetts, and at the undergraduate level, California) have lower proportions. The University of Illinois had eight per cent out-of-state undergraduate students in 1964. Wisconsin, which has been rather unique among the Big Ten in its high proportion of out-of-state students, has now been forced by the adult backlash to cut back to fifteen per cent.

[3] See Appendix F-1.

[4] See Appendix F-2.

[5] These scores place Oakland among the "Selective Schools," the fourth level of selectivity in Cass and Birnbaum, *Comparative Guide to American Colleges*, putting Oakland on the same level of student aptitude as such schools as Purdue and Ithaca College, but below the category that includes Boston University and Beloit College.

ability score increased seventy-three points (compared to forty-eight points on the mathematical test).[6]

To some extent, these improvements reflected the higher proportion of women at Oakland after the first year, since women regularly have better high school records. Unlike Monteith, Oakland drew very few foreign-born or first-generation Americans, but the proportion of Jewish students grew from slightly under two per cent at the outset to a little more than six per cent in 1963. And while the majority of Oakland students continue to be drawn from families in which they are the first to attend college, the actual socioeconomic positions of their parents have risen. In 1959, twenty-eight per cent of the students' fathers were professional, business, or administrative personnel; four years later, the proportion of students from such families rose to over fifty per cent. One of the administrators, noting the increase in socioeconomic but not in educational background of the parents, suggested that there were many men in the nearby suburbs who had moved ahead in the automobile industry, but were blocked from still further advance because they lacked the social facility afforded by a college education. Anxious that their children not be similarly blocked, such men might find Oakland's combination of liberal arts and tough-mindedness especially appealing.

By the same token, the idea that Oakland would become a major source of training for Detroit industry did not materialize. By 1963, as we have seen, only seventeen per cent of entering students chose either Engineering or Business Administration, while Education was chosen by twenty-nine per cent, and Liberal Arts by fifty-four per cent (the latter group included many who were planning to become teachers).[7]

[6] High school ranks moved in a similar direction: whereas in 1959 seventy per cent of a random sample of the class came from the upper forty per cent of their high school classes, in 1963 the same proportion were in the upper twenty-five per cent. See Appendix F-3 for the full distribution.

[7] In 1968, there were more undergraduate men enrolled in the Secondary Education program (333) than in either Engineering (261) or Business Administration (261). In giving one third to one half of its graduates teaching certificates in any particular year, Oakland's vocational profile is

If Wilson Hall's success as an admissions man helped fill the dormitories, the establishment of Oakland Community College (OCC) in 1964 relieved much of the pressure on Oakland University from the less well prepared commuter students. But, in the face of OCC's plan to have four campuses of ten thousand students each, the issue of transfer students now faces Oakland. Because Oakland's curriculum has been so tight and structured, the admission of transfer students in the early years was not easy, but Wilson Hall, in negotiations with departments, sought to make paths available for OCC graduates. Presently, slightly over forty per cent of the student body are transfer students from various two- and four-year institutions—a fact that has contributed its share to the erosion of the original required curriculum.

More difficult has been the path for entering black students. What Oakland University prized as a formidable curriculum could only have been perceived as forbidding by the black students of nearby Pontiac (whose 1960 population of 82,233 included seventeen per cent non-white and now has a number of militant factions). And of course, as a public institution, Oakland lacked the resources of such private colleges as Wesleyan or Amherst either for recruiting or for facilitating the academic passage of black students. Yet, after having had almost no black students at the outset, Oakland began Project Twenty in the fall of 1967, with twenty high-risk black students whose SAT scores averaged 360. Nineteen of them were still at Oakland a year later, and it was expected that about ten would graduate, about par for Oakland's student body as a whole.[8]

---

close to Michigan State's thirty-seven per cent average (compared to forty-eight per cent at Wayne State and twenty-nine per cent at the University of Michigan) and can be contrasted to the regional former teachers colleges, where from two thirds to three quarters of the graduating seniors qualify for teaching certificates. For postgraduate placement of Oakland students from 1963 to 1969, see Appendix F-4.

[8] Wilson Hall told us informally that in recruiting black students he looked for those who could allow themselves to be helped; these were better risks than those who resisted aid. He thinks this is why Project Twenty turned out so well. One of the Oakland psychologists suggested that SAT scores are less predictive for students who have problems in comprehending what they

Student Subcultures at Oakland

In a commuter college, student organizations have a difficult time functioning at all; everyone complains about apathy, few students volunteer for posts in student government, and small percentages vote in student body elections. Oakland's charter class, even after prodding by the Dean of Students, had shown little interest in electing class officers or even organizing a class dinner; the class of 1964 had no student officers either. These problems were heightened by Oakland's severe grading, which periodically decimated student leadership. Like most colleges, Oakland required that students holding extra-curricular offices be in good academic standing. And while freshmen and sophomores needed an academic average slightly below C (1.75) in order to avoid probation, juniors and seniors had to maintain a C average (2.00). Thus, when sophomores became juniors, a considerable number in the twilight zone between 1.75 and 2.00 found themselves automatically on probation. In 1964, the result was to leave the *Oakland Observer* without a single experienced journalist for the coming semester, while the Student-Faculty Union had only one elected student representative still eligible.

Many commuters, as elsewhere, scheduled their classes from 8:00 A.M. to noon so that they could return home or to work with a minimum of time spent on campus. When residential students came, they termed the commuters "day-goes," or sometimes "day-dogs." In the early years, we found the campus nearly deserted in the late afternoon; sometimes we would discover a sprinkling of commuters in the nearly empty cafeteria, waiting for the rest of their car pools to finish their classes. Many of these students were often invisible in other ways as well. They were not talkative in discussion sections, nor would they visit faculty in their offices. Hardly any applied for jobs as assistants to faculty.

---

read, as many blacks in the Project do have. They did well in his own course when they could take examinations home and ponder them; when time was an element, they floundered.

The sparseness of student life at Oakland was what the post-Sputnik ideology had originally called for. Commuter students will sometimes rally around athletic events, as they do in high school, but intercollegiate athletics had been barred at the outset. Commuter students may sometimes form fraternities and sororities, but these, too, had been designedly rejected. In any case, commuter students everywhere continue to play customary roles within their families, to work at jobs quite unrelated to their education, and in a number of cases, to remain part of the gang at their former high schools and neighborhoods. We have already referred to studies at Wayne State that show that almost eighty per cent of the student body held full- or part-time jobs, even though many stated that the income was not essential to their continuance in college. The commuter college competes on a daily rather than a weekly or yearly basis with other institutions that have a claim on the loyalties of their students. But at the same time, just because a strong student culture is absent, some undergraduates who loosen their ties with home and neighborhood may attach themselves all the more strongly to the faculty and to the values it aims to transmit. We have seen that at Monteith these values often included critical dissent and skepticism. At Oakland, these characteristic values were present though less salient; later on, they gradually emerged, especially under the influence of residential students who came from more cosmopolitan backgrounds. However, at the time when there were only commuters, Oakland might mean a passage into another "home," that of the discipline or department. Only recently have some of them found other sorts of homes in the religious, political, and social groups that have developed on campus.

There were a few exceptions. A small group of pinochle players could be found in the Grill as late as midnight. A teacher of Russian managed to keep a chess club going. Somehow, the *Observer* appeared weekly. But efforts to provide cultural events that would bring commuters, singly or on dates, back in the evenings or on weekends, drew disappointingly small numbers. When we asked one student about this, he said that if he were to use campus facilities for a date, he would have to drive twenty-five miles to and from Oakland in addition to the distance to and from his date. (These Michigan students did not appear to accept such driving as routine the way the Californians are said to do.)

A recognizable, though lukewarm, collegiate style arrived with the building of dormitories. A number of the residential students came from homes within commuting distance, but were sufficiently well off or sufficiently interested in college life to move onto campus.[9] But they found precious little college life. Indeed, in part because there have been so many residential students from nearby locales, the complaint of dormitory students to this day is that there are "no facilities and nothing to do on weekends." One girl from New York City told us that in the summer of 1961 there were only four girls in the dormitories on most weekends. The resident students, however, did manage a sporadic social life, and a few commuters got drawn into the dating activities of the residents. Several years later, an informal social organization had emerged, based on off-campus TGIF (Thank God It's Friday) parties. These originated with a prominent student whose parents had moved out of the state, leaving him the temporary possessor of a large suburban home. Other parties followed, sometimes as far as sixty miles from campus, with a hundred students, mixing residents and commuters. As one girl put it, "Here, the man with a car is God"; since the men with cars took the initiative, an informal fraternity system was emerging. The parties and the informal social organization that emerged around them were significant because they provided areas of life in which students were outside the University's control and in which their status did not depend on their academic standing.

Some of the commuters as well as residents questioned the ban

[9] The original surveys that had preceded the plans for Oakland did not anticipate the large number of students from within commuting distance who wanted to live on campus. Apparently, it had not been thought originally that Oakland would appeal to students in the nearby well-to-do suburbs of Birmingham and Bloomfield Hills, where students and their families would value residential experience and have the money to spend for it. Nor had it been anticipated that middle-income families within commuting distance would nevertheless be willing to spend money for student residence.

against fraternities and sororities. A number of women commuters, anxious to learn manners and proper style, asked a woman who directed the Continuing Education Program if there were any way in which they could learn how to set a table, how to walk gracefully, and how to dress. More sophisticated students and faculty might find such requests pathetic, but they illustrate the manner in which the heterogeneous worlds of the students refracted the very different aims of the faculty. In 1963, some students formed a basketball club, which officially played several of the small colleges nearby. Several years later, students were permitted to participate in varsity soccer, cross-country, and several similarly upper-middle-brow sports. Finally, in 1967, after often bitter discussion, varsity basketball was made legitimate. Its coming was opposed not only by many on the faculty, but by some of the students, who regarded it as a symbol of all they had rejected in coming to Oakland. But other faculty members, who had opposed all varsity sports at an earlier time, had concluded that, while driving out much of the collegiate fun culture, Oakland had not substituted other versions of vivacity, and that even some varsity athletics might be preferable to anemia. Some radical and liberal faculty were neutralized when it was pointed out to them that basketball would help recruit black undergraduates, particularly after a Negro from one of the Detroit inner-city high schools was recruited as the basketball coach.

The Oakland administration has been eager to diversify the student body, running considerable risks in doing so. What has recently been true of Project Twenty black students at Oakland (as in similar ventures elsewhere) was manifested in earlier years in the recruiting of students from that great spillover area of the Middle Atlantic States that has always sent Oakland a few students who were both bright and alienated. A flamboyant instance was a talented, "underachieving" Jewish student from Baltimore who had not graduated from high school; he was recommended to Oakland by his counselor after several elite colleges had turned him down. On arrival, he used his considerable ingenuity to provoke people: he refused to live in the dormitories, and the deans managed to find a cranny for him in the Administration Building. There he kept house among old rags and papers; bearded, of course, and with long hair before either of these symbols became widely disseminated stigmata of possessing an uncommon mind; moreover, he went around barefoot in a climate and on a campus where this was then highly idiosyncratic. The Chancellor and the Dean were sensitive to his qualities and respected his idiosyncrasies; the faculty delighted in his intelligence and in the evidence that Oakland could find room for non-conformists.

Somewhat later, a new Dean of Students, who had come from Michigan State with the Chancellor's original administrative staff, was not happy about unkempt and unwashed students, and was especially sensitive to complaints about the appearance of students who worked in the Oakland Center, which served the community at large. He issued an order that no student with a beard would be hired in any of the offices and facilities under his supervision. This included areas such as the dormitories, where students had no direct contact with non-academic complainers. Students, even the square and conventional ones, resented and ridiculed the action; they were joined by a number of faculty in signing petitions against the ruling. A prize of ten dollars' worth of books was offered for the best beard, and the Dean of the University refused to follow the edict of the Dean of Students in the positions under his own control. In public, the Chancellor defended the Dean of Students; privately, he saw to it that the Dean was elevated to a new office, of a more advisory sort, and the incoming Dean of Students dropped the policy. The incident illustrates the conflicts generated within Oakland by the negative reactions of a conservative area, and the student and faculty resentment of them, which made beards more popular than before.

Nevertheless, Oakland did not possess a sizable and self-perpetuating group of student activists until the past few years. The anti-war and civil right movements, which absorbed many Monteith students, came later to Oakland. Three years ago, a number of student publications appeared. The students put out a well-designed booklet, "Undiapered Moo," evaluating courses and faculty; they also attacked the parietal rules in the dormitories. A literary journal, *Contuse,* created a minor crisis with a deliberately pornographic issue, which the Chancellor felt could not be subsidized by tax moneys, allowing some students and several faculty to charge that freedom of speech had been curbed. Administrators and faculty chipped in to provide a substitute subvention for its continuation. The *Oakland Observer,* which started as a campus newssheet, now covers national affairs through the Liberation News Service and generally supports the local SDS chapter. A few students in the winter of 1968–69 founded the *New Journal,* a mimeographed, seriously written effort to reflect liberal rather than radical campus opinion.[10]

Contrary to fact and legend at many leading state universities, some of the most prominent New Left students at Oakland have been residents of Michigan, though seldom commuters. Their presence of course has greatly changed the climate. Another group that has added to the heterogeneity of Oakland are the older women commuters who hope to complete their college education or in some cases to begin it. There are almost four hundred women students over twenty-five, who come from the surrounding suburbs and often bring to discussions a liveliness and experience of life that the faculty greatly value. (The other undergraduates do not always value the ability of these women to "raise the curve.") At times, these women have been of fundamentalist outlook and have been critical of the faculty as subversive. More often, they have been wives of union leaders or professional men, who hope to keep up with their husbands and with the world of affairs. Especially in the early years, when there were no graduate students, they added significantly to diversity.

[10] The *Oakland Observer,* with its focus on national events and its often psychedelic drawings, gives rise to the complaint, heard on many campuses, that it does not give the news of the college itself. The *New Journal* is in part an effort to fill this gap, but it has been going such a short time that its viability is uncertain. More long-lived has been the *Fitz-Bits,* an occasional mimeographed product of one of the more collegiate dormitories, strongly anti-SDS and often Philistine.

Oakland has changed, but so has the United States. Political differences, and especially radical styles, have been made far more visible nationally, and it is unlikely that a student will come to Oakland today even from the most provincial Oakland County high school unaware of the fact that on the Oakland campus he will find guerrilla theater, interracial dating, psychedelic posters, and all the other insignia of "with it" modernity.

Problems of Scale

In its initial years, Oakland's student body grew by two hundred students a year, whereas between 1967 and 1968 it grew by twelve hundred. By fall 1963, Oakland had a student body of 1498; by fall 1969, it had jumped to an enrollment of 5811.[11] Between its first and third years of operation, the faculty grew from twenty-three to fifty-five; by 1968, the faculty numbered 185. As we have already noted, this growth itself was for many a betrayal of the early ideal of a small liberal arts college with a student body stabilized at perhaps two thousand. It now seems likely that the pressures of state-wide growth and the fact of ample land at Oakland will push the campus toward continued growth, so that there is now talk of a ceiling of twenty thousand students. Some faculty have left, looking for smaller colleges—there are not many—in Oakland's academic league. One man went to Harpur College, though it is also facing pressures of growth from the State University of New York system; one long-time faculty member has departed for Hampshire College, the new college opening in the Connecticut Valley in the fall of 1970. Still others, pulled by the lure of the East and West coasts and pushed by the restlessness that seems endemic among able academic men at present, have recently departed for other large locales.

But a surprisingly large number remain. Ten faculty members are left from the original charter faculty of 1959; twelve of those who came the next year remain, and five of those who joined in 1961 remain. The Chancellor is still there; the Provost has been

11 See Appendix F-1.

at Oakland for nine years.[12] The Education Department has the same head, but Engineering and Business Administration have not.

Oakland's relative success in retaining its faculty puzzles some of those who have stayed. One element is a decrease in dissatisfaction about the level of student ability. As part of a continuing effort to link recruiting with the actual offerings of Oakland, the admissions staff discuss students with the various departments, and have found that on the whole the faculty believes it is getting a better student body. Demands for student power, though beginning to be voiced, are not yet sufficiently pervasive to put the faculty at odds with each other over how to respond to them.[13]

However, one of the most important factors in reconciling innovative faculty members to Oakland's continuing growth has been the possibility of harnessing some of them to the development of the three subcolleges, two already launched and one en route, by which the University hopes to avoid the diseases of the multiversity. Pride in smallness has been endemic at Oakland among students and faculty. One student told us that she had switched from the University of Michigan to Oakland because of the friendliness of an Oakland French teacher who, in a summer course at Oakland, had troubled to find a car pool for her. She added that it was easier to speak up in class at Oakland than at Michigan, because in the smaller scale of things the instructor was not a stranger; one saw him outside the classroom as well. The beat student from Baltimore described earlier was grateful that his first efforts at creative writing were read and responded to by a full professor of English, and not by a T.A.

[12] Since our manuscript went to press, Chancellor Varner has become Chancellor of the University of Nebraska (in February of 1970), succeeding former Chancellor Hardin, who has become President Nixon's Secretary of Agriculture. Oakland's students and faculty, who had urged Varner in a rally earlier in the fall not to accept any overtures from Michigan State University, felt hurt and let down. Provost Donald O'Dowd has been made Acting Chancellor while a search for a new Chancellor proceeds.

[13] In our observation, the student personnel people, at Oakland as elsewhere, tend to support students against faculty, believing that if students do protest, there must be a cause—and perhaps fearing that they themselves are too square and therefore in danger of being out of touch.

In 1965, two veteran faculty members, one in political science and one in history, persuaded the Academic Affairs Committee to let them start a subcollege. They asked that they not be required to develop a detailed plan, but be allowed to begin with a brief, one-page statement. The Committee approved. Thus Charter College began with 150 freshmen and five faculty. The latter could offer whatever they wished within the full range of General Education, with the medium being the seminar. The idea was to avoid the usual pressures for coverage and to allow faculty to find their own route for inducting students into something their teachers cared about. Half the first wave of students were to be residents, half commuters; a sleep-in was held at one of the dormitories, in which commuters spent one week living on campus, thus getting them better acquainted with the residential group. Charter College reinforced its classroom experiences with a concert/lecture series, with required attendance at events such as the film version of *Oedipus Rex,* a concert of baroque music, and a lecture-exhibit of African and Oceanic art. The College offered a semester-abroad program, open only to its own students and led by its faculty. Originally there were to be no examinations, and all grades were to be pass-fail, but this led to a fear on the part of students as well as faculty of insufficient structure, and grades have now been restored.

Two years later, New College began with a much more prescribed curriculum than that of Charter, and with the addition of a semester of off-campus work on the Antioch College model. The five faculty recruited only seventy students in its first year, for it seemed that the Antioch ideal was not so appealing at Oakland: the romantic attraction of low-level jobs for upper-middle class students is not so readily duplicated among those Oakland students who have already held such jobs and do not find them endearing.[14]

[14] Even at Antioch, the program is in trouble today, as students want "meaningful experience" rather than any old job. The Antioch Year in Washington program and Antioch-Columbia (in the Washington-Baltimore area "new town" of Columbia, Maryland) are among the alternatives with which Antioch is experimenting.

New College also can arrange for its students to have a semester overseas, with attendant faculty, in Hong Kong or in Europe.

A third college, not yet in existence, Allport College, intends to focus on the social sciences. The hope has been to continue to recruit both faculty and students into subcolleges that would experiment with different educational plans and maintain a small-college atmosphere even as Oakland grows. One professor, who had come in 1960, has been highly critical of the pressures for growth at Oakland, especially because this would mean also increasing class size, but his resentment has been partially offset by participation in one of the new colleges, which he regards as an effective antidote to "creeping bigness."

In the fall of 1968, Oakland added sixty new faculty members, twenty-five of them replacements for departures and the rest additions. These newcomers find themselves in an ongoing university, with the administrators and older faculty struggling, not wholly successfully, to develop a sense of community and full participation. For some on the faculty, of course, growth has been something hoped for rather than something feared. It makes possible the planning of graduate programs and the diversification of undergraduate offerings; in Engineering and Business Administration, where the programs have been small from the outset, growth is hardly yet at the point to insure full viability. Here the dichotomy between the two cultures tends to reappear, with the natural scientists and engineers on the whole eager for graduate work and hence for growth. (The Teacher Education program, as anywhere else, wants to be able to give the master's degree.[15])

In some respects, the most daring ventures of Oakland have been its moves into music and drama. In the summer of 1963, Oakland presented the Detroit Symphony Orchestra and guest per-

[15] Even in the humanities, the defense of an exclusively undergraduate college is uneven. When a state constitutional reform put all Michigan educational institutions under a new State Board of Education, the Oakland Trustees insisted that a bid for graduate programs be entered before the new Board took office on January 1, 1965; nine master's programs were quickly drawn up to beat the deadline, despite some open faculty opposition. Faculty opposition to Ph.D. programs is now tending to weaken.

formers in a series called the Meadow Brook Festival. There was
no public money for this and no assurance of success. Now the
summer programs are on the cultural map, along with Tanglewood
and Ravinia, and difficult contemporary works are presented as
well as old war-horses. Sixten Ehrling, the Director of the Detroit
Symphony, is a member of the Oakland faculty, and by the
fall of 1964, the Music Department had become one of the largest departments at Oakland. Several years later, when the Provost
read that John Fernald, the Director of the Royal Academy of
Dramatic Art in London, was in the United States seeking to
relocate his theater, the Provost and the Chancellor persuaded him of
the possibilities at Oakland and gambled on the hope of providing
the necessary money and conditions of freedom requisite for bringing the company from England. Now the administration hopes to
develop a School for the Performing Arts, which would help
vitalize undergraduate education. Naturally, there are conflicts.
Performing musicians and academic musicologists, art historians
and painters, literature teachers and actors, are not always happy
colleagues. Some of the undergraduates have found the performers
arrogant and inconsiderate, and their characteristic Bohemian-
ism—and some of the plays put on—have not always appealed to
the local communities.

These are new problems for Oakland. Still in a league with
few members, it can find no easy models to emulate. It has better
students than it did, but it is not an honors college; most of its
students are still from within Michigan. It is no longer the post-
Sputnik college, and its grandiose visions of academic greatness are
gone. But with the muting of those visions has come a more realistic
and, at the same time, more ambitious and adventurous view that
avoids the disappointments and resentments of the early years.
The students are no longer being punished for belonging to Middle
America—nor of course do they belong in the old, unquestioning
way.

XI Monteith College Today:
An Experiment Stabilized

In speaking of an experiment stabilized, we do not mean to suggest that Monteith is quiescent. Far from it. A new President at Wayne State University, continuing change in the ethnic composition of Detroit, persistent problems of grading and curriculum, all contribute to a degree of turmoil at Monteith. At the same time, Monteith, now financed entirely as part of Wayne State, enrolled in the fall of 1969 a student body of 910, a gradual increase over enrollments since 1964.[1] It has had a Danforth Foundation grant of $75,000 to develop plans for a new building best suited to its particular style of learning (though it appears to have no immediate prospect of moving out of the dispersed surroundings in which it began). In 1964, the humanities staff moved to a building shared with the college administrative staff, and classes are still located anywhere space can be found on the Wayne campus.

Outside the Detroit area, Monteith is often better known than within it. As a founding member of the Union for Experimentation and Research in Higher Education, Monteith has participated in national conferences, which have brought its people into contact

[1] See Appendix G-1 for enrollment figures from 1959 to 1969.

with other educational reformers. Some Monteith faculty are active,
along with students, in tutorial projects, experiments in the arts,
and innovations in the public schools. When the Detroit riots
occurred in the summer of 1967, Alice Corrigan and other faculty
members helped to form an organization to find temporary shelter
and eventual permanent housing for displaced Negroes. While none
of these activities was planned with an eye to its possible publicity value for Monteith, which has been singularly unconcerned
with institutional public relations, they nevertheless carried the message that the College was radical, experimental, challenging, innovative. This message has not always helped recruitment in a
quantitative sense, but it has drawn to Monteith an increasing
proportion of students who apply on their own, those whom the
admissions people call "self-starters."

The Issue of Selectivity: An Honors College?

The Gray Document contained an extensive discussion of the
kinds of students who attended Wayne, their patterns of dropping
in and dropping out, and the implications of such a student body
for the Monteith plan. Yet at no time has there been a drive
comparable to that at Oakland, to recruit "better" students. Indeed, Monteith's problem from the outset was to recruit sufficient
students, for in its early years it was not free to choose its students
from a large number of applicants clamoring at its gates. This
meant in due course the abandonment of the quotas for the
professional schools, which it had trouble filling, and of the method
of random invitations,[2] which were not being accepted in large
enough numbers to fill the freshman openings. The problem of
sufficient enrollment was intensified by a large, and increasing, number of "no-shows" among students who were admitted.[3] Until the fall

[2] The early recruitment procedures are described in Chapter III.
[3] This is a reflection of a general problem at Wayne, where the proportion
of "no-shows" has increased in recent years, due in part (and in combination)
to the flight of the white population to the suburbs, the riot of 1967, and
the expansion of junior colleges and the branches of MSU and the University
of Michigan.

of 1969, the large proportion of no-shows combined with those who turned down the invitation kept entering-class enrollments to an average of around 270 students.

When it was decided to abandon the random invitations and the quota system, the Wayne Admissions Office mailed "informational" letters to all prospective students (with a few minor exceptions) until an entering class was filled. In the early years, some faculty members and a few of the abler, more committed students occasionally visited Detroit area high schools to talk about Monteith, but the College itself did not have a sustained campaign of recruitment. In 1966–67, however, the Dean's office carried out an intensive program of counselor luncheons, contacts with high school editors, college night programs, and so on, resulting in a larger volume of both self-starters and acceptances. The proportion responding affirmatively to the invitation seems to have peaked at about seven per cent of all those receiving the letter, but the proportion of the entering class who were self-starters rose to a high of sixty-seven per cent in 1968 (compared to sixteen per cent in 1959 and forty per cent in 1962). Throughout the life of Monteith, the fluctuation in student choices has meant that it has never been possible to plan the size of classes in advance— or to have the secure validation of Monteith that a plethora of applications would imply.

All this suggests to us that there is a certain degree of accident in who comes to Monteith, but also a certain degree of choice on the students' part, which has increased as Monteith has become better known. We have made a systematic examination of test scores and other data to see whether or not Monteith has become a *de facto* honors college in spite of itself. (Many faculty members at Wayne believe that it has, as do many who are familiar with its General Education program and assume that such a program will appeal only to the bright—and indulged—children of the middle class.) We know that Oakland in the course of time attracted more academically adept students and repelled the less adept. Did the same thing happen at Monteith?

The data assembled on these matters in Appendix Tables G-2 and G-3[4] are complicated, and their interpretation is not automatic. From the very outset, Monteith students appear to have come from families of marginally higher socioeconomic background than those in the College of Liberal Arts at Wayne and to have had somewhat higher test scores. In measures of personality, there were again slight differences, which suggest that Monteith students have been somewhat more liberal, religiously and politically, somewhat more impulsive and, as we would expect, somewhat more willing to be exploratory in the college years. At the outset, Monteith (and Wayne) attracted a significant stream of Jewish students (eighteen per cent in 1959), predominantly from Mumford and Cass Technical high schools. The latter was a city-wide high school comparable to the Bronx High School of Science or the High School of Music and Art in New York City, but presently is no longer elite. The Mumford area has become increasingly black in recent years, and Monteith now attracts fewer Jewish students than it did in its early years.

At the same time, reflecting a national secularization, there has been an increase at Monteith of Catholics from parochial and secular high schools, for whom the Jesuit University of Detroit or the three Catholic women's colleges (Mercy, Marygrove, and Madonna) are no longer *de rigueur*. It seems reasonably clear that Monteith and the College of Liberal Arts at Wayne currently draw from the same pool of metropolitan-area students, although the changes in this pool were apparent at Monteith earlier than at Wayne. Thus, as the white population has moved to the suburbs, the proportion of students drawn from suburban high schools has increased since 1959 at Wayne generally, but at Monteith the increase has been sharper (from thirty-one per cent in 1959 to forty-two per cent in 1963). So, too, Monteith has been ahead

---

[4] We are grateful to Sally Cassidy, Paul Bluemle, and Kay Engle for making these data available. For a detailed analysis of the characteristics of Monteith students, particularly the 1959 entering class, see the report from the Monteith Program Study by Sally Cassidy and others, *Impact of a High-Demand College in a Large University on Working Class Youth.*

of Wayne in its appeal to a cadre of Negroes, small in absolute numbers but increasing each year. In 1969 Negroes constituted thirteen per cent of the Monteith entering classes, compared to nine per cent at the University as a whole.[5]

The demographic shifts have not meant an increase in the proportion of students from elite backgrounds. Indeed, Monteith in later years has attracted fewer students who stood in the top two fifths of their high school classes (although the average entrance test performance has gone up); the proportion of students from college-educated families has not increased dramatically; and a slight gain in students from professional families has been accompanied by gains in blue collar families and losses in white collar families. Thus we conclude that Monteith from the beginning has been self-selected but not select: it has drawn a certain kind of student, but, in terms of aptitudes or social background, it has not become an honors college. It remains, as it began, a school for the average student from a non-elite background. In the statistics, there are glimmers of a special sort of student Monteith has been attracting. We draw attention to the disparity between high school performance (which has decreased) and aptitude (which has increased) as an indication that Monteith (and perhaps the College of Liberal Arts also) in later years attracted the more erratic, underachieving youngster, who often makes the most interesting—and troubling—kind of college student.

Of course, it does not follow that Monteith did equally well with all its students. To understand this process, we turn to another indicator of selectivity—statistics on attrition.

[5] Wayne has always attracted more Negroes than any of the state-supported universities in Michigan; indeed, its 1967 enrollment of nine per cent is the second highest (Temple University is first) of all four-year public colleges and universities in the country, not including Negro colleges. For a compilation of statistics, from a 1967 survey conducted by the U. S. Office for Civil Rights, of Negro enrollments in U.S. colleges with five hundred students or more, see "White, Negro Undergraduates at Colleges Enrolling 500 or More, as Compiled from Reports to U. S. Office for Civil Rights." Wayne now has a visible group of black students whose numbers, and demands, have escalated greatly since the Detroit riot.

Attrition and Graduation

Between the fall of 1959 and the spring of 1964, 1631 students had entered Monteith; by 1968, 359, or twenty-two per cent, had graduated from the College. The charter class had a considerably better record than any of its successors: it graduated nineteen per cent after four years, whereas the classes of 1961 and 1962 graduated eleven per cent and thirteen per cent in the same time period; after six years, slightly more than one third of the charter class had received Monteith degrees, as compared to seventeen per cent and eighteen per cent of the 1960 and 1961 classes after six years. Although these graduation rates were somewhat lower than Wayne overall,[6] direct comparison of the status of the 1959 Monteith and Liberal Arts freshmen in the winter of 1963 shows great similarity (Table 4).

Attrition was particularly serious after two years for the 1960 and 1961 classes; sixty-three per cent of the former and sixty-six per cent of the latter did not register at Monteith in their third year, as compared to forty-three per cent of the charter class. (Of course, as Table 4 demonstrates, many students who would be counted as dropouts in these figures were transferring to other colleges at Wayne after having taken the bulk of their General Education courses at Monteith.) In recent years, attrition has dropped somewhat, settling to around the low 40s after one year and the mid-

[6] A ten-year follow-up study of students who entered Wayne State University in 1949 showed that twenty-four per cent graduated after four years, thirty-eight per cent after six years, and forty-six per cent after ten years. Cf., Wayne State University: Office of Divisional Studies. *The Wayne State University Student.* The national graduation rate for college entrants in 1950 after four years was forty per cent for all institutions and thirty-three per cent for public institutions. The latter category includes residential schools as well as commuter schools, which possibly accounts for Wayne's lower graduation rate. For national figures, see Robert Iffert, *Retention and Withdrawal of College Students,* Table 8, page 16. Both the Wayne and Iffert statistics are dated, but are in line with a more recent national study of students who entered higher education in 1959, which reported a four-year graduation rate of thirty-six per cent for public universities. Cf. James W. Trent and Leland L. Medsker, *Beyond High School,* p. 79.

Table 4

Fate of 1959 Entrants to Monteith and Liberal Arts
(as of Winter 1963)[a]

	Monteith	Liberal Arts[c]
Graduated	b	3%
Registered in Monteith (Liberal Arts)	44%	36
Registered in another college at Wayne State	21	24
Dropped out of the University entirely	35	37
Total	100%	100%
N	265	214

[a]Source: Monteith College Advisor's Office.
[b]Less than one per cent.
[c]Based on a random sample.

50s after two—still considerably higher than the 1959 class.[7] We
know that the charter class did not differ appreciably from subsequent classes; if anything, its average aptitudes were a little lower.
At work here, we suspect, was the famous "Hawthorne effect,"
named for the discovery by Elton Mayo and his fellow researchers
at the Hawthorne plant of the Western Electric Company, that
the subjects of an experiment respond to the attention paid them,
regardless of the content of the experiment. By its very nature, the
Hawthorne effect tends to dissipate with time, although it is not
clear to us why it should have dropped quite so rapidly in view of
the continuing enthusiasm and energy invested by the faculty. No
doubt, the high attrition at Monteith after the 1959 class reflects the
greater casualness of a student body almost entirely composed of
commuters. It is clear that Monteith was unable to overcome the
pulls on commuter students that occur at Wayne generally. Some
students drop out of the University entirely, perhaps to return later.
Some treat the College as a General Education program, to be abandoned for a more specialized college after they take all or part of
the core curriculum. Indeed, this is often the case among students
with definite vocational plans: students heading for Education often

[7] The national attrition rates for public institutions are thirty-one per cent
after one year and forty-seven per cent after two years. See Iffert, *Retention
and Withdrawal of College Students.*

transfer after two years, and those going into Law School and Medical School, until recently, could enter these professional schools after three years of college. Despite Monteith's strenuous attempts to keep its students through various combined General Education-preprofessional programs, it has not been successful. Part of the reason lies in the senior essay requirement, a problem we will take up later in the chapter.

In a sense, Monteith becomes selective by attrition—but selective in what ways? We examined data showing the kinds of students who survived in the charter class, to see whether Monteith was able to graduate only those who as freshmen might have been admitted to a more selective college, and compared them to students who entered the Wayne College of Liberal Arts that year. As one would expect, those freshmen who later became seniors in both colleges were by and large students who entered with better academic credentials and from more educated, higher-status families. In comparison with the College of Liberal Arts, Monteith held onto fewer of the students from homes where a foreign language was spoken and from Slavic backgrounds. But Monteith increased its proportion of students from the inner city and from families in which both parents were foreign-born, and it lost relatively fewer students whose fathers were in the lower-status occupations. The materials provide fragmentary evidence that Monteith was able to hold onto at least some students from the "underdeveloped" strata of the city to a greater extent than the College of Liberal Arts. On our visits to Monteith, we have always encountered students, both white and black, who had been truck drivers or were the children of laboring men—students who, though often inarticulate, felt comfortable at Monteith.

There are fascinating differences between freshmen and seniors at Monteith and the College of Liberal Arts on some personality tests.[8] At both colleges, those who made it to the senior year started out more reflective and intellectual, more mature and flexible. How-

[8] As measured by the Omnibus Personality Inventory. See *Omnibus Personality Inventory Research Manual,* developed by the Center for the Study of Higher Education, University of California.

ever, people who became seniors at Monteith were less rebellious[9] (and also less authoritarian) than their freshman peers, while the reverse was true for seniors in the College of Liberal Arts. Monteith seniors were more restrained than Monteith freshmen, whereas in the College of Liberal Arts, those who became seniors started college notably less repressed and restrained, less introverted, and less anxious than others in their entering class.

Thus although there was no great overrepresentation in the Monteith senior class, compared to Liberal Arts seniors, of those who as freshmen might have seemed better suited to its program in terms of background and preparation, it required different kinds of personalities. Those students who managed to get through in four years at Monteith, in addition to being more intellectual and more mature—characteristics they shared with Liberal Arts seniors—were also more inhibited. Put another way, freshmen who were impulsive and uncontrolled did not last as long at Monteith as they did in Liberal Arts, either because they lacked the self-discipline to handle the academic demands[10] and to direct themselves in a partially unstructured program, or because the College itself discouraged such people. We think the latter is clearly not the case. One could even argue the contrary, that it encouraged them too much, to the point at which even the permissive restraints of Monteith seemed stifling—perhaps an illustration of the Tocquevillean principle that people are apt to revolt when things are getting better, when the lid is off.[11]

[9] We are referring here to the Developmental Status index of the Omnibus Personality Inventory, which measures "rebelliousness toward authority, especially when it is institutionalized within the family, school, church, or state." High scorers are "less authoritarian than the low scorer, and at the same time, freer to express impulses." Cf. *Omnibus Personality Inventory*, p. 5.

[10] Trent and Medsker report a similar finding for their national sample of high school graduates. Dropouts from college scored slightly higher on the Complexity scale of the Omnibus Personality Inventory than did persisters. They were less likely to adjust to the demands of college: "At least temporarily, the withdrawals thereby forego experiences which are at first unpleasant but which ultimately could provide the opportunity for greater development and satisfaction." *Beyond High School*, p. 126.

[11] This observation is based less on the experience of Monteith than of other experimental colleges, which often experience very high attrition in spite

The Survivors as Seniors

There were 116 students from the charter class enrolled at Monteith in the winter of 1963; of these, fifty graduated in the spring, many of the others being held back by failure to complete their senior essays. Given the rather small number of seniors in 1963, the measures of performance that we have must be interpreted cautiously. Monteith seniors in 1963 placed somewhat above the seventieth percentile on the area examinations of the Graduate Record Examination (GRE). These scores were considerably higher than those achieved by the only available comparison group of Wayne Liberal Arts seniors in 1954 (not really comparable, because of the generally rising levels of performance) and also higher than the 1963 Oakland University seniors.[12] At Oakland, the average GRE score was highest in the humanities. Of all majors, Oakland social science majors scored lowest on all three area examinations, including their own major (suggesting the relative unattractiveness of the social science programs in the early years). At Monteith, average performance was quite similar in humanities, social science, and natural science. These differences may mean that at Oakland it was possible for a student who did well in a particular area to become encapsulated within his department and pulled along to graduation, whereas the more integrated Monteith experience made such uneven development less likely.

At Oakland, freshman entrance test performance was a fairly good predictor of senior performance on the GRE: what college

---

of allowing their students great leeway. Antioch would be one example, New College (Sarasota) another.

[12] The GRE scores for these three groups were:

	Wayne Liberal Arts Seniors, 1954	Oakland Seniors, 1963	Monteith Seniors, 1963
Social Science	63	53	72
Humanities	61	68	74
Natural Science	63	53	78

did for students was a function of how they had begun. Entrance test scores at Monteith were not clear predictors of eventual graduation or of GRE performance. Of all the Monteith freshman aptitude and social background measures that we have examined, a test designed to measure the level of "critical thinking" predicted best for the GRE. Indeed, Monteith seniors from the charter class showed large gains on this test.

The outcome measures may reflect a phenomenon we have already observed: although it took a more controlled, less expressive, and perhaps more tenacious person to stay with the Monteith program for four years, the impact of the College as a whole was to counterbalance the very qualities that enabled students to stay with it. The personality tests taken by freshmen were readministered to the seniors in 1963. They show that the seniors, who had begun more intellectual and less authoritarian than their classmates, exhibited further increases in these qualities. These changes are in general characteristic of college students, who move toward less authoritarianism, more autonomy, and greater intellectualism; indeed adolescents not in college may also develop in the same direction, though to a lesser degree.[13] We cannot say that Monteith had a greater impact than other colleges, but it obviously had an impact similar to the overall trends at other colleges, particularly the elite colleges.

The faculty point to the small cadre of graduates of the first several classes who can be found in leading graduate schools and on the early rungs of careers as college teachers, building a second generation devoted to educational reform. With some students, Monteith was stunningly successful on two fronts—maintaining itself as an intellectual, non-vocational undergraduate college and at the same time transmitting aspirations for graduate school. Eighty per cent of the first graduating class continued in graduate or pro-

[13] See, for example, John C. McCullers and Walter T. Plant, "Personality and Social Development: Cultural Influences," which has some data on non-college students. For the most comprehensive analysis of college impact studies to date, see the text, appendices, and bibliography in Kenneth A. Feldman and Theodore M. Newcomb, *The Impact of College on Students*. See also Trent and Medsker, *Beyond High School*.

fessional school, some with handsome fellowships or grants. The trend over the years has been away from graduate school and toward education or industry and government service: by 1968–69, the percentage of graduates planning to go on immediately to graduate school was down to thirty.[14] Nevertheless, this percentage (which for Monteith is its lowest) is considerably higher than Oakland's and that of other commuter schools. The University of Cincinnati, for example, sends one fourth of its men and one seventh of its women on to graduate or professional school immediately after graduation. Brooklyn College sends on twenty-three per cent of its graduates.[15]

We followed the career of one student who completed graduate work at Harvard, became a leader in movements for curricular reform, and did his Ph.D. dissertation on a new urban college in Massachusetts. Another was one of the first graduate students at the Danish campus of the Friends World Institute. Still another, an education major, became the innovating chairman of the science department in a Detroit inner-city high school.

The ambivalence of some Monteith faculty—even the most apparently dissident of the social scientists felt some allegiance to academic as well as intellectual values—may have been responsible for imparting a sufficent sense of academic discipline to these students, along with the stimulus of intellectual excitement. The faculty had a desire to see students succeed, even in a game about which they themselves had misgivings. In either case, the

---

[14] See Appendix G-4 for postgraduate intentions of Monteith graduates.

[15] On Cass and Birnbaum's four-level grouping of colleges, Monteith in its early years would appear to be in this respect somewhere between "Highly Selective" (level 2) and "Very Selective" (level 3) colleges. Of the "Highly Selective" schools, sixty-six per cent of Antioch graduates and fifty-four per cent of Bowdoin graduates continue in graduate or professional school. Of the "Very Selective" schools, the percentage for Hofstra and Rollins is thirty-five per cent. Cf. James Cass and Max Birnbaum, *Comparative Guide to American Colleges*. See also James A. Davis, *Great Aspirations: The Graduate School Plans of America's College Seniors*.

At some elite colleges, a decline has begun in the percentage of students intending to continue in graduate school, reflecting lessened opportunities, alterations in draft deferments and plans, and a growing belief that graduate schools are corrupt and stifling.

choice of graduate school for many Monteith students was a continuation of the intellectual values to which they had been exposed, not the vocationalism such a choice often means for comfortable middle class students. Rather than leading students into standard social mobility careers, the faculty pulled those who remained long enough at Monteith out of their initial vocational channels into the academic channel, and toward the cultural transformation such a choice implied for them.

For other students, the first shock of confrontation was too much, and they dropped out. And among some who stayed, there were many who wanted more structure and direction in their courses rather than less. The uneasiness some students felt about the Monteith program could be exacerbated by hearing the criticisms of the program on just these grounds from faculty in other parts of the University. While for some of the Monteith students, these criticisms served to intensify their dedication, more marginal students felt their own doubts confirmed. At the price of losing many students, this elite program for non-elite students had certain elite effects, even some that anticipated the "Young Radicals" whom Kenneth Keniston describes.[16] Perhaps even for some of the students who departed, Monteith opened doors and represented an alternative way toward which they could grope. To put it more drastically, Monteith was an acquired taste—poison for some students and ambrosia for others. These contradictory reactions were apparent in the student community, which was so much the creation of the charter class.

The Legacy of the Charter Class

Members of the class who entered in 1959 were asked in the following spring whether they considered themselves involved in Monteith student activities. A quarter said they were; three fifths said that they sat around and talked very often with friends at the College; two fifths that they very often stopped in at the Student Center, while a third did so occasionally.

A later study by a Monteith social scientist of those students ac-

[16] Kenneth Keniston, *Young Radicals: Notes on Committed Youth.*

tive in the student culture showed that they were also more likely than non-involved students to take special courses and tutorials—indeed, often to initiate them.[17] In what turned out to be a *de facto* honors program, a few of the better students from the first two classes organized a series of student-run courses, termed the Co-operative Self-Education Project, in which students, with faculty help, created their own bibliographies, ran their own seminars, and invited their own speakers. One of us vividly recalls being invited to visit such a seminar in 1962, devoted to the topic of Revolution, in which seven or eight students discussed whether activities in the Deep South aimed at compelling compliance with federal law could be termed revolutionary in comparison with revolts of decoloniali-zation elsewhere. (The students concluded that it was revolutionary for Mississippi, but not for the United States as a whole.) The same group of students formed their own Senior Colloquium the first time it was taught and formed a nucleus of students who pressed for curricular changes in the natural science and humanities divisions. This interest in educational innovation preceded the Experimental College of San Francisco State and the free universities elsewhere; undoubtedly, it reflected the faculty's educationally avant-garde wing, especially among the social scientists.

This core group seems in retrospect a precursor of the New Student of today. Its members started out as freshmen more intellectual, more liberal, and more academically capable than their classmates. They were highly visible and did not always favorably impress their peers: asked less than six months after the College opened if there were a particular group associated with the Student Center, a third of the Monteith student body described the Student Center "crowd" as not serious; a fifth termed them snobs; a tenth saw them as non-conforming and aggressive. But "that crowd" was also seen as the carrier of the distinctive values of Monteith in contrast to the more pallid commuter campus of Wayne.

The College Characteristics Index[18] (which measures the "aca-

17 See Paule Verdet, "Relationships Among the Seniors."
18 For a description of the College Characteristics Index and its scales, see G. G. Stern, "Characteristics of the Intellectual Climate in College Environments" and *People in Context.*

demic press" of colleges and universities), administered to seniors in 1963, indicates that the charter class had received the message (see Appendix G-5). On all the subscales, Monteith students perceived their college in ways that were more similar to descriptions given by students at seven selective independent liberal arts colleges than they were to student responses at other university-associated liberal arts colleges. Monteith was seen as less demanding academically, less hard-working and serious than the independent liberal arts colleges (though more so than the university-connected colleges), but high in aspiration level, intellectual climate, and student freedom. To an even greater extent than at the liberal arts colleges, Monteith was viewed as unconcerned with order, neatness, detail, deference, social forms, and group life.

The impact of the first group of students lingers on at Monteith, demonstrating that there can be a golden age within such a short time. The student community that formed in the first year renews itself as students are recruited and socialized into "Monteithy" ways. Some dropouts live or hang around in the immediate area. After the fashion of many commuter colleges, those who remain often take considerably longer than four years to complete their B.A.s. Failure to complete the senior essay enables many students to remain in an academic limbo—still students working on their essay, yet not carrying classes. In this way, Monteith generated on a small scale the fringe community of "permanent students," with which residential universities have been familiar. On return visits, we would occasionally discover students we had known in earlier years who were still around, as either slowdowns or returnees. While slowdown was a block for some students, it presented an opportunity for others to continue their identification with the College. Monteith has always had a few veterans of the first years around to instruct the new recruits—no doubt a mixed blessing, since the veterans tend to be the offbeat, dissident students who have taken to heart the model of some of the more flamboyant social science faculty.

Students continue to request the formation of special classes and tutorials and to criticize the curriculum.[19] A group of black students from Monteith formed the nucleus of Wayne Negroes who initiated an Institute of Black Studies, which may eventually become a college at Wayne. Special courses on Afro-American studies, planned by a committee of faculty members and black students, were introduced recently at Monteith.

In the decaying neighborhood surrounding the University, some hippie communities flourish but, somewhat surprisingly, current Monteith students do not seem to be as involved with them as one might expect. As we have suggested, there has always been an offbeat quality about the student core at Monteith, but perhaps because Monteith manages in some measure to bridge the academic and the intellectual, its students do not seem to have fled to the hippie fringe. In the past few years, a small cadre of Monteith students have put out occasional mimeographed journals. One, called *Mystique,* is an intellectual forum for students preoccupied with race, war, and civil liberties.

Differential Adjustment to the Students in Monteith's Three Divisions

The staff system continues to be the main focus of teaching at Monteith, in part reflecting the paucity of upper-division students in tutorials and seminars. With communication among the staffs kept at a minimum and the joint Senior Colloquium abandoned, conflict softened after 1962. This was partly because the most vociferous and abrasive of the early staff members in the social sciences had left. More important, the faculty has gradually withdrawn from concern with the operation of the College as a whole to preoccupation with intradivisional activities. This has meant the relative retreat of the social science division from interventionism to competitive coexist-

---

[19] Monteith, and Wayne State generally, avoid arguments with students over their extracurricular lives; only a tiny fraction of students live in dormitories. But the university is still under attack from the watchdogs of the community and the Legislature for bringing in "Communist" or black militant speakers. The *South End,* the militant student paper that replaced the Wayne State *Collegian,* has come under severe attack from within as well as outside the University.

ence, if not isolation. Correspondingly, the humanities staff, as it increased in size to meet the larger number of students taking its sequence in the middle of the sophomore year and beyond, has had a growing influence.

The basic plan of Monteith has remained stable, with a prescribed program taking up half the freshman, sophomore, and senior years, and a quarter of the junior year. A one-credit freshman practicum has been introduced into the first two quarters, as a means of introducing new students into the ways of Monteith and the University. A senior essay is required of all students taking a Monteith degree. Beyond the required sequences (six quarters in natural science, five in social science and in humanities), the practicum, and the two-quarter Senior Colloquium, students may shop around in the University to complete their degree requirements or may stay closer to home in the special courses and tutorials offered as Monteith electives.

The Grading Crisis in the Natural Sciences

The natural sciences sequence from the beginning has been preoccupied with the historical development of science and with the relation between scientific theories and discoveries and their social contexts, combined with material on the philosophy and logic of scientific thought. The course was designed explicitly to communicate the mutability and relativity of science, rather than the Baconian model of inductive cumulation. The story was told dramatically, through the juxtaposition of different scientific theories or "cases": Copernicus confronting Ptolemy, Dalton confronting Lavoisier, Darwin confronting Lamarck.

In the original plan, these matters were set out in four sequential courses. The first course was in formal logic, deductive systems, and the mathematical concepts necessary for the understanding of the substantive sciences ("sets," "relations," "function"). The second course traced the development of selected problems in astronomy and chemistry, particularly from Aristotle through the Middle Ages to Newton and Darwin. The third course and part of the fourth course picked up where the second course stopped, with the development of the sciences since Darwin and Newton. The final course, in addition to dealing with modern physics, ended with a study of scientific inquiry in general—a combination of philosophy of science, sociology of science, and psychology of science.

What we speak of as the "grading crisis" occurred in the spring of 1962 in the fourth course of the natural science sequence. It reflected a pulling back by the natural scientists from what they felt was the excessive leniency of grading the previous year, when they had given relatively few As and few Ds and Es but many Bs, Cs, and Incompletes (the same pattern that the social scientists employed, as we saw in Chapter IX. The result was that, in 1962, fewer than half of the students achieved grades of C or above, and hardly any were given the option of taking an Incomplete. It was then that the inability of students to meet the faculty's demands became absolutely clear, and the course was correspondingly simplified.

The impact of this crisis and of student criticism led to replacing the first course in logic with a course on the development of astronomy, while a less technical and abstruse version of mathematics and logic was taught later; indeed, the elimination of much of the mathematical material pushed the course in the direction of more substantive concerns. As one natural scientist said, "You want to make a nice impression on the students when they first come in." Another natural scientist put the matter as follows:

> The math-logic course was more isolated from the rest of the sequence. It was very sophisticated. We were too subtle, too complicated, too difficult for freshmen. It's far more interesting to teach the Copernican Revolution and biological evolution to students than abstract math. The students had very little motivation for the math course.

Along with the shift in the content of the course was a change in the span of coverage. Throughout the sequence of courses, there were many attempts to structure, to organize, to make the course more coherent. Genetics and evolution, taught in different semesters during the first two years, were put together in the third year. Large sections of the sequence were completely eliminated, thus allowing more time to cover the remaining subjects.

An even more dramatic change was the decision to use texts to transmit scientific information. (Monteith's original ideology had shared the highbrow animus against textbooks.) Related to the increased reliance on textbooks was the way the Independent Study program developed:

> The first time, we let students be completely independent. The second time, we made independent study more structured because students didn't do their work until the last minute. The third time, we asked them to give feedback throughout so they wouldn't be left to pace themselves.

Natural scientists found that students left completely on their own could not meet their expectations, so they became more directive. Indeed, whenever they tried to encourage "creativity" and "independence," they felt forced to pull back. One mathematician said:

> I asked for oral reports this semester and it was absolutely disastrous. I told them they could choose their own topics if they were related to the course, but they chose far-removed topics which the class couldn't follow.

There is no doubt that the changes in the natural science sequence were adjustments to the students.[20] The elimination of much of the material in the sections on the theory of numbers, logic, and Daltonian atomics (cited by students as the three most difficult sections) and the expansion of the material in astronomy and evolution (cited by students as the sections having the greatest impact) fit student reactions exactly. One of the natural scientists, describing

[20] See Appendix G-6 for the reaction of Monteith students to different parts of the natural science sequence as it was taught the first year.

the change, said that they had moved away from "those fields that are important to us, like relativity and quantum mechanics," to those suitable for average students. Since it was generally recognized in the first years that a large number of Monteith dropouts had trouble in the natural science sequence, and since not only the administration but the social science faculty put pressure on the natural science division to fail fewer students, the natural scientists responded to the situation by changing course content (and to a lesser degree, by changing grading policy).

This resolution of the conflicts satisfied the large bulk of the students, but satisfied neither the scientific and academic superegos of the natural scientists nor the critical demands for less rather than more structure among the group of students who identified with the social science staff. These students saw the new natural science program as a departure from the ideals with which Monteith had begun, in the direction of a pedantic sequence of quizzes, lectures, and appeals to memory rather than imagination. They felt that they now had no chance to discuss what they were doing, only to cough it up again on demand. The chairman of the natural science division recognized that the model these students were using was that of the social science program, but he refused to respond to their requests. Lacking a tracking system such as many high schools with a heterogeneous student body have had, the natural scientists felt that each student counted one and no more than one, even if he was bright.

The Stability of the Social Science Curriculum

It is perhaps more surprising that the bright students who were so visible to the social science faculty could not influence that curriculum either. At one time, they asked to send a student representative to staff meetings planning curricular changes. In an unusual display of solidarity, the whole staff rejected the request. Some of the faculty who were regarded as most "student oriented" were most antagonistic. George Green, for example, commented that the curriculum was "sacred ground"—while granting that everything else was fair game for student intervention. And Howard Rich, almost to his own surprise, commented:

> Nobody went along with having students in on faculty meetings. . . . What are one family's problems is no one else's business. Nor would I go along with them evaluating the program. They can make suggestions, but it's not their role to go beyond that. Certain people have more experience and they should take heed of what the students say. . . . We used to laugh and say students determined the curriculum. Now, looking back, despite questionnaires, asking students how they felt, etc., my instinct says that it didn't make a damn bit of difference. It would have gone along pretty much the same, no matter what the students did. It doesn't make much sense, but our complaint that the other divisions don't take students into account may not be right.

Protected by more lenient grading, the social scientists were under less pressure to consider modifying their syllabi. Furthermore, the social science curriculum was less open to student recalcitrance than the natural science program, since from its inception the social science course started off with a contemporary problem that could appeal to a wide range of students. This more inductive overture represented a rejection of the Gray Document's specification of a social science sequence that was to be *about* the social sciences, heavy in the writings of the "great men," largely historical and philosophical. Instead, the course concerned itself with contemporary problems and concepts in the social sciences, moving from the simple to the increasingly complex: from relation to small group, and then, via socialization, differentiation, complex organizations, and social movements, on to the concept of civilization. These concepts were described and illustrated in books of readings compiled and edited by members of the staff.[21] Reflecting the continuing debate among

---

[21] For many, these syllabi constituted their chief "publications" during their Monteith years. In our opinion, they were often imaginative collections, thoughtfully assembled, and we regret that they have not had wider academic distribution.

members of the staff about the emphases in the readings and discussions—some faculty thought the course should become more concrete, while others felt the curriculum was too concrete and not sufficiently analytic—no syllabus ever stayed nailed down for long. Yet the changes overall in the course of years have been relatively minor. One exception was a major change in the handling of economic theory—everywhere a stumbling block to ambitious interdisciplinary efforts. Thus the section on economics, which was taught originally like a traditional "principles" course, was abandoned in favor of a course on underdeveloped nations, where some of the principles of economics came in inductively.

Alterations in the empirical tasks with which each of the three courses in the sequence opened have varied over the years without changes in the basic approach. In the first course taught in 1959–60, students studied the problem of "brainwashing" in a section on Korean prisoners of war; in the second course, they studied the problems of Detroit; in the third course, they did a survey of political behavior at the time of the 1960 elections. A discussion of the impact of the religious question on the Protestant Negro voters of Detroit was sufficiently vivid to find a place in subsequent syllabi, a demonstration to students that what they did even as amateurs could add to knowledge—particularly to the self-knowledge of Detroiters about the significance of family backgrounds like their own.

In addition to these introductory problems, many of the topics in the sequence were taught by means of research assignments. For example, in the section on small groups, students observed group interaction, using the Bales category system and sociometric methods. In the section on socialization, they observed preschool children in the nearby Merrill-Palmer Nursery School. In the second semester, individuals or teams of students worked on semester-long research projects that involved the collection and analysis of field data.

It is clear that students did not find in these inductive approaches an easy highway into the more abstract sections of the course.[22] The sections on Complex Organization, particularly the one on formal

[22] Appendix G-6 shows student reactions to the social science courses at the end of the first year.

theory, were found to be the most difficult and also of lesser impact than the empirical sections of the course. Students also complained more in social science than in either of the other two divisions about lack of structure and not enough direction by the faculty.

There was, however, one area where the social science staff had to give way in the face of student criticism. This was the attack on the retroactive grading system based on a cumulative examination given at the end of a three-semester sequence. The system worked as follows: students were given "temporary advisory grades" at the end of the first two courses in the sequence. After the cumulative examination in the last weeks of the third course, a single permanent grade was assigned for all three courses, which superseded the earlier, temporary grades. One half of the grade was determined by the final grades in the three courses (i.e., each course counted one sixth), and the other half by the grade in the cumulative examination. This practice had been imported from The College of the University of Chicago by the social scientists and only by them: it was hoped that the cumulative examination would unify the sequence and turn the exam into an educational rather than a certifying instrument.[23]

At Chicago, this system meant that students could pace themselves and make use of their very considerable powers of concentration and review, but the radical faculty at Monteith soon realized, as Howard Rich put it, that "the students can't delay gratification for so long . . . this isn't the University of Chicago." Indeed it was not. Few Monteith students gained from the retroactive grading system, and a large number lost ground by one or even two marks. The indulgent grading system as such and the giving of Incompletes were fragile protection against student resentment when As and Bs were "taken back": whatever the rationale, students felt cheated of something they had legitimately earned. Even the better students were unhappy with retroactive grading. In the end, the

---

[23] Actually, the system had been modified from Chicago's, where all rather than half the grade was determined—more or less in British style—at the very end of the course.

faculty committee on examination policy declared against retroactive grading (but not the cumulative examination), and it was reluctantly abandoned.

The Emergence of the Humanities

Since it came just as the other sequences were ending, the curriculum in the humanities was expected to build upon some of the experiences students had had in natural sciences and social sciences. In the original design outlined in the Gray Document, the humanities sequence was to open with a course in the fundamentals of the arts, which treated the materials and forms in each of the arts separately. The second course was to analyze the arts in selected historical periods—Athens in the fifth century and Western Europe in the thirteenth and fourteenth centuries—in order to "illuminate the reciprocal relationships between the content and the form of the arts . . . and the environment." The third course was to continue these historical-cultural concerns down to the present.

The first time around, the second and third courses were given pretty much as planned, while the first course was modified somewhat. The emphasis was on analyzing the arts in terms of four categories, which could be applied to each separate art: creative process, form, symbol, and value. Although many primary materials were also used, and although students were exhorted to go to concerts, plays, and museums, they found the analytical approach too abstract. Even with the emphasis on primary experiences, students were asked to appreciate the arts but not to work *in* the arts; there was nothing comparable to the social science election survey of 1960.

As in the case of the natural sciences, a small group of students was dissatisfied with the humanities course, and seventeen of them published an open letter asking that they be allowed to "experience" art, rather than learn about it in a detached way. One of these students, in an article entitled "Unhumanistic Non-Studies" complained:

The student proceeds through the course and finishes with a most proper education enabling him to discourse over a bottle of beer or olived martini about "man's reflections on his experience." Though I would rather have it over beer, there is nothing wrong with this kind of education, for most. But for those who wish to be truly educated or even "intellectual," this goal is unsatisfactory. . . . A "truly educated man," as it has been so often called, is not one who knows all "around" the humanities; it is a man who is able to appreciate and explore with delight the mysteries of art, literature, etc.

Like the natural scientists, the humanities faculty recognized that this critical group was composed of the very best students. To be sure, the humanities staff was not pleased about being forced to face the fact that most students were unable to handle abstract philosophical concepts. When the humanities faculty finally recognized the opacity of the analytic approach for the majority of their students, they altered the first course to make it less analytical, less sophisticated and demanding. One of them put matters bluntly:

The course is a series of defeats, catastrophes, compromises. The first course was dropped almost completely . . . because it went badly. The course became more ordinary, more operational. We separated music, literature, art, and philosophy. We changed from an analytic to a more concrete approach.

The humanities staff in the course of time came to adopt some of the suggestions for greater participation in the artistic experience made by the early group of student critics. Individual and group art projects were introduced; an artist, for example, has set up a print shop where students work as apprentices. Presently, students increasingly elect to take their independent quarter in the humanities, and since the senior essay has been reinterpreted to allow submission of musical performances, paintings, films, poems, and other creative writing, the humanities curriculum has become one of the most interesting and vivacious programs in the University.

The Viability of Monteith

The experimental colleges with which we are familiar have often been marked by schisms reminiscent of the history of some of the Protestant sects after the Reformation. Black Mountain College, in some ways perhaps the most creative experimental college in American history, was the outcome of a schism and endured several before it disappeared; Marlboro and Goddard in Vermont, New College in Sarasota, Shimer College in Illinois, have all been marked by bitter intramural fights. Yet in spite of sharp disagreements within and among staffs, Monteith has had the same key senior people from the very beginning, and of all those who taught in the first two years, half were still on the scene in 1967.[24]

Although it lost its special status in 1964, when the founding Ford grant was exhausted, Monteith is still protected by its membership in the larger University. As a separate unit of its University, Monteith has secured tenure even for several faculty members without the doctorate and, in a number of cases, without publications; by going directly to the central administration and not carrying its recommendations through the departments in the College of Liberal Arts, Monteith has been able to promote faculty members on the basis of their pedagogic as well as their scholarly contributions. By maintaining its emphasis on teaching and valuing faculty also for their contribution to curricular development, Monteith has made it evident that a large state university need not be geared entirely to the norms of the graduate schools.

To the extent that its Dean has had a mission, it has been to seek allies within Wayne—a mission often made difficult by the freedom with which the more dissident students at Monteith express their contempt for what they regard as pedantic in the Liberal

[24] Since joining the faculty, seven of the present instructors received their Ph.D. degrees, bringing the total proportion of Ph.D.s on the teaching staff to fifty-eight per cent. This is exactly the national average for public universities. Cf. Ralph E. Dunham, Patricia S. Wright, and Marjorie O. Chandler, *Teaching Faculty in Universities and Four-Year Colleges, Spring 1963*, p. 60.

Arts College at Wayne and middle-brow in the University as a whole. By the same token, Monteith has excited the hostility of some of the faculty in the College of Liberal Arts and professional schools, who regard it as sloppy or arrogant and resent the modest resources devoted to it. Largely devoted to intramural concerns, the Monteith faculty have not established ties with colleagues in the wider world of Wayne, which might soften hostility. The survival of Monteith in this state of competitive coexistence reflects the low-pressured, good-natured work of Dean Donald Pearson, his many friends in the College of Liberal Arts, and the belief that something with which he is associated can't be all bad. His relaxed manner, though often frustrating to activist Monteith faculty, serves as a buffer between the College and the University.

There has been virtually no effort to recruit students from outside the metropolitan area, yet in 1967, ten per cent of the students came from outside Detroit and its suburbs. Whatever the special qualities of these non-Detroit students, the viability of Monteith nevertheless depends largely on the willingness of the staffs to experiment with a curriculum and a set of standards that best come to terms with the local students the College can attract. Examples of this throughout Monteith's history have been handled in different ways by the three staffs. Consider the willingness of the humanities and natural science staffs to beam their program at the average students in the face of criticism from precisely those more avant-garde students who generally become teachers' pets. The changes that took place in these two divisions were intended to cope with the faculty's estimation of the backwardness, recalcitrance, and unresponsiveness of most of the students. They represented a victory over elitism in fields where such elitism is commonly defended by all sorts of good (and bad) rationales.

In another aspect, however, Monteith never sacrificed its focus on General Education as distinct from what might be called the higher vocationalism of the academic departments. If students wanted to prepare themselves for graduate school or for an undergraduate vocational program, Monteith did not have to make the sort of adjustments that the teacher education program required at Oakland: such students had ample room to find their way in the University at large. Monteith faculty on the whole were not snobbish about the careers their students might pursue, and because their program was not all-embracing, they happily accepted students headed in many different directions after their baccalaureate. What they did not do was to try to create a set of mini-Ph.D. undergraduate programs parallel to the Wayne academic departments in Liberal Arts. They kept aloft the flag of General Education at a time when introductory courses in most colleges of high academic quality continued to be geared to the departments. The movement away from a more historical or philosophical approach at Monteith has been toward induction and immersion in experience— field work in the social sciences and the studio in the humanities (but not the laboratory in the natural sciences). Monteith was looking for relevance—that "in" word of today—and for connection with the students' own experience, including their ethnic and provincial experience, quite a while before either black or white students were demanding programs tailored to their versions of personal destiny.

Monteith has also retained its program of Independent Study. Some members of the faculty were led to re-examine whether Independent Study, so strongly stressed in the Gray Document, could really live up to the billing it now has among educational reformers, and some restructuring has taken place in the independent quarter and the Senior Colloquium, particularly in natural science and humanities. One might ask why Monteith held on to its requirement of a senior essay in the face of the fact that many students could not go through with it, especially since attrition has always been extremely high. Since Monteith has taken the position that it is not an honors college, why does it retain a requirement that even selective colleges like Swarthmore and Harvard ask only of honors students? In part, the line has been held on the senior essay by lowering the threshold required for adequate performance (as one of us discovered in reading through a number of undistinguished pieces of undergraduate work), in part by broadening the kind of product that could be approved (films, works of art, poetry, and so on). Monteith could escape the consequence of blocking students from the B.A. because in this and other respects it has been protected by the ability of students to transfer to other colleges at Wayne. Beyond all this, we are inclined to think that many Monteith faculty, perhaps especially in the social science division, have been unwilling to compromise their original belief that all students can be led to independent work.

As those who have tried it know, teaching of this sort, whether or not it involves extracurricular ties also, is enormously demanding. It is demanding for an individual teacher with the need to relate, on the one hand, to his own training and interest and, on the other hand, to the changing mix of students. As the number of staff increases, particularly in the absence of a structured hierarchy of authority, the problems of mutual adjustment tend to go up exponentially. It is no surprise that Monteith faculty have had little interest or energy for evangelizing their sort of teaching elsewhere at Wayne State University.

The result has been to render its existence an open question. As two recent observers stated:

> . . . [Monteith] is subject to all of the hidden rivalries, professional jealousies, and financial infighting of competing constituent college deans for their "fair share" of the financial, staff, faculty, facilities, and general academic pie.[25]

We think it would be a loss to higher education in general, as well as to Wayne itself, if Monteith should not continue to be supported. Monteith is the only bid Wayne is presently making for undergraduate experimentation, although it hopes to play in a league with Michigan State, which has three new subcolleges under way, and the University of Michigan, which has its Residential College. The extraordinary expansion of facilities for higher education in the past decades has been aggregative at best, and few of the new state colleges that have been founded to meet the tide of students have

[25] See the vignette of Monteith in Morris Keeton and Conrad Hilberry, *Struggle and Promise: A Future for Colleges.*

sought to do much more than mimic already established ways. Monteith's failures, as well as its successes, are a contribution to the small store of cumulative knowledge about educational innovation, its costs, and its benefits. Monteith makes a contribution to the development of its students—to the majority that pass through a portion of its program as well as the minority that graduate—in the only terms that count: value added.

XII The Crucial Role of the Administration

It is interesting to compare the kinds of problems that faced Oakland and Monteith when they began ten years earlier, with the radically different overture of the State University college of Old Westbury on Long Island, which opened in the fall of 1968 with eighty-seven students. In the State University 1966 Master Plan, Old Westbury had been given the mission of ending "the lock-step march as one semester follows on another . . ."; the College stated its readiness to "admit students to full partnership in the academic world and grant them the right to determine, in a large measure, their own areas of study and research."[1] A year before the College had opened, President Harris Wofford, a former lawyer, civil rights activist, and Peace Corps official, had recruited student planners from places like Antioch, Goddard, San Francisco State, and Berkeley; some of these then stayed on at the college in its first year. The locale of all this is a conservative Long Island community and an estate, handsomer than Oakland's Meadow Brook, that had once belonged to F. Ambrose Clark. Counterposed to the exurban locale, Harris Wofford began with a commitment to community action and field work, whether in the non-white poverty areas of metropolitan

[1] See *Catalogue*, 1967, State University College of New York at Old Westbury, p. 2.

New York or on an Israeli kibbutz or elsewhere overseas; he seemed prepared to accept whatever risks would occur in involving faculty and students at a public college in almost inevitably controversial local actions.[2] Long before the College opened for its trial run, it had become highly visible to student and faculty educational reformers and activists all over the United States, drawing them to where the action seemed to be while scaring off some more scholarly or less venturesome faculty and students.[3]

Wofford soon discovered that in an era when the ideology of student power possesses weight, not only for undergraduates but also for many faculty, the concept of "full partnership" was interpreted to mean more than he had bargained for, greatly constraining his own freedom to shape the institution's future.[4] Given Wofford's own style and that of students and faculty attracted by the promise of innovation, this might have occurred in any event. It appears that a student-faculty alliance with veto power over admissions policy, faculty recruitment and retention, curricular organization, and governance made it difficult for the President and other administrators to maintain their hoped-for dialectic between field work and Great Books and seminars, between the model of St. John's and Monteith with their coherent programs and that of Antioch with its "university in dispersion."

Most new public colleges, of course, begin (at the rate, it is said, of one a week) with nothing like the contentiousness or glamour of Old Westbury. New commuter colleges open with the kind of local fanfare that a new supermarket might have. Many have all they can manage in simply finding the physical plant and recruiting faculty to keep up with each successive wave of students. When the University of Massachusetts opened a branch in Boston in 1965 with an entering class of twelve hundred, the planner-recruiters

[2] See Harris L. Wofford, Jr., "Agent of Whom?" In W. John Minter and Ian M. Thompson, *Colleges and Universities as Agents of Social Change*, pp. 13–24.
[3] Cf. Michael Novak, "Experiment at Old Westbury: Trying to Talk" and "The College That Students Helped Plan," by various authors.
[4] Wofford announced his resignation from Old Westbury and accepted the presidency of Bryn Mawr College in the fall of 1969.

from the Amherst campus had had barely eight months to convert
an old downtown office building into a makeshift campus and to
recruit a faculty; pressure of student numbers and limited capital
and annual budgets have made planning extremely difficult, even
while the first waves of students were inclined to feel, in an area
where private education has hegemony, that they were at a second-
class institution, even if it *was* new.[5]

When Oakland was being planned, it did not occur to anyone,
so far as we know, that students should have a hand in designing
the new institution. Chancellor Varner thought that the best way to
begin was to pick a first-rate faculty, give them autonomy subject to
a vestigial veto, and protect that autonomy against legislators,
trustees, and other constituencies—students were not then a vocal
one. We have described the way in which a headstrong faculty
imported from elsewhere was inclined to disregard the locally defined requirements for mass education. We have seen how the first
Dean of Faculty regarded himself as a spokesman for the faculty,
and beyond that for the embattled humanities, rather than as a
buffer between faculty and the locale. Neither the Dean nor many
of the charter faculty had had direct experience with public higher
education; they were willing to make only grudging and minor
concessions to student vocationalism and to the expectations of the
local secondary schools and potential employers.

President Clarence Hilberry of Wayne State, once he had played
the role of midwife to Monteith College and chosen its Director,
lost further initiating power to his appointee. He remained in the
background as a potential support against opposition from other
Wayne colleges, but he no longer had any direct influence over
Monteith. He did not have to worry about what dissident students
today call co-optation, or about community pressures outside
Wayne vis-à-vis a small experimental college.

Indeed, when one looks at both of these top administrators, one
sees how marginal their power was as soon as they had made their

[5] For an account of the formation of student subcultures in the first year,
see Michael Weinstein, "On Students Educating One Another." Michael
Weinstein was a member of Monteith's first graduating class.

first appointments. Many American Presidents have discovered this too, once they have made their first appointments to the Cabinet or to such non-Cabinet posts as Director of the Bureau of the Budget. While these officials are subject to presidential removal, the actual problems of turmoil and morale that would come from doing so have given pause even to the most strong-willed of men. In a college or university of any distinction, the situation of the top administrator often seems more powerful than it is, while as Clark Kerr observed in *The Uses of the University*, he frequently has only the influence possessed by a good mediator.

Moreover, a career administrator like Chancellor Varner is a bit like a ship's captain: the professors can take to the boats, but he is stuck with the institution. Higher education in the United States has hardly any career administrators who begin as such: that is one of its many dilemmas. In community colleges or ancillary posts like dean of students, people are recruited rather less from regular scholarly departments and more from some of the newer centers for the study of higher education, such as at Berkeley, Claremont, Oregon, Minnesota, Michigan, Columbia Teachers College, Michigan State, and elsewhere. Although there are great variations, academic administrators are generally trained, like college classroom teachers, on the job, usually after having started on a career of doing something else.[6]

How one describes the reaction of the charter faculty at Oakland toward the first waves of students depends on one's perspective—whether one sees it as an insensitive disregard for both the students and the viability of the institution, or as an idealistic and brave adherence to principle against the temptations of popularity. We ourselves see nothing especially courageous in those faculty who did not want their colleagues to judge them as lacking in rigor,

[6] See Herbert A. Simon, "The Job of a College President."

The American Council on Education has a program of internships for young faculty who can spend a year as assistants in the office of an established administrator in the hope of preparing themselves for a call to higher administration that may never come. One of the Assistant Provosts at Oakland was an ACE intern in the office of the President of Rice University a few years ago.

and we find much to criticize in the policy of sinking the ship to defend a particular—and not especially sacred—grade-point average. In any event, we think it likely that the administration saved Oakland from some of its initial faculty. It introduced departments into what had been a divisional structure, in part to hasten and facilitate the recruiting of new faculty; but this change also served to restrict the power of junior faculty, whose lack of experience and commensurate eagerness to prove themselves made them especially severe.

Yet the very fact that the Chancellor encouraged the recruitment of conventionally excellent faculty from conventionally excellent institutions gave Oakland the kind of éclat it needed when it began to look for other roads to distinction, such as work in the performing arts. Oakland is better known than most of the state colleges that have begun in the past ten or fifteen years. In our experience of talking about Oakland in quite diverse academic settings, we have found that it is widely visible through faculty members who have considered going there or who have read something by an Oakland professor.

Monteith's visibility, through the networks of the academic disciplines and through faculty publications, is lower. Its audience, as we have seen, is in the league of experimental colleges, and there, the fact that it is not a separate institution has lowered the visibility of its Dean, whose initial reluctance to assume that title in part reflects the fact that Monteith has never been in the hands of someone who considered himself an administrator by profession. Taken as a whole, Monteith still has an underadministered air about it (in contrast to the brisk, knowledgeable air Oakland exhibits, even when its administrative resources, as often happens, are strained by pressure and expansion).[7] Indeed, the Dean's will-

[7] Underadministration, as well as the lack of a professional cadre, resembles the amateurism once prized in the federal civil service (although not always achieved even under Andrew Jackson). Student and faculty antagonism to "bureaucracy" is internalized by those who become administrators; in their self-deprecation they are prone to overwork rather than to expansion of their staffs. See Mark H. Ingraham, *The Mirror of Brass: The Compensation and Working Conditions of College and University Administrators.*

ingness to give energetic and talented women their due, as heads
of both the social science and humanities staffs, is an illustration
of his light rein.[8] Considering the fact that discrimination against
women in university life is far more endemic than discrimination
against other minorities, this is remarkable.

If there had been efforts at stronger leadership, it is doubtful
whether the Monteith faculty would have stood for it, perhaps
especially in the social sciences. If, after the retirement of Donald
Pearson and Sidney Karr, the new dean who comes to Monteith
seeks to establish a "taller" hierarchy rather than the present broad
and egalitarian structure, he can expect to encounter the antagonism
of a faculty accustomed to a loosely permissive setting, as well as
the resistance of students who can readily mobilize for attacks on
administration. Protected by its parent and to some degree by
inertia, Monteith has not had to find strong leadership at the "federal" level to sustain itself; it has had such leadership unevenly at
the divisional level. Whatever the sniping between Monteith and
the Wayne College of Liberal Arts, most of the Monteith battles
have been internal, seldom reaching the mass media and never the
state Legislature. In terms of faculty retention, student traffic, and
general standing, Monteith has been fairly stable as an entity,
despite the turbulence and conflict within its staffs. Given protection by Wayne's top administrators and a willingness to stay
small, Monteith has been able to afford a relaxed decentralization.

To be sure, this relaxation has had its costs, and not all of them
are easily visible. Lack of a consistent admissions policy has led
to instability in enrollments and hence in class size and faculty
staffing. Indeed, staffing has sometimes had a helter-skelter quality,
and, especially on the social sciences side, recent Monteith graduates have been added at the last minute despite the College's
stern opposition to the use of teaching assistants; there has not
been an effort at a national canvass for prospective faculty. In
these circumstances, the burden of such central planning as has to
be done for budgeting, classroom assignments, and similar logistical

[8] Furthermore, in the early years a woman librarian with many ideas about
educational innovation was a driving force at Monteith.

issues has fallen on a devoted but harried and understaffed executive officer, who has to negotiate with the Wayne central administration with little support from Monteith faculty. Conceivably, the considerable attrition of Monteith students, who drift out of the College and into other colleges at Wayne, may reflect the uneasiness of some at the lack of structure and planning, even while this improvisational quality appeals to other students. Nevertheless, given Monteith's original faculty cadres, it seems doubtful whether a stronger administration could have brought about a reconciliation among the three curricular divisions or enforced a tighter overall policy.

As we have seen, the Oakland administration was considerably tighter; and so were the faculty. Yet at the outset the Oakland administration did little to focus the attention of the faculty on teaching ordinary students in extraordinary ways. Instead, they modified the original definition of the ordinary student by recruiting more of the kind of young people the faculty felt they could teach. Beyond this, the administration played both a protective role vis-à-vis the students and an educative or socializing role for the faculty, feeding back to the latter the consequences of their standards of grading and seeking to give them some sense of the reaction of area high schools to those standards and the consequences for recruitment that might follow. They also worked to provide a kind an ancillary net under the high wires students were asked to walk which now includes a Reading Center, a Writing Center, and an elaborate Office of Psychological Services. Oakland has always paid a great deal of attention to advising, especially for freshmen, making special efforts to link them with faculty who were both conscientious and knowledgeable—and thus providing still another form of feedback to faculty from students. Similarly, the program of Freshman Exploratories linked individual faculty to freshmen in groups small enough to allow for a good deal of individual attention and ancillary advising. In this respect, Oakland, and Monteith too, have always been more careful about advising than most colleges, public or private.

The Administrative Role in Faculty Recruitment and Training

Deans and presidents of primarily undergraduate institutions are constantly complaining that they have to hire Ph.D.s who have little experience of teaching and little interest in it. In the large universities that emphasize graduate training to do research, T.A.s are thrown into the (usually lower-division) classroom with little grounding in their subject matter and even less development of self-awareness as college teachers.[9]

Currently, much propaganda and a few new structures are being devoted to the efforts to develop a greater interest in teaching on the part of prospective college teachers. One proposal is to create a new degree, the Doctor of Arts, which would be a teaching degree, as against the Ph.D., seen as a research degree.[10] Conceivably, as its proponents hope, the Doctor of Arts degree would not be a second-class degree for those cooled out from Ph.D. programs, but a first-choice degree for those whose commitment would be to college teaching and whose doctoral program would be as demanding as but different from a more research-oriented one. It would include consideration of problems of teaching and learning, practice teaching, and work outside one's immediate field of specialization. Yet, unless major universities hire men, including their own graduates, with Doctor of Arts degrees, it is likely that in fact it will be a less valued degree, somewhat limiting the opportunities of its possessors. Moreover, while deans and presidents of colleges want to hire teaching-oriented faculty, a department chairman may be more ambitious for national visibility—or occasionally vice versa. But beyond such considerations, we think that the emphasis on the purity and virtue of the college teacher who does no research can

[9] For an incisive discussion of the resentments T.A.s often develop in their role as "double agents" as between undergraduates and senior faculty, see Martin Trow, "The Teaching Assistant"; see also Charles H. Monson, Jr., "Teaching Assistants: The Forgotten Faculty."
[10] See the discussion in E. Alden Dunham, *Colleges of the Forgotten Americans: A Profile of State Colleges and Regional Universities*, pp. 157–64; Stephen H. Spurr, *Academic Degree Structures: Innovative Approaches*.

be overdone. A faculty member who has no constituency other than his own students easily becomes a captive to the latter, and of declining benefit to them. He needs them too much, too long. Frustrated charisma easily gives rise to despotism or despair.

When Riesman was a student, he spent a summer with the Grenfell Mission in Labrador, and soon discovered that non-celibate missionaries whose families had to make many sacrifices were inclined to demand more of the populations they served in the way of gratitude than was forthcoming, leading to heightened bad feeling among the missionaries themselves. Obviously, an experimental college is not as isolated as a mission station, but some of its faculty, who have devoted "the best years of their lives" to the institution, gain a kind of moral estoppel which makes it difficult to part with them when they have apparently surrendered their opportunities for alternative careers. Administrators in such colleges have to consider how their faculty's personal growth can be encouraged and how an appropriate balance between opportunistic transiency and excessive risk of failure can be maintained in the lives committed to the institution. For some faculty, this may mean pressure on them to achieve visibility in their disciplines or in other intellectual pursuits by an extremely generous sabbatical policy, perhaps with more provision for research than experimental colleges generally consider necessary. For other faculty, especially perhaps in the social sciences but not only there, encouragement may be needed to leave academic life altogether for a spell in government work, business, the Peace Corps, or in myriad other areas which can increase understanding of society and the chance to contribute to it. (There is much to be said, of course, for such in-and-out careers in general, quite apart from the problems of experimental colleges.)

Unless such flexibility can be maintained, academic institutions are likely to have a short half-life, because of the very dedication demanded of men and women primarily engaged in teaching. There is the danger for them of being cannibalized by their students, a possibility made more poignant by their immobility: although students come and go, teachers who gain tenure or its equivalent in under-graduate colleges cannot easily consider going elsewhere.[11] There is the danger for the institution as well as the faculty that time and events may pass them by, and what once were innovative ideas and practices may become frozen.

When we have discussed these problems with the presidents and other administrators of the more experimental liberal arts colleges, they have reminded us of their common penury, which makes it difficult to grant frequent sabbaticals to men who would like to renew their disciplinary ties, for example, by a leave at a major university. Postdoctoral fellowships may make this possible for a few, but it was pointed out that there was difficulty in persuading some of the "saints" of academic dedication to surrender their prized invisibility. We were told by one president that if he intro-duced a policy of sabbaticals he could not confine it only to those faculty members with an interest in and capacity for doing scholarly work, because egalitarianism would insist on all sharing alike. But he felt that the majority of his faculty, faced with an unwonted sabbatical, would only become alcoholics! He was, of course, exag-gerating. He had in mind both the older type of small college zealot, unworldly and devoted to the young, and the newer type of faculty who prefer political activism and evangelism among the young.

Some flexibility might be won through institutionalizing an ex-change program among experimental colleges so that these institu-tions could serve as adult education centers in a way that now occurs only by chance. The small number of experimental colleges

[11] The problems of mobility and visibility we are discussing bear some resemblance to those of a religious or political sect that protects its young people from the corruption of the world by offering them opportunities within the sect and by inculcating in them attitudes that make the outside world seem unalluring. By limiting the higher education of their young people, the Amish, Mennonites, and Hutterites go further still in binding their children, making it difficult for them to navigate outside these intentional communities. But one of the costs of such a policy is that if the young people decide to leave in spite of it all, they enter the economy of the wider world on its lower rungs.

in the United States—perhaps several dozen—means that something on the order of fifteen hundred faculty have had exposure to one or another version of explicitly experimental teaching. Unlike the situation in England or on the Continent, where faculty positions are formally advertised and applied for, the American academic market is chaotic to the point of anarchy, and the chance, for example, that someone may hear of Monteith and (against the normal grain of things) apply for a job there is most unlikely.[12]

At both Oakland and Monteith, the obvious supplement to graduate training for faculty concerned with innovation in the undergraduate curriculum is on-the-job training. Most new enterprises start that way. The first psychoanalysts trained themselves on the job and then supervised others who were trained while on the job; the psychoanalytic institutes of the present day still focus principally on a one-to-one relation of this sort, supplemented by seminars and readings. Staff-taught courses like those at Monteith or The College of the University of Chicago encourage learning on the job as faculty members observe each other in the open discussion sections and in the highly visible lectures. Nevertheless, Monteith did not *require* a faculty member to learn about teaching in the ordinary course of things, and there was nothing to prevent the interminable arguments about the students and what they were like from remaining merely gossip or polemic. Thus although Monteith has seen itself as something of a laboratory for educational change, it has had no systematic way of inducting its faculty into the problems of undergraduate teaching for its specific type of student.

[12] The new University of California at Santa Cruz has had exceptional success in recruiting faculty members capable of satisfying both the boards of study in the several departments and the expectations of the provost of the colleges that faculty can contribute to the specific core programs of these colleges. In a luminous setting and with the prestige of the University of California behind it, Santa Cruz has drawn both some nationally visible stars and younger men with Ph.D.s from top institutions in the United States and the United Kingdom. Whether this success will continue as the boards of studies develop greater numbers and hence greater strength vis-à-vis the provosts of the colleges is an open question.

A small group of faculty at Oakland did make an effort in this direction when they attended (in 1965) the National Training Laboratory in Bethel, Maine, to help them become sensitive to group process. On returning to Oakland, they conducted a seminar on teaching and learning; there was hope for a time that they would spark the founding of a new subcollege, but this did not occur, and their effort has tapered off. As already suggested, part of the problem lies in the individualism of faculty, which makes men attracted to academic life especially resistant to overall direction and explicit re-education. This same individualism generally means that faculty are recruited one by one, not even on a Noah's ark basis, so that the kinds of teams that have sometimes developed for research are rarely available for pioneering in undergraduate educational reform.

Such reform must also face the obstacle of how to assess the quality of teaching. Many administrators would like to promote "good teachers" if they only knew how to make qualitative judgments with the self-confidence that academic colleagues often have in judging another man's research.[13] A former president of Bennington, the late William Fels, once described his college's procedure for faculty assessment. Each course had a designated student evaluator selected by the student government. The evaluator announced herself as such, and it was up to her to collect the judgments about the course from her fellow students and to write a report. This went to the instructor, who had the opportunity of discussing it with the students and, if they could not agree, of filing his own report. Both reports would then go to the president. Over the years, it was Fels's conclusion that the best teachers were those who remained related to some constituency other than the students—not necessarily through an article in a professional journal or monograph,

[13] For a discussion of some of the problems of citation counts and other methods of measuring the impact of work in mathematics and the natural sciences, see Warren O. Hagstrom, "Departmental Prestige and Scientific Productivity." Journals often referee articles anonymously, a practice hard to institutionalize with respect to classroom teaching, even if the privacy of the classroom could be broken down.

but through a poem in *Harper's,* a concert in Pittsfield, a book review in the *New Republic.*[14]

In judging the significance of research or scholarship that is neither obviously original nor obviously routine, colleagues make implicit assessments about the intellectual sophistication of the work, the knowledge of the relevant paradigms, and the long-run relevance for further understanding in the field. In the case of the impact of teaching, the assessments are again more difficult. Scholars are apt to be skeptical about the exceptionally popular teacher, fearing that he panders to student passivity and sets a model of charismatic excitement that is unhealthy and indeed impossible to maintain. But how is one to weigh the importance of a teacher who connects with an otherwise sullen and self-mistrustful student, even though he has no appeal for the cognoscenti, or even the ordinarily engaged students? How do we assess the teacher who, like Thorstein Veblen, regards students as a nuisance and does his best to fend them off, yet responds creatively to the one or two who are willing to put up with him? In principle, an administration could work out a division of labor among faculty in which students could be matched with a variety of mentors in the hope of genuine interchange. Depending on the local context, the administration may need to protect the faculty member who, even with the best will, appeals only to the esoteric, while at the same time encouraging other faculty to enlarge the constituency of students to whom they speak.

Yet faculty, even those most open to students, have generally made it difficult for administrators to monitor the quality or, in many cases, the amount of their teaching. Their very definition of

---

14 In a study at Tufts University of the correlation between, on the one hand, publication and success in obtaining support for research and, on the other hand, teaching effectiveness, Bresler reports that faculty members who published were rated more highly by students as teachers than were faculty who published less. Cf. Jack B. Bresler, "Teaching Effectiveness and Government Awards." See, however, the less clear-cut conclusions on the same issue reached by William M. Stalling and Sue Shila Singho, "Some Observations on the Relationships Between Research Productivity and Student Evaluations of Courses and Teaching."

academic freedom protects their right to conduct their classes as
they think best, to grade and respond to students as they think
best (subject to review only in the most flagrant cases of injustice,
and seldom even there). Despite the elaborate Program Study, which
made it possible to trace the trajectory of individual students through
the College, Monteith faculty could speak only in a general way
about the effectiveness of specific strategies of teaching. At Oakland
the group of teachers who had visited Bethel did sometimes visit
each other's classes, but as a general rule Oakland faculty lacked
the regular observations of each other's performance as teachers
that the Monteith staff structure made available. Thus they were
often in the position of relying on the kinds of hearsay and impressions that outstanding institutions employ in judging whether or
not a teacher falls below the threshold of minimal performance.

The presidents who initiated Oakland and Monteith were concerned about undergraduate education long before most undergraduates became selfconscious as a class. The power of John
Hannah at Michigan State and Clarence Hilberry at Wayne State
to "do something" for undergraduates reflected the fact that they
headed growing institutions: the growth allowed them to satisfy
and indeed to spur their faculties' upward mobility while making
use of some of the new resources for experiments in undergraduate
life. However, in raising the scholarly level of their institutions, they
introduced into them the kind of nationally mobile faculty whose
orientation had been to the model of the leading graduate schools
and not to innovation at the undergraduate level. As we write
these lines, John Hannah has left Michigan State at a time when
his own power to innovate there had already been curbed. The
faculty he helped gather are proceeding to disregard his efforts
to focus attention on undergraduates. The nearly independent operation at Oakland has not suffered from the loss of its founder, but
it is too soon to know whether it should feel secure about the future.

Monteith lost its founding patron when Hilberry died, but his
successor has allowed the enterprise to stay afloat, apparently without intervention and without curtailment. However, Wayne as a
whole and Monteith in particular are involved in the new student

radicalism, especially that of black militants who are linked to adult counterparts in the inner city. Those who come in as successors to Donald Pearson and Sidney Karr will find strong administration regarded as illegitimate by many students and considerable numbers of faculty. Room for maneuver within Monteith is therefore limited, as it was not at the outset.

It is also limited increasingly from without, as conservative reaction to black and white student protests, and to the apparent inability of administrators to curb them, grows. In Michigan, as in other states, major public universities are suffering from an adult and taxpayer backlash of gathering momentum, and this is also being felt in Congress. The Michigan Legislature has a committee investigating student radicalism and pornography, a committee that began with a special focus on Oakland and that has been broadened to investigate student radicalism and pornography in other state universities. At the same moment, colleges and universities are being subjected to new demands for social responsiveness, demands that in some instances may be productive of curricular reform but in other instances divert the energies and resources needed for such reform. Guilt, opportunism, good will, and fear combine to push programs of urban studies, black studies, and other new imperatives without time for the normal processes of the academic timetable to sort things out or to develop new models of what may possibly work. Yet there are new models around, some of them arising from the recent demands—as in the pressure to respond to new cadres of black students. We turn in our final chapter to look briefly at some of these alternative models.

XIII The Search for Alternative Strategies in Mass Higher Education

Looked at in comparative and historical perspective, American higher education is astonishingly pluralistic. No central Ministry of Culture or Education determines who is to teach what to whom at what level. Neither the Federal Trade Commission nor the regional accrediting agencies police the way in which American colleges advertise themselves (including their use of such terms as "college" and "university"). Student customers lack the assurance that if they pay more tuition, they will get a better academic buy, in terms of either prestige conferred or personal growth. Faculty members wander over the academic landscape, seduced here by early tenure, there by a fading reputation, in a seminational marketplace that lacks rational mechanisms for bringing together colleagues who can help each other, advance scholarship, and contribute to the education of young people.

The entrepreneurial energy and lack of central control in this non-system mean that new academic and para-academic fields will get a hearing faster than anywhere else in the world.[1] The inception

[1] See the account by Joseph Ben-David, "The Universities and the Growth of Science in Germany and the United States." Ben-David describes American academia as highly competitive, therefore providing for innovation in research methods and diverse sources of funding, in contrast to the more centralized Continental model. Cf. Riesman's comment.

in just a few months of myriad programs in Afro-American Studies, or Third World Studies, are illustrations. New scientific fields will also get a hearing: oceanography at the University of California at San Diego, Rhode Island, and the University of Miami (Florida); desert sciences in Texas Tech; microbiology and ecology in old as well as new institutions. New fields can, as it were, migrate eastward, like sociology, which came late to Ivy League colleges, or scatter to diverse institutions, as American Studies has done.

In comparison with more centralized societies, there are virtually no provinces left in America; thus, academic luminaries (and energetic university presses) can be found almost everywhere—at Southern Illinois and Oklahoma, the University of Houston and Washington State at Pullman—and novel undergraduate degree programs can be found at the state college at Brockport and Western Michigan University, at Chico State College and Florida Atlantic University. Among the fastest-growing segments of American higher education is the group of the 150 or so state colleges and universities, none of them the major public institutions in its respective state, that have hopes of developing doctoral programs and joining the academic leaders.[2]

All this has been happening at the same time that access to higher education has widened to include almost anyone who wants some form of college. Both to create and to meet this demand, many states started to build commuter colleges several decades ago that would be available to any high school graduate or, as in California, to anyone eighteen years old. Whereas the state university, whether or not it was also the land-grant college, was often, like the state capital, located in a rural or small-town environment, the new commuter colleges had to be where the people were: in the cities or their environs. They had been preceded by private commuter colleges—for example, the network of Jesuit colleges, which

2 These institutions are described by E. Alden Dunham in *Colleges of the Forgotten Americans: A Profile of State Colleges and Regional Universities.* Typical examples would be many of the state colleges of California and New York; some of the regional universities of Michigan, Illinois, Florida, and Texas; and in the less wealthy states, one or another of the state colleges that is neither a land-grant institution nor the state university.

were finding themselves compelled to raise both admission standards and tuitions, or the more traditionally elite network of once-Methodist universities such as Boston, American, Northwestern, and Denver. The new commuter colleges were also designed to take some of the heat off the state universities, which had neither interest in nor room for every student who could be tempted by higher education.

Looked at in terms of the sheer magnitude of the job, these commuter colleges are an extraordinary success story. It was possible to draw on the secondary schools and in lesser degree on skilled technicians or local professionals for administrators and faculty. Needless to say, there are enormous differences among the community colleges in the degree to which they have been able to meet the demand both for transfer and for terminal programs; there have been differences also in the disposition to avoid or accept invidiousness among faculty members engaged in more traditionally academic as against more technical kinds of teaching. As elsewhere in higher education, this kind of status integration has proved at least as difficult as the racial integration some of the new colleges are also facing.[3]

[3] While we take it for granted now in the United States that the provision of equality of educational opportunity means making colleges available to commuters in every population center, it is interesting to notice that the British decision has been very different. English policy since the Second World War has held that every student should have the same privilege of residential living that the elite have enjoyed at Oxford and Cambridge. Thus, there is no financial pressure on the young men in Manchester to attend the excellent University of Manchester: they are free to apply for places anywhere in England. (Only in London is there any sizable group of commuters, and this is principally by choice.) Though not all universities are alike in prestige, they supposedly hold to identical academic standards, which are enforced in part by the practice of external examiners and in part by the slow growth of the student population and hence of the faculty. Cf., however, a conservative critique of the British policy of subsidy by Edward Mishan, "Some Heretical Thoughts on University Reform: The Economics of Changing the System."

The Carnegie Commission on Higher Education believes that full funding for students from impoverished families might increase college enrollments, mainly in commuter colleges, by as many as a million students. See *Quality and Equality: New Levels of Federal Responsibility for Higher Education*.

The California Master Plan of 1960 sought to deal with what we have termed status integration by a division of labor among institutions rather than a catch-as-catch-can division of labor within them: it assigned the mission of research and graduate instruction to the branches of the University of California; undergraduate, professional, and liberal education (and master's degrees in such fields as teaching) to the nineteen four-year state colleges; and postsecondary technical training or preparation for transfer to college or university to the ninety community colleges. Yet the experience of California in recent years dramatically illustrates the difficulty of maintaining a commitment on the part of able and energetic faculty to working intensively and imaginatively with non-elite students. A great many state college faculty are bitter at being confined by the Master Plan principally to undergraduate teaching. Not satisfied with their right to give the master's degree (generally in fields related to education) they insist on their right to give the doctorate and, at the more developed institutions such as San Francisco State College, San Diego State College, and San Jose State College, they pursue the aim of full university status through efforts to reduce their teaching loads to levels commensurate with those of elite universities such as Berkeley. Holding degrees from "good" institutions themselves, they do not see why they should not also have doctoral programs and join the upwardly mobile ranks of their counterparts in other states.[4]

Only if students could borrow money (perhaps to be repaid over a lifetime through the income tax) would many of these commuters be free to travel wherever they could get in rather than to go to the local college. Yet lack of money is not always the barrier to attending college that young people claim it to be; it provides a useful alibi, a cover for low interest or motivation. Cf. Jencks and Riesman, *The Academic Revolution* pp. 107 ff.

[4] It should not be assumed from the foregoing that all the faculty members of the branches of the University of California insist on their monopoly of the doctorate or on their exclusiveness as far as undergraduates are concerned. Particularly, of course, when it comes to recruiting black and Chicano undergraduates, they are moved by egalitarian ideals in much the same way that state college faculties have been.

There is less bitterness among the regional universities of Michigan, such as Eastern Michigan or Northern Michigan, which are not forbidden to give the doctorate. They face instead the problem of finding resources and

The Problem of Faculty Supply

In recent years, a number of major universities have set up centers or institutes for research and development in higher education. In some measure, they supply faculty and administration for community and for four-year colleges; but as yet there is certainly no regular supply of faculty whose concern is with experimentation at the undergraduate level. The fifteen hundred faculty or so involved in such experimentation is a minute number in comparison with the some three hundred thousand in all of American higher education.

Among these great numbers, there seems to exist what Sumner might have called a strain to consistency in American academic life—a strain that goes contrary to the apparent pluralism. In *Constraint and Variety in American Education,* Riesman described American higher education as a snakelike procession in which the bulk of institutions followed what they took to be the models set by the most prestigious leaders; the creation of a national academic market and the decline of provincial values have made such models seem attainable at many different levels.[5] Looked at from below, the academic leaders are universities whose more eminent faculty concentrate on research and on the training of graduate students. Some academic men would perhaps prefer to have only other academic men as clients, that is, as people on whose judgments they depend not only as a model and as a reference group, but also as the

persuading the State Board of Education and the accrediting agencies that they can do an adequate job.

Florida has tried still another system of articulation, setting up Florida Atlantic University with an upper division (that is, junior and senior years only) to be fed by community colleges or transfers from four-year colleges. Many students, however, transfer to Florida Atlantic in one field and then want to begin studies in another, and they have been able to compel the university to accommodate them by laying on introductory courses it thought it could surrender to the junior colleges. America has been too diverse to make assignment of explicit academic missions easy at any level, or to hold students to one set of ladders. (Again, England is different: one enters a university in a particular field, and transfers without starting all over again are virtually impossible.)

[5] See Riesman, *Constraint and Variety in American Education,* Chapter 1.

only people with whom their intellectual exchange relations are carried on. But the majority of faculty in elite universities are willing to include graduate students, and of course postdoctoral fellows, among their preferred clients.[6] Because of the enormous expansion of higher education, it has been possible for many new Ph.D.s to hope that they can begin their teaching at institutions hardly less eminent than those where they were trained—and eminence here means that one's students can become apprentices who can help with one's research.[7] To be sure, many new Ph.D.s have neither the energy nor the self-confidence to aim for such a goal, at least not immediately; or they get their degrees in a bad year for their particular discipline, when all the attractive posts are already filled. Thus, many must begin by teaching only undergraduates. But here, too, there are preferred clients.

Not everybody wants to teach the better students in the better places. Some have a missionary calling to teach the less privileged, especially, perhaps, if they are black. Another kind of academic may feel that "better" students will be too competitive and critical. He may fear that he cannot maintain authority over them, or that in the setting where he finds them, there will be other drawbacks, such as constant pressures for visible publication or the rivalry of colleagues. He may prefer to be a big man in a lesser place, or to be his own man in a quieter place. He may have some of the outlook of those academic and non-academic people who value their leisure or their extracurricular life more than the work they get paid for.

Some faculty who made these non-combative decisions turned up at Oakland and Monteith and were extremely useful teachers.

[6] Everett Hughes has taught us to see that all professionals have preferred clients. The physician wants as a client someone who has a curable but not redundant disease, does not smell, and is preferably young and well educated but not arrogant. The lawyer wants someone intelligent enough to appreciate his own acumen but not so meddlesome as to second-guess him, who is well-off, responsible, and able to spread his fame where it will help.
[7] Critics often put this in terms of exploitation of graduate students by faculty, and of course some of this goes on. But much more important is the desire of the faculty member for validation of his own line of work, because bright students find it interesting and carry the torch elsewhere.

Teaching at such colleges requires people of the very highest attainments, who are willing to devote themselves to less than the ablest or most specialized student clients. Models exist, and we shall come to them later, but first we must notice a logistical problem facing all public colleges that want to devote lavish resources to non-elite education.

The way in which most state systems of public education have been financed has permitted the development of graduate instruction and research through persuading state authorities to abide by a set of norms about FTE—Full Time Equivalents. These are the rules of thumb by which faculty time is allocated in large state systems. A consensus has developed (somewhat analogous to fixed piecework rates in industry) about the span of control that may be asked of professors in terms of student/faculty ratios. At the doctoral level, a ratio of one faculty member to seven or eight Ph.D. candidates has come to be considered a proper load for supervision in state universities. At the master's level, the load is somewhat higher; at the upper-division level of majors, somewhat higher still; in the lower division, or freshman and sophomore years, a proper load for one faculty member may be twenty or thirty students. (Evening or continuing-education programs are sometimes even worse off: they are almost invariably conducted in such a way as to make money for the institution.) These ratios have permitted the great state universities to build programs of graduate instruction and research in the face of Populist insistence that they devote themselves to a mass clientele and give service to the state in less esoteric fashion.[8] Without such formulas, universities like Illinois or Michigan or Berkeley could not attract a large faculty of world-class distinction. Yet one consequence of these formulas is that lower-division work tends to be consigned to teaching assistants, to junior faculty who have not yet established claims to "their own"

[8] Some state colleges and universities put into a discretionary fund the overhead on government grants and contracts for their faculty members. This money may then be used to pay the expenses of prospective faculty, to bring visiting lecturers or artists to the campus, or to pay for other amenities that the state in its Spartan wisdom or neglect fails to provide. Without such devices, many state colleges would be a good deal less vital than they are.

courses, or to the occasional distinguished man who is willing to introduce his subject to freshmen and sophomores.

Monteith proceeded from the beginning against such state-wide formulas. Its plan assumed that, at the freshman level, faculty should be more plentiful vis-à-vis students than later on. It could hold to this course in part because attrition reduced upper-division loads more than had been allowed for, and in part because its cost could be spread out in Wayne's overall budget (of course, as we have seen, not without objection from Wayne's College of Liberal Arts). Oakland was never able to reduce classes and seminars to a size as low as Monteith's, but it had a similar aim of keeping classes small and faculty/student ratios high at the lower-division level. Furthermore, freshmen and sophomores were to be taught without discrimination by senior faculty as well as by younger faculty; and even now, although graduate work has begun, this practice continues. Indeed, Oakland's move into graduate work has in part been motivated by the necessity to exploit the FTE formulas in order to have the basis for acquiring more faculty, whose major energies will still be devoted to undergraduates.[9]

Two Cultures, or Perhaps Three?

So far, we have been talking as if an interest in undergraduate teaching were spread evenly over the academic disciplines, but of

[9] To the extent that state colleges are pushed by FTE formulas to want to become graduate-oriented universities even apart from the drive for more prestige and for more and better research, it becomes clear that one of the major problems of the future in American higher education is how to preserve those elite functions—principally research and graduate training—that the FTE formulas support, while at the same time doing a less shabby job for the undergraduates. The FTE formulas have the advantage of appearing impersonal and therefore not requiring invidious distinctions to be drawn among bitterly competitive public institutions, no one of which is willing to accept the fact that it cannot become an eminent institution. It would seem well-nigh impossible to devise nationwide or even state-wide formulas that would favor both a very small number of research-oriented universities and also a small number that were experimenting expensively at the lower-division level—at a cost per student (like Oakland's) greater than that of apparently competitive community colleges.

course this is not true. At Monteith from the start, and at Oakland in the course of time, the social scientists accommodated themselves with particular energy to the mandates of mass education. Empirically minded social scientists possess, in principle if not in practice, the "right" to be interested in the lives and backgrounds of their students. At its worst, one kind of social science becomes a low-level coffeehouse discussion, but at its best, an enterprise like the Monteith study of the 1960 election provides the faculty with a non-intrusive opportunity to confront their students with the world in which they and their families live, and to discuss contemporary issues in the light of scholarly traditions of craftsmanship and theoretical work.

In contrast, mathematicians and physicists have no such ready opportunities to gain a purchase on obvious relevance. The athletes of academic life, so to speak, they often rise early to the height of their capacity and later may be ready to range into other areas, including teaching methods for high school math, or new curricula for colleges, at an age when professors of history or literature or politics have only begun to read, observe, and reflect enough to do seasoned work. Men in these fields, as in some branches of economics and psychology, are quickly able to distinguish a fraud from a genius (or at least believe that they are able to); and those graduate students who have early concluded that they will not succeed in the big academic leagues may be ready at an early age to teach in other leagues, in a good liberal arts college or a less eminent university, with relative freedom from the feeling that, if they worked a bit harder or had better luck or patronage, they might after all get the Nobel Prize.[10]

[10] We are suggesting here that while mathematicians and natural scientists are often fairly sure of where they stand, free of the fratricidal conflicts that rage in fields like English or sociology, those near the top nevertheless engage in the races for priority that Robert K. Merton and others have described, sometimes with the sort of rivalry James Watson portrays in *The Double Helix*. (Cf. Merton, "Behavior Patterns of Scientists.") Furthermore, those scientists who resign themselves to entering industry as a second-choice career are sometimes quite embittered. They are less likely than those who enter college teaching to feel that they are their own

The natural scientists attracted to Oakland had on the whole not given up the hope of careers in research. But because departments at the outset were small and facilities slender, some were required to shift from one specialty to another, as did one physicist who had come from a major university and then entered a field of interest to the motor industry. Such men, of course, did not regard themselves as "mere" college teachers. Having themselves made it through tough competition, they were quite explicitly meritocratic in dealing with undergraduates. They were far less prepared than the Monteith natural scientists to adapt the curriculum to the students; they insisted on better students.[11] When Oakland students referred to the natural science faculty, they often called them punitive, but ordinarily this was an error. These were men without malice, generally quite willing to help those students who, if they extended themselves, had the potential to do the work; if the natural scientists had a failing, it was insensitivity to the way their own reactions deflated self-mistrustful students and overpersuaded them of their incompetence for academic work.

A boyhood interest can lead a man to become a chemist or a zoologist, but rarely into French literature or anthropology. In comparison with the natural sciences, the road into the humanities and some of the social sciences is a more involuted one. These areas tend to attract people who want to become all-purpose intellectuals and yet eat regularly; the particular field they enter may be a ques-

---

masters, and they lack the traditional status of an academic position as well as feedback from students. Perhaps more important, they are apt to feel that they are rewarded only for useful and not for interesting work. See Simon Marcson, *The Scientist in American Industry; Some Organizational Determinants in Manpower Utilization;* Warren O. Hagstrom, *The Scientific Community.*

[11] There were notable exceptions at Oakland, and this picture should not be overdrawn. We think of one member of the mathematics department in particular, trained at Dartmouth under Kemeny (one of the leaders in the revision of secondary school curricula), who was principally concerned with the place of mathematics in General Education. Other natural scientists at Oakland have given seminars on problems of pollution and environmental hazards.

tion of the accidents of personal encounters.[12] Eleven years between the baccalaureate and the doctorate is not uncommon in these
fields. Subsidy is somewhat more rare than in the natural sciences,
and finding a dissertation topic is not simply a matter of pursuing a
track in conjunction with an already established team, but depends more on the luck or ability to discover some academic turf
where the grass has not yet been worn completely down by others.
(In a department of English, it may mean discovering a recondite
author whose work has not been exhumed, or a minor work by a
better-known writer. In history, it may mean archival research, always time-consuming, frequently a kind of detective work in the pursuit of leads that turn out to be false.) Wisdom takes time—and may
never come. By the same token, however, in areas of qualitative
work a researcher is not likely to be pre-empted by a discoverer
who got there first: there is room for any number of books on
Shakespeare or the philosophy of history, although it may matter a
bit who gets there first with a biography of John F. Kennedy. Yet,
lacking the team support (and frustrations) such as many natural
and some social scientists have, the teacher of the humanities is
perhaps more likely to feel that he stands alone vis-à-vis barbaric
students and the materialistic, tasteless community. While many
natural scientists have until recently been able to turn materialism
to account by linking basic research to technological payoffs
(whether they believe in the linkage or not, or simply regard it as
good public relations),[13] men in other fields must often earn their
way by teaching students who regard them as purveyors of cultural
bull, unfair obstacles to earning a credential or postponing the draft.
Thus, while the self-mistrust of natural scientists tends to be overcome by collegial and societal support, for the scholar in the humanities support from colleagues may seem more indeterminate, and his
students often speak for a society that regards what he does as un-
important, or at any rate not central.

[12] Cf. Howard S. Becker and James Carper, "The Development of Identification
with an Occupation" and "The Elements of Identification with an Occupation."
[13] On the moral ambiguity and political risks of this linkage, see Carl
Kaysen, *The Higher Learning, the Universities, and the Public.*

We have seen that the humanities faculty recruited to Oakland in the first few years reacted to this situation by collective defensiveness, defining their academic freedom as total control over the curriculum, including such issues as the language requirement and the hurdles to be cleared by those students aiming to be schoolteachers. Even so, as Oakland grew and as its student body increased in both quantity and quality, the faculty in the humanities became more differentiated and less defensive. While some scholars were not especially impressed with the stagecraft that John Fernald brought with his Royal Academy troupe or with the musicianship of the Meadow Brook Festival, these artistic endeavors lessened the feeling in the early years that Oakland consisted of a few scattered buildings surrounded by dreary parking lots. Faculty became more willing to experiment with ways of connecting contemporary student concerns with avant-garde interests, as in the Freshman Exploratories introduced in recent years.

The humanities faculty at Monteith never possessed the initial Oakland attitude of in-country expatriation; recruited originally by Donald Pearson from among his own former students at Wayne, they did not believe that they were living in a cultural desert in exile from the more cosmopolitan East and West coasts. Many were quite content to work hard with first-generation students. Because they came late on the scene and discovered that the social scientists dominated what there was of student culture, they allied themselves with the natural scientists, less to defend culture against *kitsch* than to defend appropriate academic standards against what they regarded as the sentimentality of personalism. In recent years, thanks to the recruitment of staff talented in painting and music, a strengthened and diverse humanities group has found its own constituency among students who, as we have noted, choose to do their senior essays by presenting fiction or a film or some other work of art. While some professional painters and musicians would prefer to teach in their own studios or in a school principally devoted to their art, the broadening of the concept of the humanities at both Oakland and Monteith has widened the orbit of recruitment for faculty.

Models of Undergraduate Education

Just as many critics of American higher education have neglected the differences among the fields of knowledge in the degree to which they envisage undergraduates as colleagues or as necessary evils, there is also a tendency to gloss over those forms of academic enterprise that out of conviction or *faute de mieux* have been concerned with undergraduates as persons rather than specialists. The denominational colleges have from the beginning had this concern, although seldom exclusively so. Their *raison d'être* was often to look after the spiritual welfare of their students, even though preparing them for professional careers other than the ministry. Down to the present time, some of these colleges have continued the traditions of the frontier Protestant churches in counterposing cleverness and sophistication by the virtues of warmth, piety, and plain style. It is easy to overstate the moral claims of the earlier church colleges, whose students periodically rioted while enduring pedantic drill sessions. But it is also possible to condescend to the surviving church colleges and ignore the possibility that an institution like Brigham Young University, for example, may combine a faculty oriented to teaching, with opportunities for mobility and spiritual development of students. Yet such cases are rare, and most faculties have come over time to prefer learning to piety, or rather to regard them as moral equivalents.[14]

In some ways, it was easier to secularize a devotion to learning

[14] Cf. the excellent account by Thomas H. A. LeDuc, *Piety and Intellect at Amherst College, 1865–1912.*

The Catholic colleges have developed in a somewhat different ambiance. Many of them could count on a tradition of classical scholarship in the priesthood, but the urban Jesuit and other universities, much like the land-grant colleges, have tended to adapt to a mass clientele by having different standards in their different undergraduate colleges, with the less capable men shunted into business programs, the less capable women into education or nursing. Again, these undergraduate professional curricula did not create a new educational plan for the non-elite, but rather provided some elite trim in the nature of service courses (English, history, some science) for the students kept out of the classical program.

than a devotion to students. And, of course, a devotion to students per se contributed motivation but not talent to the intricate tasks of stimulating non-middle class and not especially ambitious undergraduates to develop a thirst and capacity for learning. More literate and cohesive cultures than ours, such as the Japanese and the French, have been able to force entire age-grades through the discipline of demanding secondary schools, allowing very few to fail or wander by the wayside. They have had the asset of the almost complete legitimacy of culture in these two societies—a legitimacy which has meant that efforts to establish socialist countercultures invariably seemed to have a no less literate and cultivated style. Even where European cultures have had nationalist movements along ethnic lines, they have not developed hostility to literacy as such, nor has there been a specifically male rejection of culture as something belonging to the distaff side. Given the ethnic, social-class, and sexual antagonisms to high culture in the United States, the community college movement has had to work within the American grain and has not sought to bring its students to learning after the fashion of the French *lycée* or the Japanese secondary school. It has been willing to provide vocational and technical programs or sufficiently relaxed general programs to create in many cases an upward extension of high school, but not much of a shift of pace or style. Yet because, as in the high schools, the focus is on teaching, the situation exists in a number of states, notably California, that students will find better teaching of the same subjects in the community colleges than in the lower division of the state's major universities—with the result that those few who transfer from the former to the latter at the junior-year level often have a relatively easy time of it accademically.

In general, however, commuter colleges have not ranked high in the American scheme of things, and they have needed some special pull to attract talented faculty and to sustain morale. As already suggested, urban denominational colleges have sometimes founded such morale on a religious base—witness, for example, urban Jesuit colleges such as St. Louis University or Boston College, or such secular-Protestant enterprises as Northeastern and Roosevelt, both of which were started by the YMCA.

An interesting light is cast on the meaning of these examples by the secular accomplishment of that group of public commuter colleges whose glittering record in sending students on to professional and postgraduate work has not been equaled elsewhere: the city colleges of New York during the period when the children of mostly Jewish immigrants brought to their studies a fierce energy and intellectual ambition. With a certain degree of extravagance, many of these students were prepared to accept high culture on high culture's own terms, and while they went home again at night, they often did so to a milieu where they could continue to argue over issues raised at the college. To be sure, there is a fair amount of legend about all this; most of the students were not like Alfred Kazin or Morris Raphael Cohen but bore more resemblance to the older teachers now in the New York City school system, or the accountants and lawyers now practicing in the city. As everywhere else, it was the minority who gave flavor to the city colleges. Yet the city colleges made doubly clear what has always been evident: that a first-generation student of high ability and motivation is capable of sustained take-off into intellectual growth while still in his teens. The teachers during that epoch at the city colleges had little doubt about the ends to be achieved by higher education or about the values of the (mainly Protestant) cultural tradition of which they were the carriers. The residual legacy of these colleges in their heyday has been to give an image of intellectual vitality to the unwashed—a romantic view that misled several of the early recruits both to Oakland and to Monteith.

Only among residential students is there an opportunity to link curricular innovations to a home-base—an opportunity that is absent at commuter colleges. For example, the experimental Grove Program at Stanford is a coed living unit that is also the home of a special curriculum (directed by Mark I. Mancall, Associate Professor of History). Yale has experimented with the use of its residential colleges as curricular units, giving the college masters the budget and leeway in recruiting faculty from outside the University. The first-year core courses in the cluster colleges of the University of California at Santa Cruz are built on a tie between residential propinquity and the attractiveness of a special curriculum. Raymond College of the University of the Pacific and the Residential College at the University of Michigan have also tied a coherent curriculum to a residential locale.[15] A student-faculty-administration committee at Stanford has proposed setting up a General Education college to serve as a counterweight both to increasing professionalism and to the anarchic temptations among students and faculty who want to do their own thing. Monteith is taken as a model here, seen as allowing "both the personalized, immediate relationship between student and teacher available at a good, small, liberal arts college, and the broad range of coverage and depth offered by the departments of a university."[16]

Innovations such as these in elite university colleges reflect both the willingness of some faculty to teach freshmen (when they have already been carefully screened) and the realization that many freshmen today are not only more sophisticated than their predecessors but also much better prepared. At the same time, beginning with the wave of World War II veterans, many of the elite colleges have sought to diversify their student bodies and hence have recruited freshmen from non-college backgrounds, whose preparation was decidedly poorer. One motivation for Harvard College's General Education program after the Second World War was the hope of bringing these new constituencies into contact with the Western heritage in courses analogous to the Columbia (and later Oakland) Western Civilization program and to cultivate and unify in this way a prospective national elite.

Yet with the limited exception of part-time jobs often provided by the college itself (as in many work/study enterprises), the freshman in these residential colleges is a full-time student and the General Education courses have been taught by leading faculty

[15] See the report by Jerry Gaff, describing the Raymond College experiment in the context of the cluster college concept, *Innovations and Consequences: A Study of Raymond College.*
[16] "The Study of Education at Stanford," Volume II, Appendix IX, pp. 97–98.

members. "General Education" means something different at a largely commuter institution, where students are channeled into the General College for interdisciplinary courses taught by a second-echelon faculty. Commuter colleges cannot count on a spillover from classroom to dinner table; as at Oakland in the early years, students melt away after class, and in many such places General Education programs have been a way of providing low-cost service courses for students whose focus lay elsewhere.

These differences naturally raise the question whether the experience of the elite private colleges has any bearing on the very different problems of the large public commuter institutions. When Riesman spoke in 1964 at the annual meeting of the American Council on Education on the need for innovative centers of research and development on large state university campuses, the presidents of some of the larger state universities pointed out that places like Swarthmore, Chicago, Reed, and Columbia had a combined student body smaller than the freshman class in their own colleges of liberal arts. Their implication was that these pint-sized models were of minimal significance, since they educated a tiny fraction of the population, under very special conditions—but it then turned out that several of the college presidents making this point were themselves graduates of these private colleges.[17] In fact, the influence of the small liberal arts college as a model bears little relation to its size, its wealth, or even the éclat of its student body.

The wide influence of ideas originating in elite schools is a consequence of democratization. Sumptuary laws have never governed dress or other forms of conduct in the United States. One of the

[17] Cf. David Riesman, "Alterations in Institutional Attitudes and Behavior," in Logan Wilson (ed.), *Emerging Patterns in American Higher Education*, pp. 66–73. Clark Kerr's belief as President of the University of California that Berkeley and UCLA had grown beyond optimal scale may not have been unrelated to his experience as a Swarthmore undergraduate; the collegiate plan emphasized at Santa Cruz and less strongly pushed at the University of California at San Diego reflects the explicit impact of Swarthmore as well as the model set earlier by Oxford and Cambridge. Similarly, much of the planning for the new residential college at the University of Michigan was done by Theodore Newcomb, who had taught at Bennington—whose population of 350 would hardly fill a Michigan dormitory.

consequences of affluence and of mass higher education is that a great many students, and not only the notably privileged ones, feel entitled to make their own claims on significant adults.[18] Once an idea such as personalism is launched, it may spread far beyond the circles that have experienced it firsthand, like any social or technological innovation. However, we know from the Monteith experience that not all students are eager for close student-faculty relations: they prefer to keep their footing in their families, their peer groups, and other protective enclaves. Futhermore, the Monteith social science faculty worried at times that they might be too protective, as when they feared lest their backing of a student government in the College's first year would militate against the very autonomy they hoped would develop in the students.

Our observations do not support the conclusion that the smaller the faculty member's span of control, the better job of teaching he necessarily does. It is true that it is hard to be personal with sixty freshmen if one is hoping to have each of them develop a style of oral and written expression suited to his idiosyncratic talent. In the supervision of writing and in the first steps of research, one-to-one tutoring may be requisite. But, for the development of cognitive and imaginative breadth, small seminars are not necessarily superior to large lectures. Today many faculty share the judgment common among students that large lectures are necessarily impersonal and pompous, a view that then becomes self-fulfilling. The desire for close student-faculty contact and small classes becomes regressive if it is seen as the principal problem of higher education and not as simply one strategy for developing the variety of cognitive and affective styles among students that we see as one ideal aim of education. The advising function is decisive in helping students make the best uses of their own potential as well as of the institution, and this requires individuation and hence a manageable

[18] For an unsympathetic account of this world-wide tendency, see Edward Shils, "Plenitude and Scarcity: The Anatomy of an International Cultural Crisis." See also, S. M. Lipset, "The Possible Political Effects of Student Activism on International Politics," in S. M. Lipset and Philip Altbach (eds.), *Students in Revolt*.

number of advisees. Nevertheless, the doctrine of personalism can become as rigid as the FTE rules in public colleges, which make no allowance for the fact that some faculty are better in a small and some in a large setting, that students can learn in both if they believe they can, and that—almost ominously—there will be no abundance of gifted teachers for either sort of setting in the years ahead.

The Impact of Black Undergraduates

A number of colleges and universities are discovering the distance between what their faculties are prepared to teach and what their students are prepared to learn in the dramatic and visible case of the new cadres of black students they have been recruiting. The University of Illinois, which has had few black students on either its Urbana or its Chicago Circle campus, inaugurated a program to recruit five hundred black freshmen at the former campus for the fall of 1968. It was a crash program—and it faced enormous difficulties and some turbulence during orientation sessions at the beginning of the year. Discussing the effect on the university, Chancellor Jack W. Peltason declared that, while Illinois was not a junior college, it was capable of doing something for these high-risk black students; he continued, "The time and effort we're spending is also making people sensitive to improving instruction in the whole university. Faculty members used to say, 'I'm a good teacher, but the students are too dumb.' They can't say that about these kids, or anyway they don't. They know they've got to find ways to teach them."[19] Likewise, the City University of New York has been under intense pressure from within and without to extend its reach in order to recruit into experimental transition programs more black and Puerto Rican students than the relatively small numbers who had in the past been able to make it in the regular course of things. In several articles, Leonard Kriegel, a white professor of English at CCNY, has described his efforts to reach such students without being patronizing; he assumes that his students can

[19] William Trombley, "College Plan for Negroes Passes Test—But 'Project 500' at Illinois U. Meets Obstacle."

respond to Conrad as well as to Richard Wright and to such transcendent works as Camus's *The Stranger* and Tolstoy's *The Death of Ivan Ilyich.*[20]

Whether or not the entry of underprepared black students into colleges will reshape these institutions in such a way as to make them more accessible to underprepared students of whatever color, elite faculty are more ready to move away from their preferred clients or to find other reasons for preference than academic aptitude and discipleship when it comes to black (and to a somewhat lesser degree, other non-white) students. In part, this interest in black students illustrates the easy alliance between members of the upper social and intellectual strata and those they like to believe have come from the lower depths; middle class academics who have learned to look down on the lower-middle class, who seem in no way exotic, may much prefer to work with black students. The large black enclaves at Wayne and other urban universities stand as a partial bulwark against these efforts by white faculty, serving perhaps some of the same functions for their members that fraternities and sororities have in the past served for both white and black students. They help to overcome feelings of self-deprecation on alien academic turf; they provide alibis for not fully entering that turf; they create a student subculture resistant to faculty expectations and demands.

Both Monteith and Oakland were unusual in their ability to attract faculty willing to work with unselected white students, since they enrolled virtually no non-whites at the beginning. In the past several years, Oakland has made the considerable effort required to tie itself to the militant black leaders of Pontiac and to find its own entree into black high schools both there and in Detroit, competing for black students against Wayne's traditional appeal and the full-blast recruiting of Michigan State, the University of Michigan, and Eastern Michigan University. At first, Oakland seemed too academically high-brow and astringent to attract blacks, and it became necessary for the faculty to make clear that they would look after

[20] See "Teaching the 'Pre-Baccs': Headstart for College" and "Playing it Black."

the black students who did come.[21] Black freshmen can now be channeled to faculty who will take a special interest in them, who will provide extra tutoring and so on. Yet as far as we know, these new recruits have not had a direct impact on teaching styles other than to bend them a bit in individual instances.

When Monteith began, it had, in comparison with its parent university, relatively few blacks; perhaps, it was thought, because its General Education program was too highfalutin and insufficiently vocational. It was observed a year or two later that the College brochure had no photographs of black students, and efforts were then made by faculty to recruit more blacks. Some of the social science faculty in particular had easy rapport with black students in the early days—especially a sociologist of French origin, who had the advantage of being outside the American racial dichotomy. Now, as we have mentioned, about a seventh of the student body at Monteith is black. Monteith's black students are part of a radical network that includes some of the editors of *South End,* the militant student paper that is tied to black radicalism in the Detroit area. Yet the presence of so many blacks at Monteith and in the other colleges of Wayne does not necessarily spare any individual black from the conflict between being a student and being an activist, and some drop out because they cannot bridge the gap. The social science program at Monteith at least allows this gap to be raised as an appropriate topic within the curriculum.[22] Yet Monteith, like Oakland, has made no special effort to change its teaching methods to accommodate black students, although courses in Afro-American studies have been added recently.

In many universities, the new black militants have helped persuade white faculty that black students need their own special thing, such as Afro-American studies, or that they need what is "relevant," meaning some kind of swinging, unstructured teaching.

[21] As elsewhere, the office of the Dean of Students has moved to provide support to black students. There is a black Assistant Dean of Students; there is a new black basketball coach; there are several black faculty members.
[22] One social science faculty member was a black graduate of Morehouse with a doctorate in sociology from the University of Chicago who stayed at Monteith for two years.

Such hortatory generalizations lose sight of distinctions that have to be made. To illustrate, a *program* in Afro-American studies that offers courses in various departments, depending on local initiative and potential, is likely to have different consequences for students than a *major,* which may lead to pressures on all black students to enroll. What kind of teaching is really needed for black students from city and country, North and South, male and female, from professional families and ghetto matriarchies, needs discovery and experiment no less than similar questions about white students. Personalism may not always be the right strategy, for some students wish not to be noticed until they are more sure of their capacity to respond: they may prefer the safety of the lecture hall to the risks of the seminar or tutorial. Already there is some evidence that first-generation black commuter students prefer fairly structured, unexperimental teaching (whether or not this is what they in fact need). As some students at Federal City College explained to us after FCC's opening in the fall of 1968, they sought a conventional academic program that would prepare them in an immediate vocational way and not confuse them by pedagogic experimentation.[23]

In general, black nationalism on the campus, whether fostered by blacks or whites, has been more concerned with problems of psychological identity as a basis for academic learning than with discovering ways to teach basic skills to high school graduates who may often read at a seventh-grade level. The rationale has sometimes been that black pride will be conducive to learning, that ghetto youth will take to a book more readily if it has been written by Eldridge Cleaver or Malcolm X than, let us say, by Ernest Hemingway or Norman Mailer. Enthusiasm often does act as a semi-

[23] On the experience of Federal City College, the land-grant college of Washington, D.C. that opened in the fall of 1968 with two thousand students chosen by lot, ninety-four per cent of them black, see David Dickson, "Higher Education for One World or for Two?"; Barbara Raskin, "Federal City College: Militancy in Microcosm," and "A Racial Split Hits New College."

For a survey of black studies programs in white and Negro colleges see Tobe Johnson, "Black Studies: Their Origin, Present State, and Prospects"; also the autumn 1969 issue of *The Massachusetts Review* for a symposium on black students and black studies.

conductor between teachers and students. Furthermore, curricula geared to black identity, though presently often anti-intellectual in temper, have the potential for developing a wider intellectual reach because of the demands they make on the imagination of students and faculty. Indeed, such curricula might hopefully supplement more vocational curricula, allowing black students in college to acquire both the security of vocational training and the reflectiveness made possible through a focus on their own lives and backgrounds. Yet experience to date does not justify the belief that there is any all-purpose hook that can connect particular cultural materials to the cognitive and emotional development of the enormous variety of black students now entering college. Certainly, black faculty *per se* provide no all-purpose answer for the learning problems of these students, as the experience of the District of Columbia schools and of many Negro colleges suggests.[24]

The Hazards Facing Educational Innovation

Pressure on colleges and universities to recruit and then respond to increasing numbers of black students has far outrun the ability of most of these institutions to recruit or train faculty who themselves have been acculturated to such students, or who know how to cope with them either separately or in classes that also include both more adept and less adept white students. To be sure, the spread of such demands on colleges is uneven, and many state universities and rural or suburban private and public colleges have neither been attractive to black students nor successful in recruiting them. When such students do come, they often need more in the way of scholarship aid than comparable lower-income whites attending the same

[24] Some militant black propagandists contend that this is because the teachers and faculties are "Negro" rather than "black," but this begs the question at issue, which is whether the curriculum the nationalists prefer will take hold with all the different forms of personal and vicarious experience with which students come. The fact that French was the second most popular subject in the Mississippi Summer Freedom Schools of 1964 would indicate some caution about jumping to conclusions. For general discussion, see Christopher Jencks, "Private Schools for Black Children."

colleges.²⁵ The new cadres of black students, as already suggested, may require special tutoring and other facilities. These very privileges can contribute to these students' feelings of guilt vis-à-vis those less well-off, and hence to demands that still more black students be recruited.

The pressures to respond to new and demanding constituencies come upon the universities at a time when their sources of public and private support have become increasingly restive and indeed ungenerous. The major state universities were once regarded as secular cathedrals, where the children of influential local citizens could be subsidized and readied for careers that would help them become loyal alumni. When such state universities actively recruit black students who then appear ungrateful, white alumni feel that their children would not be similarly courted. Certainly the parents of South Side Chicago, and East St. Louis black students at Illinois or Carbondale, are not about to replace white legislators or philanthropists who have supported (if not always understood) the universities. Furthermore, the dissident, unruly white radical students and their faculty sponsors have now heightened a backlash that runs from the blue collar class to the very edge of the elite. The colleges and universities most likely to suffer are exactly those that have been the cathedrals, not the more tranquil local colleges, which have made fewer claims and taken fewer risks.²⁶

The pressure today is to shift research priorities and, to a lesser

²⁵ In an unpublished paper, "Black Student Life," Richard Scott, of the Columbia Students Afro-American Society, has discussed why black students may require more financial support than whites of similar economic background. He notes their inability to count on support (even from parents who in principle could afford to supply it) and the need to supplement the earnings of parents and fellow siblings if one is not to feel too guilty about being in college at all. Furthermore, black students until very recently have maintained a higher standard of spending on dates and clothes than whites, and have often had to start with a smaller accumulation of the student capital equipment of typewriters, automobiles, and high-fi sets.
²⁶ See for fuller discussion, David Riesman, "The Collision Course of Higher Education." Sputnik can no longer be used to press the case for putting more money into academic science, which now seems as linked to demonic dangers as to magical benefits.

extent, to shift away from research altogether, toward a new preoccupation with undergraduate instruction. The Right hopes this will keep students in line and faculty from agitating, while the Left hopes that it will turn faculty attention to the students' preoccupations. But of course the pressure for a return to the classroom does nothing to create financial and human resources that would make this return significant. It is important to emphasize again that the work that began at Oakland and Monteith was not initiated because of pressures of the sort just mentioned, either from students or from state legislators; here as elsewhere, social invention was the mother of necessity rather than the other way around. Indeed, Populist pressures had nothing whatever to do with the origins of Monteith, which grew as an idea within academic circles and, as we have seen, depended on a grant from the Fund for the Advancement of Education. Oakland's origins, too, go back to private money: the donation of an estate and matching money by Mr. and Mrs. Wilson, and supplementation by local philanthropy. The post-Sputnik ideology was always an elitist rather than a Populist one, confined mostly to successful Puritans who were worried about the slackness of the nation as a whole and of *la jeunesse moyenne sensuelle* in particular.[27]

[27] What made Oakland and Monteith notable was precisely the combination of public and private resources, for both could begin with the backing of state universities, thus minimizing the insecurities that haunt so many private experimental colleges and make them dependent on high-income, high-risk, students. Private moneys have been just as essential in the inauguration of the college plan at Santa Cruz. Even though California, by national standards, has been munificent in its provisions for public higher education, the Regents of the University did not believe that they could provide Santa Cruz with the amenities necessary for a college plan at the taxpayers' expense. (These amenities included senior and junior common rooms in each college; a home in the college compound for the Provost; additional library and other facilities for the college.) No college was supposed to begin unless a million dollars had been raised for it in private money, although the fund drives have had to curtail their aims to half that amount. What a state legislator or budget officer may consider a frill depends on prevailing ideologies as well as stringencies, so that a new stadium or cyclotron may not be thought of as a frill (or even a fantastically expensive medical school), while the facilities mentioned for Santa Cruz could not be justified as a public expense even though they have been

With state legislatures and the Congress less and less sympathetic to the more troubled campuses, and the alumni and other donors becoming restive, we are pessimistic about how the university can support both its research and graduate training functions and also its new service functions.[28] If one could count on a rational division of labor among institutions so that some devoted themselves principally to pedagogic exploration, others to community service, and still others to the specific problems of minority students, one could hope for a *modus vivendi* between financial stringency and competing demands. But, as many critics have pointed out, pluralism in American higher education does not necessarily produce diversity: it can produce what Harold Rosenberg once called "the herd of independent minds," all moving in the same direction.

One immediate consequence of increasing democratization of decision-making in both public and private universities is to enlarge the agenda to include issues raised by activists concerning war-related or other research, as well as the effort to make colleges and universities behave as moral corporate citizens locally and nationally. In the first flush of confrontation or convocation, many participants find plebiscitary democracy not only exciting but also educative. For while students everywhere reject the already dissolving doctrine of *in loco parentis,* many do see the universities as a home away from home that can serve as a substitute for family, church, or precinct. Allan Silver, a sociology professor at Columbia, writes of "the desperate search [by the most academically inclined and politically sensitive students] for a livable home in America, for if not at the universities, then where? The options thus far are few and unsatisfactory: the 'free university,' counter-cultures parasitically attached to campuses, various ways of dropping

crucial to the development of cohesiveness in the college plan itself. The importance of the additional moneys is reflected in the difficulty of bringing the natural scientists into close contact with colleagues in other fields because it has not proven possible to build offices and laboratories for them in the colleges, even on a small scale, but only in the Science Building.

[28] For a brilliant discussion of some of these dilemmas, see Martin Trow, "Reflections on the Transition from Mass to Universal Higher Education." We have profited greatly from this paper and from discussions with its author.

out. . . . Some of the strains within the universities would be relieved if the rest of the occupational landscape did not look as bleak as it does to many sensitive students."[29]

Allan Silver is sympathetic to the demands of students for a "livable home," but he is also alert to the strains imposed on the university by the effort to turn it into an intentional community, like Mennonite or Hutterite settlements. We noticed in the Monteith style of personalism that it proved exhausting and often disappointing to faculty members—particularly when, as in the repeated episodes of plagiarism, students insisted on behaving not as peers, but as evasive subordinates. The rhythms and demands of youth and of adult life are different, and synchronization can occur for only rare periods, or for exceptionally energetic, free-floating adults.

Monteith has had an atmosphere that struck many at Wayne as unduly free from the very outset, but of course this has been a matter of style and not of curriculum: the curriculum has always been a largely required one. And just now some of the students are beginning to make the same demands for freedom from the curriculum that are appearing elsewhere, most vehemently vis-à-vis the natural sciences sequence, which is regarded as too technical. Both activist and vocational students can rally to such a cry—the former for student power, the latter to pursue a less demanding degree. A curriculum premised on the insistence that there would be no "spoon feeding" may be jeopardized by students' view of all curricula, all adult expectations, as spoon feeding. In that sense, the student-run Senior Colloquia and Co-operative Self-Education Project, which began with energetic and academically eager students, may have less happy sequels, analogous to some of the free universities, where many courses and programs dissolve into nothing and an anti-institutional ethos minimizes the possibilities for curricular planning.

In his book *Experiment at Berkeley,* the philosopher Joseph Tussman describes a two-year integrated program in General Education, which he initiated in the fall of 1965 in the wake of the Free

[29] See Allan Silver, "Who Cares for Columbia?"; see also Walter Metzger, "Academic Freedom in a Delocalized University."

Speech Movement disturbances.[30] The inspiration for the Experimental Program was the Experimental College founded by Alexander Meiklejohn at the University of Wisconsin forty years earlier, a college that had a short life at Wisconsin, but whose influence has spread and continues to have an impact. Tussman faced opposition from faculty colleagues who wondered how the first year could be devoted to Ancient Greece when those who would teach could not read classical Greek (and were not preparing students for careers in the classics). He faced opposition from activist teaching assistants, who sided with the undergraduates in opposition to a structured program they had not themselves chosen. The teaching was intended to be dialectic rather than personalistic, topic-centered rather than student-centered. In spirit and style, it seems to us similar in many ways to some of the work in the humanities at Monteith and to a lesser degree in other fields there. Tussman's book discusses many of the issues mooted at both Monteith and Oakland concerning the optimal size of discussion groups, the proper length of a class "hour," the proper length of a reading list, and the need for continuous work with students on their writing. Students were allowed to take one course outside the Tussman program, and some were allowed to transfer out into the Berkeley College of Letters and Science. Tussman's Report to the Faculty shows, however, that the program suffered less attrition than Berkeley regularly does.[31]

Tussman's book is honest about the difficulties of putting such a program over—for example the shambles that the Tuesday lectures became on many occasions when too much weight had been put on them and when lecturing sometimes went against the grain of faculty members as well as students. Each of the authors could testify to comparable experiences: any experimental teaching runs the risk of failures, which are often more obvious—because more is

---

[30] See Tussman, *Experiment at Berkeley*.
[31] Similar to Monteith, the Experimental Program possesses only an old, run-down house as its physical locale. For the second run of his program, Tussman recruited among his former students and others outside of Berkeley, on a short-term basis, rather than trying to pry additional faculty away from their departments.

attempted—than in more standardized teaching. And as these last remarks have suggested, changes in student temper have altered the ground rules within which experiment can be carried on.

Oakland and Monteith had a head start on student activism. The struggle over bearded student workers in the Oakland Center in the early years now seems pleasantly archaic. Indeed, the early Oakland faculty would have borne the penalties of student activism gladly to assure themselves that they were at a real college. Now the campus faces many of the issues of troubled campuses elsewhere, although most of the fire has been directed against the administration and MSU officials.[32] Those students who try to organize others at Oakland, Monteith, and other commuter colleges know that most of the student body is not explicitly political. Commuters come to get a credential, because it is easier to come than not to come, because the draft is an unhappy alternative. Yet, even though many commuters come for reasons that faculty members and activist students tend to find crass and self-centered, it does not follow that the students come exclusively from such motives or that they are completely closed to other definitions of the college experience than those with which they arrived. In our own observation, a good many commuter students are more open than they appear—less mindlessly insistent on getting their credential and not being bothered—than were comparable students in an earlier day. We know from the various studies of the effects of college attendance that something happens to these students just by virtue of being in college, no matter what the institution explicitly does or does not do. We also know from our study of Oakland and Monteith that a great deal more can happen in a few cases, but that this takes enormous, detailed, continuous effort on the part of the faculty.

[32] During a student campaign against the Board of Trustees, a professor of psychology sought to set the students straight as to who the enemy is: Donald C. Hildum, in a letter to the editor of the student paper, wrote: "Dammit, you guys, wake up! It's the faculty that runs the day-to-day business of this place, and the students have, right now, far more influence with this 'ruling clique' [of Trustees] than they realize. If there are things wrong with Oakland—no doubt you can find a few—don't let us off the hook by tilting at the East Lansing windmill. Use the influence you already have. . . ." (*Oakland Observer*, p. 10.)

We also know, from the record of these two colleges, that the effort can have less happy outcomes as well. At Oakland, there was the kind of ruthlessness toward many students who were cast into outer darkness with no concern for what would become of them. In an earlier, less meritocratic era, the damage to a young person's career chances was probably smaller than would be true today, and the damage to his ego was probably smaller too.[33] Today, as Chancellor Peltason of Illinois said, one cannot blithely flunk out with newly invited black students, and probably it is harder to do with whites also.[34]

Faculty Ambivalence and Academic Values

Before the post-Sputnik wave of reforms had been thoroughly tried and tested in various settings, a new and quite different agenda was spreading at the end of the 1960s. Both the post-Sputnik and the now prevailing agendas are immensely critical of bureaucracies, professional guilds, and educational establishments. There the resemblance ends. Now the demand is for affect-oriented education, with the student at the center of things and the teacher an undemanding, benign resource person responding to the student's wants as these unfold. Students are seen as hard-pressed by tiresome credentialism, and student rebelliousness is interpreted as justified resistance to having been programmed in irrelevant and boring directions. We ourselves in other writings have contributed to this chorus of complaint, but the major voices have been louder ones: John Holt and Paul Goodman, Judson Jerome and Edgar Friedenberg, George Leonard and Harold Taylor, and many, many more.

Unquestionably, there are institutions where the effect of this critique has been salutary, much like the opening of windows that

[33] In a series of studies, Bruce Eckland followed a cohort of University of Illinois entering freshmen and showed that some returned to the University of Illinois for a second chance and made it, and many transferred elsewhere and made it; it took a long time for all the returns to be in. Cf. Bruce K. Eckland, "Social Class and College Graduation: Some Misconceptions Corrected" and "A Source of Error in College Attrition Studies."

[34] For a brilliant discussion of analogous problems, see John McDermott, "Campus Missionaries: The Laying on of Culture."

Vatican II provided for the more entrenched enclaves of the Roman Catholic Church. In many public schools and in some colleges, however, the effect of the critique has been demoralizing: the goals seem so often beyond realization, and the teachers feel caught in many places between the demands of students hostile to constraint and the attacks from high-brow adults contemptuous of all routines. It seems to us nearly inconceivable that the public schools or most institutions of mass education can ever muster the geniuses of empathy who come at us from the pages of these skillful writers. To the degree that the standards they set in their writings are taken seriously as ideals, most teachers and most schools fail so abysmally as to be tempted to reject such idealism altogether. In this situation, it is necessary to say that it is vital throughout the educational process for students to learn how to learn from less than ideal teachers and settings, and not anticipate utopian settings as the only ones in which they can flourish. Indeed, a more adventurous attitude on the part of the students would allow them to profit from all sorts of teachers, if only in some cases to expand their understanding of the range of adults to be found in the world and in their corner of it.[35]

Correspondingly, it is an illusion to believe, as some of the initial faculty at Oakland and Monteith did, that it would have been better to start completely from scratch than to start as a branch or colony of exisiting institutions. In fact, no human enterprise ever does start from scratch, whether it be a commune, a college, or a co-op. A new college, in fact, may need more safeguards than one already established, because if it has ambitions for novelty, it becomes a magnet for a large and mobile group of disaffected faculty and students who bring with them their individual agendas, only to discover irreconcilable differences among themselves. Moreover, as has happened at Old Westbury, the newcomers will be tempted to read into the plans for the college their own definitions

[35] When we have talked to students in this vein, the response has often been that learning can only go on in settings of intimacy and utter mutuality. Students are then unwilling to discover that it might be otherwise. Such a view leads to the countervailing demand for excitement, a passive waiting to be pulled out of boredom by personal charisma or group action.

of what ails America and its institutions of higher education; and they will demand their own prescriptions for reform or revolution which turn out to be unacceptable to legislators, donors, parents, and other sponsors. (Of course there will always be some friction here, and some need for buffering and compromise; it is a question of degree.)

With great variation among fields and faculties, academic traditionalists are today on the defensive and doubt their missions. Recent products of the major graduate schools are not likely to start teaching at a new college with the simple mission of rigor that inspired some of the early recruits to Oakland. On the contrary, they are at least as likely to assume that academic reform is relatively simple, being defined as doing away with academic vested interests, prefabricated curricula, hierarchical structures, budgets and other controls, and all "irrelevant" requirements.

Under these conditions of altered educational climates, there are evident advantages in starting new colleges with support from existing institutions. On its three new campuses at San Diego, Santa Cruz, and Irvine, the University of California could enter bids along three quite different intellectual and pedagogic lines, in each case with the backing as well as the restraints of the overall University administration. The new university and college centers in the State University of New York have likewise been able to diversify, with Old Westbury taking one road for example, and a new college focused on the arts to open in Purchase in Westchester County in 1971, quite another.

Oakland and Monteith began in what was then the quite decentralized non-system of public higher education in Michigan with the advantages, however uneasily viewed by most of their faculty, of financial, administrative, and logistical support from their parent universities. With that support, along with private support, neither college faced premature cost-effectiveness judgments, nor did either have to fear instant legislative disaster because of a momentary mistake. For a time, modest budgets could be buried in the larger budgets of the parent, and while of course this could provide an excuse for slipshod work, it could also give greater leeway for experiment. The dramatic drop in Oakland's recruitment after the first year, and a lull in publicity after the fanfare of its inauguration, could both be endured while reorganization occurred, dormitories were built, and an altered symbiosis achieved between the faculty and the students.

Another "lesson" we would draw from our observations is that all educational change must be incremental and must take full account of the local terrain. To create a single genuinely new course, even within a discipline (let alone among disciplines), is a large accomplishment. Administrators, faculty, and students all talk much too glibly about interdisciplinary programs, urban studies, ecological studies, and so forth. Yet if one examines urban studies programs even in major, well-financed universities, one sees how seldom there has been success in connecting serious and well-supervised work in the field with the academic disciplines; those who are capable of such supervision are rare, the pull of the field is great, and such pioneering and exploratory work is exhausting for all concerned.[36] The quality of the social science program at Monteith as a curricular creation depended on a coterie of individuals who had studied together and could work together at least for a few seasons. It was not simply the outcome of an evangelistic belief in "General Education."

If programs must be tailored to the specific faculty who are there or who can be recruited, similar warnings must be issued concerning the variety of students who turn up even in a non-selective commuter college.[37] In such a college, some students will

[36] For two examples from Cornell University, see William F. Whyte, "On Making the Social Sciences Relevant to Students," and William H. Friedland, "Making Sociology Relevant: A Teaching-Research Program for Undergraduates." A further consideration is that, whereas a large business can find room for emotionally or intellectually exhausted executives in the warehouse division or can buy out their contracts, rules of tenure (and the feelings that lead to estoppel) rob academic institutions of comparable flexibility.

[37] To take an obvious but often disregarded example, we believe that, in the present cultural climate, the same programs may have very different consequences for men and women students. Women students, regardless of social-class backgrounds, seem to us to need protection, by a greater degree of undergraduate professionalism, against the chances or mischances of matrimony

be focused principally on an immediate vocational goal, sensible
if short-run, while others will have their eyes on a more open
and indeterminate future. Many, like young people everywhere,
will want to insure their futures by paying minimal premiums while
enjoying their present. Any good educational plan must place a
far greater emphasis on the advising function than is common even
in highly selective undergraduate colleges, let alone in large commuter colleges.[38] The college that in some ways comes closest to
this model is Sarah Lawrence, where there are virtually no curricular requirements, where the adviser or don carefully counsels
a student in terms of her—and now his—particular qualities, suggesting paths through the available courses (the normal load is
three courses) where the student can be persuaded, although not
compelled, to abandon self-protectiveness and to venture into areas
of previous weakness as well as previous strength.[39] What Sarah

than may be suitable for talented men who are likely to go on to graduate
or professional school. We know many men who drop out of college and
return at their wives' expense! If the wives drop out too, they may not get
the second chance that is somewhat easier for their husbands: the United
States is still a second-chance country for men much more than for women.
A liberal arts program that encourages young women to graduate from college
as English or philosophy majors is more of a threat to their future independence than would be the case for men. At its best, Oakland University
prepared the majority of its women graduates with a teaching credential as
well as a liberal arts major, allowing them to have their pick of secondary
school teaching positions or to choose to go on later for more education.
For further development of this theme, see David Riesman, "Observations on
Contemporary College Students—Especially Women," *Interchange*.

[38] We have drawn in this section on David Riesman, "The Search for Alternative Models in Education."

[39] Sarah Lawrence does not give grades but rather furnishes students with
detailed evaluations. To the extent that its students have been high-status
women, a don with detailed knowledge of the curriculum and a close relation
with his students could readily encourage them to break out of their narcissism
or their excessive humility, since the chances they would take in areas
previously avoided would not be serious in career terms. Furthermore, Sarah
Lawrence's location on the outskirts of New York has allowed it to recruit
faculty, especially in the arts, but also in other fields, who would not be
available to most commuter colleges. Even so, the Good Soldier Schweiks of
the student body can defeat such arrangements, as they can any other, winning
in the end the battle over requirements that Willard Waller described many
years ago—saying in effect to the faculty: "You can't make me!"

Lawrence can just barely afford for its five hundred students and $4500 tuition is plainly not a model for large, public commuter colleges. Yet at any college where resources must be divided between formal teaching in courses and advising, some faculty energy spent on advising might be more productive than further energy expended on coursework.

A curriculum must be seen as a rough-and-ready substitute for an advising system. It allows some students to continue to coast on any momentum gained in secondary school, while facing others with the kind of formidable barriers that Oakland presented at the outset for many of its ill-prepared entrants. When we have talked with faculty and officials at large public universities about the role of advising, we have been told that it is impractical to ask faculty to do the job even if time were released from teaching, because they would never know or learn enough about the campus, or careers, or the draft, or anything else to be helpful. Indeed, it is mostly in large public institutions that advising has been delegated to counselors responsible to the Dean of Students Office or the Vice President for Student Affairs. These counselors are often devoted men and women who try to protect the young people in their charge from the traumas that the institution and life itself can transmit. But since they have very little standing with regular faculty, they do not serve as feedback to faculty concerning the impact (or lack of it) of the curriculum on particular categories of students; they may serve the faculty by "cooling out" unwanted students or, in some few cases, they may "turn on" students— even against the faculty. Faculty could do much more in the way of advising, even without becoming experts in career planning or the draft or other such areas: they could act as general practitioners, referring students for advice on special topics to the professional counselors but using the occasion of advising as a way of increasing their own understanding as well as providing for the students one sort of model of the contagion of intellectual life.

Where the curriculum is highly structured and channels the students regardless of individual variation, an advising system as a way of encouraging students to venture into new areas seems to be less important, but it is still essential to help students remove blocks, and perhaps even enjoy the fields they cannot avoid.

In one of his essays, the psychoanalyst Leslie Farber mentions therapeutic despair: the haunting sense in the therapist that rarely, if ever, does he really succeed in helping someone, with the consequent inability to sustain his work in the face of repeated failure.[40] A similar despair can overtake faculty members whose students can be unwittingly, as well as wittingly, cruel or indifferent to their efforts. Such faculty misgivings are especially strong now, when all adult authority is under attack and when the worth of humane understanding is called into question by eloquent and apocalyptic voices. However, just as a psychoanalytic institute helps sustain therapists by allowing them to pool failures as well as successes, so Oakland and Monteith helped some of their faculty respond to the trials of teaching in a less isolated and more rewarding fashion than is possible at most comparable institutions.

The two colleges described in this book are far from solving all the problems with which they began in 1959. One of the questions now on the horizon—for American higher education generally—is whether faculty resourcefulness can be renewed to cope with the issues raised by increased student participation and by the entry of greater numbers of black students, even when the old problems of education are far from being understood, let alone resolved.

Given the diversity of educational settings in America, we must again insist that there are many institutions where pressures from students—and from outside critics—are the only leverage to support educational reformers surrounded by academic timeservers. There are colleges where faculty need to believe that they are not crazy to take a genuine interest in students and their development. Yet when one tries to look at the whole academic spectrum in America,

---

[40] See Leslie Farber, *The Ways of the Will; Essays Toward a Psychology and Psychopathology of Will;* also Allen Wheelis, "The Vocational Hazards of Psychoanalysis," in *The Quest for Identity,* Chapter VII.

one wonders whether movements for reform may not bear some resemblance to the boom and bust characteristic of the business cycle. The danger we see is that hubris on the one side and desperation on the other may short-circuit the time required to struggle with tentative models of education for students whose heightened expectations will be encountering limited, and relatively shrinking, resources.

References

"Abundance into Excellence" (editorial), *Life*, 1959, *47* (Oct. 5), 50.

ADELSON, JOSEPH. "The Teacher as a Model." In Nevitt Sanford (ed.), *The American College*. New York: Wiley, 1962.

ARENDT, HANNAH. *The Origins of Totalitarianism*. New York: Harcourt, Brace, and World, 1951.

ASTIN, ALEXANDER. "Undergraduate Achievement and Institutional 'Excellence,'" *Science*, 1968, *161*, 661–68.

ASTIN, ALEXANDER. *Who Goes Where to College?* Chicago: Science Research Associates, 1965.

AXELROD, JOSEPH. *Model Building for Undergraduate Colleges*. Berkeley, Calif.: Center for Research and Development in Higher Education, 1969.

BARZUN, JACQUES. *The American University: How It Runs, Where It Is Going*. New York: Harper & Row, 1968.

BECKER, HOWARD S. and CARPER, JAMES. "The Development of Identification with an Occupation," *American Journal of Sociology*, 1956, *61*, 289–98.

BECKER, HOWARD S. and CARPER, JAMES. "The Elements of Identification with an Occupation," *American Sociological Review*, 1956, *21*, 341–48.

BECKER, HOWARD, and OTHERS (eds.) *Institutions and the Person: Essays in Honor of Everett C. Hughes*. Chicago: Aldine Press, 1968.

288   *References*

BECKER, HOWARD S.; GEER, BLANCHE; AND HUGHES, EVERETT C. *Making the Grade: The Academic Side of College Life.* New York: Wiley, 1968.

BELL, DANIEL. *The Reforming of General Education: The Columbia College Experience and Its National Setting.* New York: Columbia University Press, 1966.

BEN-DAVID, JOSEPH. "The Universities and the Growth of Science in Germany and the United States," *Minerva; a Review of Science, Learning, and Policy,* 1968–69, *7,* 1–35.

BEN-DAVID, JOSEPH and COLLINS, RANDALL. "Social Factors in the Origins of a New Science: The Case of Psychology," *American Sociological Review,* 1966, *31,* 451–65.

BERELSON, BERNARD. *Graduate Education in the United States.* New York: McGraw-Hill, 1960.

BERGER, BENNETT. "On the Youthfulness of Youth Cultures," *Social Research,* 1963, *30,* 319–42.

BERGER, BENNETT. "Sociology and the Intellectuals; an Analysis of a Stereotype," *Antioch Review,* 1957, *17,* 275–90. Reprinted in Seymour M. Lipset and N. J. Smelser (eds.), *Sociology: The Progress of a Decade.* Englewood Cliffs, N.J.: Prentice-Hall, 1961.

BERNARD, JESSIE S. *Academic Women.* University Park: Pennsylvania State University Press, 1964.

BOWERS, W. J. *Dishonesty and Its Control in College.* New York: Columbia University, Bureau of Applied Social Research, 1964.

BOYLE, MARYBELLE. "The Measurement of Some Self-Concepts of Entering Students." Unpublished paper, Wayne State University (1965).

BRESLER, JACK B. "Teaching Effectiveness and Government Awards," *Science,* 1968, *160,* 164–67.

BROWN, DAVID G. *The Mobile Professors.* Washington, D.C.: American Council on Education, 1967.

CALIFORNIA, UNIVERSITY. Center for the Study of Higher Education. *Omnibus Personality Inventory Research Manual.* Berkeley: 1962.

CALIFORNIA, UNIVERSITY, Santa Cruz. *So You're Thinking of Coming to Santa Cruz.* Santa Cruz: 1967.

CAPLOW, THEODORE and MCGEE, REECE. *The Academic Marketplace.* New York: Basic Books, 1958.

CARNEGIE COMMISSION ON HIGHER EDUCATION. *Quality and Equality: New Levels of Federal Responsibility for Higher Education.* New York: McGraw-Hill, 1968.

CARTTER, ALLAN M. *An Assessment of Quality in Graduate Education.* A Study for the Commission on Plans and Objectives for Higher Education, American Council on Education. Washington, D.C.: American Council on Education, 1966.

CARTTER, ALLAN M. and FARRELL, R. "Higher Education in the Last Third of the Century," *Educational Record,* 1965, *46,* 119–28.

CASS, JAMES and BIRNBAUM, MAX. *Comparative Guide to American Colleges for Students, Parents, and Counselors.* 1968–69 ed. New York: Harper & Row, 1968.

CASSIDY, SALLY W., and OTHERS. "Evaluating an Experimental College Program with Institutional Records: An Interim Report." Unpublished manuscript (1965).

CASSIDY, SALLY W., and OTHERS. *Impact of a High-Demand College in a Large University on Working Class Youth.* Final report to the U. S. Office of Education for project no. 5-0818. Detroit: 1968.

CLARK, BURTON R. "The 'Cooling Out' Function in Higher Education," *American Journal of Sociology,* 1960, *65,* 569–76.

"A Clean Slate and a Free Hand: Michigan State University—Oakland," *Michigan State University Magazine,* 1959, *5* (Nov.), 9–24.

COLEMAN, JAMES S. *The Adolescent Society: The Social Life of the Teenager and Its Impact on Education.* Glencoe, Ill.: Free Press, 1961.

"The College That Students Helped Plan," by Ralph Keyes and others, *Change in Higher Education,* 1969, *1* (Mar.–Apr.), 12–23.

DAVIS, JAMES A. "The Campus as a Frog Pond: An Application of the Theory of Relative Deprivation to Career Decisions of College Men," *American Journal of Sociology,* 1966, *72,* 17–31.

DAVIS, JAMES A. *Great Aspirations: The Graduate School Plans of America's College Seniors.* Chicago: Aldine, 1964.

DICKSON, DAVID. "Higher Education for One World or for Two?" Address at the 1968 annual meeting of the Association of State Universities and Land-Grant Colleges.

DOERMANN, HUMPHREY. "Baccalaureate Origins and Performance of Students in the Harvard Graduate School of Arts and Sciences." Unpublished manuscript (1968).

DUNHAM, E. ALDEN. *Colleges of the Forgotten Americans: A Profile of State Colleges and Regional Universities.* New York: McGraw-Hill, 1969.

DUNHAM, RALPH E.; WRIGHT, PATRICIA S.; and CHANDLER, MARJORIE O.

Teaching Faculty in Universities and Four-Year Colleges, Spring 1963. (OE-53022-63), Washington, D.C.: U. S. Department of Health, Education, and Welfare, 1966.

ECKLAND, BRUCE K. "Social Class and College Graduation: Some Misconceptions Corrected," *American Journal of Sociology,* 1964, *70,* 36–50.

ECKLAND, BRUCE K. "A Source of Error in College Attrition Studies," *Sociology of Education,* 1964, *38,* 60–72.

ERIKSON, ERIK H. "Inner and Outer Space: Reflections on Womanhood." In Robert J. Lifton (ed.), *The Woman in America.* Boston: Houghton Mifflin, 1965.

FARBER, LESLIE. *The Ways of the Will: Essays Toward a Psychology and Psychopathology of Will.* New York: Basic Books, 1966.

FELDMAN, KENNETH A. and NEWCOMB, THEODORE M. *The Impact of College on Students.* San Francisco, Jossey-Bass, 1969.

FENSKE, ROBERT H. "Who Selects Vocational-Technical Post-High School Education?" In *The Two-Year College and Its Students: An Empirical Report.* Iowa City, Iowa: American College Program, 1969.

FLAX, SUSAN. "'Everybody Has to Do His Own Thing': Life-Styles of College Youth." Unpublished paper done at the Merrill-Palmer Institute by a participant-observer from Michigan State University, June 1968.

FRIEDLAND, WILLIAM H. "Making Sociology Relevant: A Teaching-Research Program for Undergraduates," *The American Sociologist,* 1969, *4,* 104–10.

GAFF, JERRY G. *Innovations and Consequences: A Study of Raymond College, University of the Pacific.* U. S. Office of Education Research Project no. 6-1257. Berkeley, Calif.: 1967.

GAMSON, ZELDA F. "Social Control and Modification." Unpublished Ph.D. dissertation, Harvard University, 1965.

GLAZER, NATHAN. "'Student Power' in Berkeley," *Universities Quarterly,* 1968, *22,* 404–24.

GOODMAN, PAUL. "The Present Moment in Education," *The New York Review of Books,* 1969, *12* (Apr. 10), 14–24.

GOODWIN, LEONARD. "The Academic World and the Business World: A Comparison of Occupational Goals," *Sociology of Education,* 1969, *42,* 170–87.

GUSFIELD, JOSEPH R. *Symbolic Crusade.* Urbana: University of Illinois Press, 1964.

HAGSTROM, WARREN O. "Departmental Prestige and Scientific Productivity." Paper presented at the American Sociological Association meetings, Boston, 1968.

HAGSTROM, WARREN O. *The Scientific Community.* New York: Basic Books, 1965.

HALSEY, A. H. "British Universities," *Archives européennes de sociologie. European Journal of Sociology*, 1962, *3*, 85–101.

HAMMOND, PHILLIP E. *The Campus Clergyman.* New York: Basic Books, 1966.

HARVARD COLLEGE. Office of Tests. "Testing and the Freshman Year: A Handbook for Harvard Advisers." Cambridge, Mass.: 1968.

HILDUM, DONALD C. Letter to the Editor, *Oakland Observer,* 1968 (Nov. 15), 10.

HIRSCHMAN, ALBERT O. *Development Projects Observed.* Washington, D.C.: The Brookings Institution, 1967.

HOFSTADTER, RICHARD. *Anti-Intellectualism in American Life.* New York: Knopf, 1963.

HUGHES, EVERETT C. *Men and Their Work.* Glencoe, Ill.: Free Press, 1958.

HUGHES, EVERETT C. "Stress and Strain in Professional Education," *Harvard Educational Review*, 1959, *29*, 319–29.

HUGHES, EVERETT C.; BECKER, HOWARD; and GEER, BLANCHE. "Student Culture and Academic Effort." In Nevitt Sanford (ed.), *The American College.* New York: Wiley, 1962.

IFFERT, ROBERT. *Retention and Withdrawal of College Students.* Washington, D.C.: U. S. Department of Health, Education, and Welfare, 1958.

INGRAHAM, MARK H. *The Mirror of Brass: The Compensation and Working Conditions of College and University Administrators.* Madison: University of Wisconsin Press, 1968.

JACOB, PHILIP E. *Changing Values in College: An Exploratory Study of the Impact of College Teaching.* New York: Harper, 1957.

JENCKS, CHRISTOPHER. "Private Schools for Black Children," *The New York Times Magazine*, 1968 (Nov. 3), 30+.

JENCKS, CHRISTOPHER and RIESMAN, DAVID. *The Academic Revolution.* New York: Doubleday, 1968.

JOHNSON, ALVIN S. *Pioneer's Progress.* New York: Viking Press, 1952.

JOHNSON, TOBE. "Black Studies: Their Origin, Present State, and Prospects." Proceedings of the Twenty-fifth Annual Meeting of the American Conference of Academic Deans, 1969.

KATZ, JOSEPH. "Personality and Interpersonal Relations in the College Classroom." In Nevitt Sanford (ed.), *The American College*. New York: Wiley, 1962.

KATZ, JOSEPH, and ASSOCIATES. *No Time for Youth: Growth and Constraint in College Students*. San Francisco: Jossey-Bass, 1968.

KAYSEN, CARL. *The Higher Learning, the Universities, and the Public*. Princeton, N.J.: Princeton University Press, 1969.

KEETON, MORRIS and HILBERRY, CONRAD. *Struggle and Promise: A Future for Colleges*. New York: McGraw-Hill, 1968.

KENISTON, KENNETH. *Young Radicals: Notes on Committed Youth*. New York: Harcourt, Brace, and World, 1968.

KERR, CLARK. "New Challenges to the College and University." In *Agenda for the Nation: Papers on Domestic and Foreign Policy Issues*. Kermit Gordon, ed. Washington, D.C.: The Brookings Institution, 1968.

KERR, CLARK. *The Uses of the University*. Cambridge, Mass.: Harvard University Press, 1963.

KRIEGEL, LEONARD. "Playing it Black," *Change in Higher Education*, 1969, *1* (Mar.–Apr.), 7–11.

KRIEGEL, LEONARD. "Teaching the 'Pre-Baccs': Headstart for College," *The Nation*, 1968, *206*, 270–74.

KUHN, THOMAS S. *The Structure of Scientific Revolutions*. Chicago: University of Chicago Press, 1962.

LAZARSFELD, PAUL F., and THIELENS, WAGNER, JR. *The Academic Mind: Social Scientists in a Time of Crisis*. Glencoe, Ill.: The Free Press, 1958.

LEDUC, THOMAS H. A. *Piety and Intellect at Amherst College, 1865–1912*. New York: Columbia University Press, 1946.

LIPSET, SEYMOUR M. *Political Man*. New York: Doubleday, 1960.

LIPSET, SEYMOUR M. "The Possible Political Effects of Student Activism on International Politics." In Seymour M. Lipset and Philip Altbach (eds.), *Students in Revolt*. Boston: Houghton Mifflin, 1969.

MANCHESTER, WILLIAM. *The Long Gainer, a Novel*. Boston: Little, Brown, 1961.

MANNHEIM, KARL. *Ideology and Utopia*. Harvest books, 3. New York: Harcourt, Brace, and World, 1955.

MARCSON, SIMON. *The Scientist in American Industry: Some Organiza-*

tional Determinants in Manpower Utilization. New York: Harper, 1960.

MARCUSE, HERBERT. *One-Dimensional Man: Studies in the Ideology of Advanced Industrial Society.* Boston: Beacon Press, 1964.

MARIN, PETER. "The Open Truth and Fiery Vehemence of Youth: A Sort of Soliloquy," *The Center Magazine,* 1969, 2 (Jan.), 61–74.

MARTIN, WARREN B. *Alternative to Irrelevance: A Strategy for Reform in Higher Education.* Nashville, Tenn.: Abingdon Press, 1968.

The Massachusetts Review, 1969 (autumn)

MCCLELLAND, DAVID C. "Wanted: A New Self-Image for Women." In Robert J. Lifton (ed.), *The Woman In America.* Boston: Houghton Mifflin, 1965.

MCCULLERS, JOHN C. and PLANT, WALTER T. "Personality and Social Development: Cultural Influences," *Review of Educational Research,* 1964, *34,* 599–610.

MCDERMOTT, JOHN. "Campus Missionaries: The Laying on of Culture," *The Nation,* 1969, *208,* 296–301.

MCKEACHIE, WILBERT. "Procedures and Techniques of Teaching." In Nevitt Sanford (ed.), *The American College.* New York: Wiley, 1962.

MEDALIA, NAHUM. "Choice of College Major by Contest Mobility," *Sociology of Education,* 1968, *41,* 282–90.

MERTON, ROBERT K. "Behavior Patterns of Scientists," *The American Scholar,* 1969, *38,* 197–225.

METZGER, WALTER P. "Academic Freedom in Delocalized Academic Insitutions." In *Dimensions of Academic Freedom.* Urbana: University of Illinois Press, 1969.

"Michigan Maps New State School," *The New York Times,* 1959 (June 7), Section 4, 11:1.

MISHAN, EDWARD. "Some Heretical Thoughts on University Reform: The Economics of Changing the System," *Encounter,* 1969, *32,* 3–15.

MONSON, CHARLES H., JR. "Teaching Assistants: The Forgotten Faculty," *Educational Record,* 1969, *50,* 60–65.

NEW YORK. State University College at Old Westbury. Catalogue. Old Westbury, N.Y.: 1967.

NEWCOMB, THEODORE M. "The Nature and Uses of Peer-Group Influence." Proceedings of Bowling Green University Conference on Residential Colleges, October 1967.

NEWCOMB, THEODORE M. *Personality and Social Change: Attitude For-mation in a Student Community.* New York: Holt, 1943.

NEWCOMB, THEODORE M., and OTHERS. *Persistence and Change: Ben-nington College and Its Students After Twenty-Five Years.* New York: Wiley, 1967.

NISBET, ROBERT A. "Hutchins of Chicago," *Commentary,* 1964, *38,* 52–55.

NISBET, ROBERT A. "Sociology and the Academy." In Charles H. Page (ed.), *Sociology and Contemporary Education.* New York: Random House, 1964.

NOVAK, MICHAEL. "Experiment at Old Westbury: Trying to Talk," *Com-monweal,* 1969, *49,* 560–63.

PARSONS, TALCOTT. "The Academic System: A Sociologist's View," *The Public Interest,* 1968, *13,* 173–97.

PARSONS, TALCOTT and PLATT, GERALD M. "The American Academic Pro-fession: A Pilot Study." Unpublished paper, March 1969.

PARSONS, TALCOTT and PLATT, GERALD M. "Considerations on the Ameri-can Academic System," *Minerva; a Review of Science, Learning, and Policy,* 1968, *6,* 497–523.

PARSONS, TALCOTT AND WHITE, WINSTON. "The Link Between Character and Society." In Seymour M. Lipset and Leo Lowenthal (eds.), *Culture and Social Character.* Glencoe, Ill.: Free Press, 1961.

PATTERSON, FRANKLIN K. and LONGWORTH, CHARLES R. *The Making of a College: Plans for a New Departure in Higher Education.* Cam-bridge, Mass.: MIT Press, 1966.

PLATH, DAVID. *The After Hours: Modern Japan and the Search for En-joyment.* Berkeley: University of California Press, 1964.

RAFFEL, STANLEY. "Some Effects of Columbia College on Its Students." Unpublished study (1965).

RAMSHAW, WARREN C. "Religious Participation and the Fate of Religious Ideology on a Resident and Non-Resident College Campus: An Ex-ploratory Study." Unpublished Ph.D. dissertation, University of Il-linois (1966).

RASKIN, BARBARA. "Federal City College: Militancy in Microcosm," *The Washington Monthly,* 1969, *1,* 52–61.

RASKIN, BARBARA. "A Racial Split Hits New College," *The Washington Post,* 1968 (Nov. 13), A-1, A-3.

RICKS, DAVID F. "Helpful and Harmful Intervention in Schizophrenic Development." Paper presented at the 7th annual research meeting of the Department of Psychiatry, Harvard Medical School, 1965.

RIESMAN, DAVID. "Alterations in Institutional Attitudes and Behavior." In Logan Wilson (ed.) *Emerging Patterns in American Higher Education.* Washington, D.C.: American Council on Education, 1965.

RIESMAN, DAVID. "The Collision Course of Higher Education," *The Journal of College Student Personnel,* 1969, *10,* 363–69.

RIESMAN, DAVID. Comment by D. Riesman on "Universities and the Growth of Science in Germany and the United States," *Minerva; a Review of Science, Learning, and Policy.* 1969, *7,* 751–55.

RIESMAN, DAVID. *Constraint and Variety in American Education.* Lincoln: University of Nebraska Press, 1956.

RIESMAN, DAVID. "The 'Jacob Report,'" *American Sociological Review,* 1958, *23,* 732–39.

RIESMAN, DAVID. "Notes on New Universities, British and American," *Universities Quarterly,* 1966, *20,* 128–46.

RIESMAN, DAVID. "Observations on Contemporary College Students—Especially Women." *Interchange,* 1970, *1,* 52–63.

RIESMAN, DAVID. "Planning in Higher Education: Some Notes on Patterns and Problems," *Human Organization,* 1958, *18,* 12–17.

RIESMAN, DAVID. A review of R. Hofstadter's *Anti-Intellectualism in American Life. American Sociological Review,* 1963, *28,* 1038–40.

RIESMAN, DAVID. "The Search for Alternative Models in Education," *The American Scholar,* 1969, *38,* 377–88.

RIESMAN, DAVID. "Some Problems of a Course in 'Culture and Personality,'" *Journal of General Education,* 1951, *5,* 122–36.

RIESMAN, DAVID. "The Urban University," *The Massachusetts Review,* 1967, *7,* 476–86.

ROSSI, ALICE S. "Equality Between the Sexes: An Immodest Proposal." In Robert J. Lifton (ed.), *The Woman in America.* Boston: Houghton Mifflin, 1965.

RUDOLPH, FREDERICK. *The American College and University.* New York: Knopf, 1962.

RUML, BEARDSLEY. *Memo to a College Trustee: A Report on Financial and Structural Problems of the Liberal College.* New York: McGraw-Hill, 1959.

SANFORD, NEVITT (ed.). "Personality Development During the College Years," *Journal of Social Issues,* 1956, *12,* 4.

SCOTT, RICHARD. "Black Student Life." Unpublished paper (1968).

SEEMAN, MELVIN. "The Intellectual and the Language of Minorities," *American Journal of Sociology*, 1958, *64*, 25–35.

SHILS, EDWARD. "Plenitude and Scarcity: The Anatomy of an International Cultural Crisis," *Encounter*, 1969, *32* (May), 37–48+.

SILVER, ALLAN. "Who Cares for Columbia?" *The New York Review of Books*, 1969, *12* (Jan. 30), 15–24.

SIMON, HERBERT A. "The Job of a College President," *Educational Record*, 1967, *48*, 68–78.

SNOW, CHARLES P. *The Two Cultures: And a Second Look*. New York: New American Library, 1964.

SPADY, WILLIAM. "Peer Integration and Academic Success: The Dropout Process Among Chicago Freshmen." Unpublished Ph.D. dissertation, University of Chicago, 1967.

SPAETH, JOE L. "The Allocation of College Graduates to Graduate and Professional Schools," *Sociology of Education*, 1968, *41*, 342–49.

SPURR, STEPHEN H. *Academic Degree Structures: Innovative Approaches*. New York: McGraw-Hill, 1970.

STALLING, WILLIAM M. and SINGHO, SUE SHILA. "Some Observations on the Relationships Between Research Productivity and Student Evaluations of Courses and Teaching." Paper presented at the American Educational Research Association meetings, Los Angeles, 1969; available from the Office of Instructional Resources, University of Illinois.

STANFORD UNIVERSITY. "The Study of Education at Stanford." Stanford, Calif.: 1968.

STERN, G. G. "Characteristics of the Intellectual Climate in College Environments," *Harvard Educational Review*, 1963, *33*, 5–41.

STERN, G. G. *People in Context*. New York: Wiley, 1970.

STORR, RICHARD J. *Harper's University: The Beginnings; A History of the University of Chicago*. Chicago: University of Chicago Press, 1966.

TRENT, JAMES W. *Catholics in College: Religious Commitment and the Intellectual Life*. Chicago: University of Chicago Press, 1967.

TRENT, JAMES W. and MEDSKER, LELAND L. *Beyond High School*. San Francisco: Jossey-Bass, 1968.

TROMBLEY, WILLIAM. "College Plan for Negroes Passes Test—But 'Project 500' at Illinois U. Meets Obstacle," *Los Angeles Times*, 1968 (Dec. 19), Part 6, 4.

TROW, MARTIN. "The Campus as a Context for Learning: Notes on

Education and Architecture." Address at Colloquium on Education and Architecture, Sarah Lawrence College, Spring 1968.

TROW, MARTIN. "Conceptions of the University: The Case of Berkeley," *American Behavioral Scientist*, 1968, *11*, 14–21.

TROW, MARTIN. "Notes on Undergraduate Teaching at Large State Universities." Unpublished paper, Berkeley, Calif. (1966).

TROW, MARTIN. "Reflections on the Transition from Mass to Universal Higher Education," *Daedalus*, 1970, *99*, 1–42.

TROW, MARTIN. "The Teaching Assistant." Unpublished paper, University of California, Berkeley (1968).

TUSSMAN, JOSEPH. *Experiment at Berkeley*. New York: Oxford University Press, 1969.

U. S. DEPARTMENT OF HEALTH, EDUCATION, AND WELFARE. *Reference Facts on Health, Education, and Welfare*. Washington, D.C.: U. S. Government Printing Office, 1966.

UYEKI, EUGENE S. "The Service Teacher in Professional Education," *Human Organization*, 1962, *21*, 51–55. (Revised version of a paper entitled "Two Degrees of Marginality" presented at the American Society for Engineering Education in 1960).

VERDET, PAULE. "Relationships Among the Seniors." Unpublished paper, Monteith College (1963).

VEYSEY, LAURENCE. *The Emergence of the American University*. Chicago: University of Chicago Press, 1965.

WALLER, WILLARD. *The Sociology of Teaching*. New York: Wiley, 1932.

WATSON, JAMES. *The Double Helix*. New York: Atheneum, 1967.

WAYNE STATE UNIVERSITY. Division of Admissions and Records. Office of Divisional Studies. *The Wayne State University Student*. Detroit: 1960.

WEBER, MAX. *From Max Weber: Essays in Sociology*. New York: Oxford University Press, 1946.

WEINSTEIN, MICHAEL. "On Students Educating One Another." Unpublished Ph.D. dissertation, Department of Social Relations, Harvard University (1967).

WHEELIS, ALLEN. *The Quest for Identity*. New York: Norton, 1958.

"White, Negro Undergraduates at Colleges Enrolling 500 or More, as Compiled from Reports to U. S. Office for Civil Rights," *The Chronicle of Higher Education*, 1968, 2 (Apr. 22), 3–4.

WHYTE, WILLIAM F. "On Making the Social Sciences Relevant to Students." Unpublished paper (1969).

WOFFORD, HARRIS L., JR. "Agent of Whom?" In W. J. Minter and
   I. M. Thompson (eds.), *Colleges and Universities as Agents of Social
   Change*. Berkeley, Calif.: Center for Research and Development in
   Higher Education, 1968.

WRIGHT, ERIK. "A Psycho-Social Study of Student Leaves of Absence."
   Unpublished senior honors thesis, Committee on Social Studies, Harvard College (1968).

YOUNG, MICHAEL and WILLMOTT, PETER. *Family and Kinship in East
   London*. Glencoe, Ill.: Free Press, 1957.

ZELAN, JOSEPH. "Religious Apostasy, Higher Education, and Occupational Choice," *Sociology of Education*, 1968, *41*, 370–79.

Appendix A (to accompany Chapter II)
Social and Academic Characteristics
of Oakland University Students, Fall 1959

Curricular Choices[a]

Business Administration	12%
Engineering Science	25
Liberal Arts and Science	28
Teacher Education	35
N	570

Fathers' Occupations[b]

Professionals, executives	11%
Small businessmen, administrative personnel	17
Clerical and sales	7
Skilled manual	18
Machine operators and semiskilled	20
Unskilled and service workers	11
No response, other	16
N	171

Fathers' Education[b]

College graduate	12%
Some college	27
High school graduate	15
Some high school	25
Less than high school	19
No response	2
N	171

High School Rank[b]

Top fifth	36%
Second fifth	35
Third fifth	22
Below third fifth	6
No response	1
N	171

[a] Excludes 44 students who transferred in with advanced standing.
[b] Based on a 25% random sample study.

Geographical Distribution[a]

Oakland County	77%
Macomb County	18
Wayne County (including Detroit)	2
Other counties in state	2
Out of state	1
N	570

Appendix B (to accompany Chapter III)
Social and Academic Characteristics of Monteith and Wayne College of Liberal Arts Students, Fall 1959

Curricular Choices		
	Monteith	*Liberal Arts*[a]
Business Administration	8%	9%
Liberal Arts	42	28
Education	22	31
Prelaw	5	2
Premedical	23	6
	N 265	N 945

Fathers' Occupations		
	Monteith	*Liberal Arts*[b]
Professionals, executives	20%	15%
Small businessmen, administrative personnel	18	13
Clerical and sales	18	19
Skilled manual	18	19
Machine operators and semiskilled	10	12
Unskilled and service workers	7	7
Other, no response	10	15
	N 265	N 342

Appendixes

Fathers' Education

	Monteith	Liberal Arts[b]
College graduate	23%	10%
Some college	13	15
High school graduate	12	23
Some high school	37	31
Less than high school	15	19
No response	0	2
	N 265	N 342

[a] Totals to less than 100% because other majors are possible in the College of Liberal Arts.
[b] Based on a random sample of fall 1959 freshmen entrants to the College of Liberal Arts.

High School Rank

	Monteith	Liberal Arts[b]
Top fifth	54%	57%
Second fifth	30	27
Third fifth	14	12
Below third fifth	2	3
No response	0	2
	N 265	N 342

Geographical Distribution

	Monteith	Liberal Arts
Detroit	62%	64%
Tri-county area (excluding Detroit)	33	33
Other Michigan counties	3	1
Out of state	2	3
	N 265	N 7,138

[b] Based on a random sample of fall 1959 freshmen entrants to the College of Liberal Arts.

Appendix C (to accompany Chapter V)
Political, Religious, and Marital Characteristics of Oakland and Monteith Faculties, 1960

Presidential Choices	Oakland	Monteith
Kennedy	86%	71%
Nixon	7	10
None	4	14
No response	4	5

Attachment to Religious Groups		
Attached	29%	43%
Unattached	68	57
No response	4	0

Marital Status		
Married, children	64%	33%
Married, no children	29	29
Single	7	38
N	28	21

Appendix D (to accompany Chapter VI)
Educational and Class Origins
of Oakland University and Monteith Faculties, 1960

Educational Levels of Parents[a]	Oakland	Monteith
College	39%	33%
No college	61	67

[a] "College" includes some college as well as college graduates and advanced degrees for *either* parent.

Class Origins		Oakland	Monteith
Working class		29%	24%
Middle class		46	57
Upper class		25	19
	N	28	21

Appendix E (to accompany Chapter VIII)
Percentage of 1959 Oakland Entrants in Each
Major Curriculum, as Freshmen and Juniors

	Freshmen Fall 1959			Juniors[a] Fall 1961		
	Male	*Female*	*Total*	*Male*	*Female*	*Total*
Business Administration	17%	4%	12%	12%	1%	6%
Engineering	38	2	25	14	0	7
Liberal Arts	28	29	28	50	27	38
Education	17	65	35	24	72	49
N	326	200	526	86	89	175
Sex ratio (M/F)		1.63			.97	

[a] Some of the entering class of 1959 were still sophomores by fall 1961, which accounts for the small number of juniors.

Appendix F (to accompany Chapter X)

TABLE F-1
ENROLLMENT AT OAKLAND UNIVERSITY, FALL 1959–69[a]

	Size of entering class (freshmen and transfers)	Total enrollment
1959	570	570
1960	511	908
1961	493	1069
1962	475	1259
1963	696	1498
1964	887	1812
1965	1054	2458
1966	1241	3143
1967	1401	3896
1968	1638	5094
1969	2050	5811

[a] Source: Annual Enrollment Reports, Office of the Registrar, Oakland University.

TABLE F-2
ENTRANCE TEST PERFORMANCE OF FRESHMEN
ENTERING OAKLAND UNIVERSITY, 1959–66[a]

*Raw Scores at Each Percentile Rank on Scholastic Aptitude Test
Equivalents Based on College Qualifications Test—Total Score*

Percentile Rank	1959	1960	1961	1962	1963	1964	1965	1966
90th percentile	556	585	595	643	630	643	636	626
75th	485	536	545	576	573	592	586	572
50th	413	463	485	490	513	539	519	510
25th	363	396	413	413	450	470	455	443
10th	316	350	363	376	396	413	403	383

Fiftieth Percentile on Verbal Ability

	443	463	480	503	516	530	523	516

Fiftieth Percentile on Mathematical Ability

	490	499	513	528	538	587	577	557

[a] Source: Office of Psychological Services, Oakland University, 1968.

TABLE F-3
HIGH SCHOOL RANK OF OAKLAND UNIVERSITY FRESHMEN,
FALL 1959 AND FALL 1963

	Fall 1959[a]		*Fall 1963*[b]
Top fifth	36%	Upper 10%	36%
Second fifth	35	Upper quarter	37
Third fifth	22	Second quarter	20
Below third fifth	6	Third quarter	5
No response	1	Below third quarter	1
N	171	No response	1
		N	490

[a] Based on a 25% random sample study.

[b] Based on questionnaires from total incoming freshmen, Office of Psychological Services, Oakland University.

TABLE F-4

IMMEDIATE POSTGRADUATE ACTIVITIES OF OAKLAND GRADUATES, SPRING 1963–SPRING 1969

	Spring 1963	1963– 1964	1964– 1965	1965– 1966	1966– 1967	1967– 1968	1968– Spring 1969	Total Spring 1963– Spring 1969
Elementary and secondary education	47%	33%	35%	36%	39%	35%	35%	35%
Industry and government service, social services	20	28	25	22	19	22	28	24
Graduate and professional school[a]	26	20	17	24	18	16	15	18
Military service	2	2	2	2	3	4	3	3
Other, undecided[b]	5	19	21	16	21	23	19	20
N	146	225	211	219	326	414	343	1964

[a] Full-time only; an unknown percentage in other categories are in part-time graduate or professional programs.
[b] Includes housewives.

Appendix G (to accompany Chapter XI)

TABLE G-1

ENROLLMENT AT MONTEITH COLLEGE, FALL 1959–69[a]

	Size of entering class (freshmen and transfers)	*Total enrollment*[b]
1959	265	265
1960	307	537
1961	268	679
1962	233	690
1963	244	708
1964	303	817
1965	281	889
1966	211	793
1967	310	894
1968	325	954
1969	272	910

[a] Source: Adviser's Office, Monteith College.
[b] Excludes students who were enrolled in another college at Wayne State University but followed the Monteith core curriculum.

TABLE G-2

SOCIAL BACKGROUND OF MONTEITH ENTERING CLASSES, 1959–64
(Liberal Arts Entering Classes in Parentheses)

	Fall & Spring 1959–60	Fall & Spring 1960–61	All Quarters 1962–63	All Quarters 1963–64
Parents' Education[a]				
Both parents with some college or more	15%	14%	16%	16%
One parent with some college or more	21	22	25	27
Both parents finished high school	7	22	17	17
One parent finished high school	23	18	18	18
Both with less than high school	24	23	21	19
No response	10	1	3	3
Fathers' Occupations[a]				
Professionals, executives	20% (15%)	16%	23%	29%
Small businessmen, administrative personnel	18 (13)	23	18	13
Clerical and sales	18 (19)	10	14	11
Skilled manual	18 (19)	22	24	21
Machine operators and semiskilled	10 (12)	16	11	16
Unskilled and service workers	7 (7)	3	3	4
Other, no response	10 (15)	10	7	6

[a] Source: Monteith Program Study.

TABLE G-2 *(continued)*

	Fall & *Spring* *1959–60*	*Fall &* *Spring* *1960–61*	*All* *Quarters* *1962–63*	*All* *Quarters* *1963–64*
Students' Religious Preferences[a]				
Jewish	18% (20%)	15%	9%	8%
Roman Catholic	25 (27)	24	30	34
Protestant	40 (43)	53	36	36
None	6 (8)	5	11	12
Freethinker, other	9 (0)	3	11	10
No response	2 (2)	0	3	0
Recency of Family in the United States[a]				
Student foreign born	6% (6%)	4%	6%	6%
One or both parents foreign born	28 (33)	22	24	17
One or more grandparents foreign born	34 (37)	44	44	42
All grandparents U.S. born	29 (18)	29	26	30
No response	3 (6)	1	1	5

[a] Source: Monteith Program Study.

TABLE G-2 *(continued)*

High School Origins[b,c]

High schools in the inner city	64%	(59%)	57%	(55%)	50%	(58%)	49%	(56%)
High schools in the suburbs of the metropolitan area	31	(28)	34	(34)	40	(34)	42	(35)
High schools in Michigan outside the metropolitan area	2	(2)	5	(3)	3	(2)	2	(2)
High schools in other states and other countries	1	(5)	3	(4)	4	(3)	7	(4)
Other, no response	2	(6)	1	(4)	3	(3)	0	(3)
N	265		301		303		308	

[b] Source: Wayne State University Office of Admissions.

[c] Data available for fall classes only. N's were:

Fall 1959—258
Fall 1960—286
Fall 1962—206
Fall 1963—192

TABLE G-3

ACADEMIC INFORMATION ON MONTEITH ENTERING CLASSES, 1959-64

(Liberal Arts Entering Classes in Parentheses)

	Fall & Spring 1959-60	Fall & Spring 1960-61	All Quarters 1962-63	All Quarters 1963-64
High School Ratings[a]				
Excellent	26%	26%	21%	22%
Good	41	40	35	35
Indifferent	25	30	39	35
Poor	6	5	5	6
No response	2	0	0	2
High School Ranks[a]				
Top fifth	54% (57%)	51%	51%	46%
Second fifth	30 (27)	29	27	31
Third fifth	14 (12)	18	19	20
Below third fifth	2 (3)	2	3	3
No response	0 (2)	0	0	1
Entrance by Certificate[b]	79% (69%)	63% (67%)	65% (60%)	56% (69%)
Test of Critical Thinking (mean raw scores)[a]	33.6 (31.9)	35.4	34.5	34.3

[a] Source: Monteith Program Study.
[b] Source: Wayne State University Office of Admissions

TABLE G-3 (continued)

Performance on Wayne State Entrance
Examinations (mean percentiles)[b,c]

	Fall & Spring 1959–60	Fall & Spring 1960–61	All Quarters 1962–63	All Quarters 1963–64
Verbal Ability	65 (53)	69 (57)	65 (57)	76 (65)
Quantitative Ability	54 (48)	65 (50)	71 (58)	61 (58)
Curricular Choices[b]				
Business Administration	8% (9%)	11% (8%)	8% (8%)	13% (6%)
Liberal Arts	42 (28)	41 (36)	38 (36)	39 (40)
Education	22 (31)	24 (24)	29 (26)	23 (22)
Prelaw	5 (2)	8 (2)	9 (1)	7 (2)
Premedicine	23 (6)	16 (7)	16 (8)	18 (9)
Proportion of Engineers[b]	16%	15%	8%	4%
N	256	301	303	308

[b] Source: Wayne State University Office of Admissions.
[c] Data available for fall classes only. N's were:

    Fall 1959—258
    Fall 1960—286
    Fall 1962—206
    Fall 1963—192

TABLE G-4

POSTGRADUATE PLANS OF MONTEITH GRADUATES,
SPRING 1963–SPRING 1969

	Spring 1963	1963– 1964	1964– 1965	1965– 1966	1966– 1967	1967– 1968	1968– Spring 1969	Total Spring 1963– Spring 1969
Elementary and secondary education	7%	18%	9%	7%	5%	19%	35%	16%
Industry and government service, social services	5	8	14	22	12	20	20	15
Graduate and professional school[a]	79	68	69	60	70	43	30	57
Military service	2	3	3	2	5	6	4	4
Other, undecided	7	3	5	9	8	12	11	8
N	41	39	58	45	59	69	83	394
Number of students who did not indicate their plans	20	14	17	26	27	27	17	148
Total graduates	61	53	75	71	86	96	100	542

[a] Full-time only. Of those who indicated their plans, the following percentages were planning to take graduate or professional courses part-time:

Spring 1963:	7%	1964–65:	14%	1967–68:	13%
1963–64:	20%	1965–66:	4%	1968–69:	29%
		1966–67:	8%		

TABLE G-5

COLLEGE CHARACTERISTICS INDEX (MEAN STANDARD SCORES)

Intellectual Climate *Factors*	*Monteith*[a]	*Seven Independent Liberal Arts Colleges*[b,c]	*Seven University-Associated Liberal Arts Colleges*[b,a]
Aspiration level	3.35	2.29	−0.75
Intellectual climate	3.41	2.90	−0.92
Student dignity	3.05	2.39	−1.48
Academic achievement	0.20	2.04	−1.58
Self-expression	1.80	2.17	−1.03
Vocational	−3.60	−3.16	1.11
Play-work	0.20	−1.64	1.94
Non-intellectual Climate *Factors*			
Group life	−2.10	−1.26	−0.08
Academic Organization	−5.80	−1.95	0.15
Social form	−3.30	−2.04	1.08
N	76	460	543

[a] Source: Monteith Program Study.

[b] Source: George G. Stern, *People in Context.*

[c] Antioch, Bennington, Oberlin, Sarah Lawrence, Shimer, Sweet Briar, Wesleyan University.

[a] University of Buffalo, Emory, Florida State, Kentucky, Miami University, University of Minnesota, Rhode Island.

TABLE G-6
STUDENT REACTIONS TO DIFFERENT PARTS OF THE NATURAL
SCIENCE AND SOCIAL SCIENCE SEQUENCES, MONTEITH, 1960[a,b]

Natural Science	Most Difficult	Greatest Impact on Student
Theory of Numbers	38%	14%
Logic	20	15
Astronomy	14	30
Dynamics	8	8
Daltonian Atomics	16	8
Evolution	5	39
All	1	5
None	7	1
N	155	155

Social Science		
Relation	3%	20%
Small Group	3	21
Socialization	3	15
Differentiation	8	4
Pattern	7	12
Complex Organization—Verstehen	26	14
Complex Organization—Formal Theory	42	10
All	11	7
None	10	8
N	155	155

[a] Two responses possible per person.
[b] Students interviewed in spring 1960.

Index

A

Academic administration. *See* Administration, academic
Academic Revolution, The, 9
Adelson, Joseph, 133n, 169n
Administration, academic, 237–238
Administrators
  readiness to innovate, xi–xii
Advising, importance of, 282–284
American Council on Education Report; *see also* Cartter, Allan, 60–61
Amis, Kingsley, xiv
Antioch College, viii, 202, 236
Astin, Alexander W., 161
Axelrod, Joseph, 129n

B

Bales, Robert F., 122
Barzun, Jacques, 32
Bell, Daniel, 44n, 95
Ben-David, Joseph, 73n, 250n

Fels, William, 246
Fernald, John, 204, 261
Florida Atlantic University, 251, 254*n*
Freshman year, as a substitute for selective admission, 10
Friedenberg, Egar, 279
Full-Time Equivalent (FTE) formulas, 256–257
Fund For the Advancement of Education, 43, 48

G

General Education, xiii, 8, 12, 93, 265–266
Glazer, Nathan, 115*n*
Goddard College, 230
Goffman, Erving, 124
Goodman, Paul, 279
Grading, 137–138
"Gray Document, The." *See* Monteith, founding
Great Books tradition, 96
Grove Program. *See* Stanford University

H

Hampshire College, 47*n*
Hannah, John, 20–21, 23–24, 27, 248
Harvard College, 265
"Hawthorne effect," 211
Henry, David, 42
Higher education, expansion of, 1–2
Higher Education in England, 252*n*
Hilberry, Clarence, viii, 39, 42, 237, 248
Hirschman, Albert O., 37*n*
Holt, John, 279
Honors Programs, 12–13
Houston, University of, 251
Hughes, Everett C., vii-viii, 26*n*, 108, 176*n*, 255*n*
Hutchins, Robert M., 12, 96